CENTER
OF THE STORM

PRACTICING PRINCIPLED LEADERSHIP IN TIMES OF CRISIS

KATHERINE
HARRIS

WND BOOKS

A DIVISION OF THOMAS NELSON, INC.
www.ThomasNelson.com

To Anders,
who always centers me.

Published in Nashville, Tennessee, by Thomas Nelson, Inc.

Library of Congress Cataloging-in-Publication Data

Harris, Katherine, 1957–
    Center of the storm : practicing principled leadership in times of crisis / Katherine Harris.
        p. cm.
    Includes bibliographical references.
    ISBN 0-7852-6443-4 (hardcover)
    1. Presidents—United States—Election—2000. 2. Contested elections—United States. 3. Contested elections—Florida. 4. Crisis management in government—Florida. 5. Political leadership—Florida. I. Title.
    JK526 2000 H37 2002
    352.3—dc21   2002012423

Printed in the United States of America

02 03 04 05 06 BVG 5 4 3 2 1

Contents

INTRODUCTION

WHEN THE STORM BREAKS

*What do you do when a time of crisis strikes unexpectedly . . .
when adversity or controversy interrupts your daily routine . . .
when you find yourself in the eye of a hurricane? When
circumstances demand action, will you demonstrate the resolve
of Winston Churchill and Abraham Lincoln or the courage of
Joan of Arc? Will you rise to the occasion like Rudy Giuliani
and President George Bush or inspire others like Susan B.
Anthony or Mother Teresa?*

In the event of sudden, unanticipated tumult, have you ever considered how you would hold up if you discovered that you were directly in the line of fire . . . decided how you might make crucial decisions without knowing the consequences . . . imagined what it would take to survive in the center of the storm?

How would you face down your deepest fears, your greatest weaknesses, and your strongest temptations? How might you handle the glare of the spotlight that publicity, notoriety, and scrutiny would inevitably bring? Could you exercise principled and effective leadership under such circumstances?

As Election Night 2000 stretched into the following morning, I realized that I might soon have to confront such questions—whether or not I particularly wished to do so. My duties as Florida's chief elections officer had thrust me into the eye of an electoral tempest of historic dimensions. The stakes were enormous. The pressure was intense. The scrutiny was extraordinary. The eyes of the world had landed upon me.

> *A smooth sea never made a successful sailor.*
> —ISAAC WATTS

How would I respond? Would I bend under the pressure? With the leadership of the world's lone remaining superpower at stake, could I resist the competing forces that assailed me from every direction?

This book chronicles how I answered those questions. It details what I learned about life and leadership in the difficult days and months that followed. I make no pretense of expertise on either subject. I was not an expert on life and leadership when the storm broke around me on November 7, 2000, nor during the turbulent thirty-six days that followed; I am still not today. Nevertheless, I learned a great deal about how to weather an unexpected storm. I discovered where to find the necessary moral reserves, where to turn for help, and how to address mistakes, while staying true to my fundamental convictions.

Thus, I have not written this book to provide a historical analysis of the remarkable dead-heat presidential election that turned on a few hundred ballots in Florida. Though most of the media and countless self-appointed "experts" have yet to accurately report an infinite number of critical facts, such details do not constitute the heart of my story.

Neither is this book an apologetic for the decisions I made during the recount period of the 2000 presidential election in Florida. I have made hundreds of speeches, granted untold numbers of interviews, issued myriad policy papers, and promoted numerous legislative initiatives since the election. I have won and lost many battles. That is politics. As important as these outcomes are to me, they do not provide the essence of my story, either.

Instead, this book offers a glimpse into the heart and the soul of a rather ordinary woman who found herself amidst an extraordinary maelstrom, who in consequence had to resolve for herself what really matters most in life. It provides a reflection of the principles I drew upon as I fought to function effectively and preserve my integrity while the pressure was on and the storm was raging, and friend from foe were difficult to distinguish. Thus, while this book obviously constitutes a lessons-learned-from-the-fire reflection, it really explores permanent values rather than temporal events.

The events of Election 2000 appear anecdotally to illustrate how my experience at the center of the storm deepened my appreciation of the power of twelve basic ideals. I have not chosen this approach because I somehow believe that I was, am, or will become any time soon a leader who employs these principles with perfect regularity. Moreover, by presenting the stories of persons whom I regard as exemplars of each leadership principle, I do not purport to equate my experiences to the depth of their struggles or to the greatness of their achievements. Instead, I seek to illustrate how their stories inspired me to think differently about my unique circumstances.

This book had its genesis in my realization early in my political life that newly elected officials receive no formal training in how they can effectively implement their vision, values, and purpose amidst the ragged, contentious, and sometimes ruthless world of representative government. Due to its very nature, a deliberative democracy thrusts its participants into a roiling cauldron of competing interests with little training or warning.

During my first days as a Florida state senator, I learned the basics of filing a bill or writing a policy briefing. I studied the structure of the committees and subcommittees, becoming familiar with their key members. But where was the guidance concerning how to employ the dizzying, surreal institutional framework of politics and personalities in the service of integrity, wisdom, and constancy? I found myself wishing for a "boot camp" for leaders, a workshop or retreat designed to help legislators look deeply into how their motives, goals, and principles could survive and prevail in the real world of government.

After the recount controversy of the 2000 presidential election in Florida had administered yet another staggering dose of revelations to my experience in public service, I wondered how I could have been better prepared for the onslaught. I was proud of the decisions I had made. I knew that I had weathered an extraordinary tempest in order to uphold the rule of law, which constituted the only proper course of action. But, how could I relate the principles that sustained me through this challenging period, in order to prepare others for the challenges of an unpredicted storm?

My jesting proposal to start a boot camp for leaders led to count-less in-depth discussions with friends, consultants, and advisors—old and young, male and female, Republican and Democrat, U.S. citizens and visitors—about the essential ways our most firmly held principles guide us all, in times of calm and in times of storm. But in order for these inner resources to be available when we need them, we must know what they are—what we value, what we feel is primary, what we live for. In other words, what are our first principles?

While inspired by my experiences at the center of a political whirlwind, my sincere hope is that this book describes practical lessons each of us can apply to our own lives. Although we might think about leadership only in political or business terms, in truth, the need for principled leadership arises in every facet and every walk of life. We all face times of crisis and decision in our lives when, with God's help, we must take charge. We all reach profound emotional or spiritual crossroads at one time or another. By sharing my sources of inspiration, I hope that you, the reader, will find information and solace to apply in the midst of your trials. After all, we all find our-selves in the center of the storm eventually. And as the shocking tragedy of September 11 reminded us, we never know when the storm may break.

The twelve principles I describe in this book can enable a person to approach a crisis with the indispensable tools of integrity and resolve. When I use the terms *principled leader* and *effective leader*, I intend for those terms to be understood in their broadest sense, to describe any person who applies a creative blend of strength, courage, judgment, sensitivity, and self-control in addressing a crisis. I do not proffer myself as a teacher. I see myself as a fellow student of the extraordinary persons I describe in these pages, some of whom I have always appreciated, and some of whom I have come to study and admire as I searched for perspective in the aftermath of my tenure in the center of the storm.

So, what is principled and effective leadership in a time of crisis? How does it differ from mere crisis management or contingency planning? Where does it come from, and how can we prepare the way for it?

I was not terribly surprised to discover that principled and effective leadership in a time of crisis is unlike anything that political consultants, academics, speechwriters, and public relations spinmeisters would have us believe. I discovered that principled leadership is simply the kind of common sense that has become all too uncommon these days.

Principled and effective leadership in a time of crisis consists of the same wisdom, honor, decency, and valor that celebrated leaders have modeled throughout history. This unique brand of sensibility ultimately enabled Patrick Henry, Frederick Douglass, Teddy Roosevelt, Martin Luther King Jr., and a host of other inspiring leaders to realize great achievements. This singular variety of common sense also fueled the quiet daring of the nameless pioneers and settlers, the humble mothers and fathers, and the quiet artisans, merchants, and traders who laid the foundations for the great American experiment in liberty. Uncompromising ideals leavened by tolerance and down-to-earth practicality will continue to secure the future of our freedom.

PRINCIPLE 1

Know what you believe. When adversity strikes, it is essential that we know what we believe, why we believe it, and how we came to believe it.

PRINCIPLE 2

Remember your raising. We always need to keep in mind from whence we came, drawing perspective from that background in evaluating our current circumstances.

PRINCIPLE 3

Stick to your guns. While effective leadership frequently requires principled compromise, tenacious adherence to a particular principle, when accompanied by wisdom, often provides the only safe harbor in times of crisis.

PRINCIPLE 4

Finish what you start. We must ascertain our responsibilities and work hard to uphold them, regardless of how difficult that task may prove.

PRINCIPLE 5

Do what is right—and the future will take care of itself. When we hold to our first principles and simply focus on doing the right thing, we can leave the outcome to Providence.

PRINCIPLE 6

Feed your mind. The development of a well-rounded, well-trained mind provides the best preparation for times of difficulty.

PRINCIPLE 7

It is amazing what you can accomplish if you don't care who receives the credit. We need to focus our concern on accomplishing our priorities and fulfilling our calling—not on achieving power, glory, or prestige.

PRINCIPLE 8

Embrace the differences. Our world contains rich diversity. Persons who appreciate and embrace this diversity are most likely to emerge from a crisis successfully.

PRINCIPLE 9

Resist the tyranny of the urgent. We must learn to stay on task and on message, even when urgent distractions clamor for our attention.

PRINCIPLE 10

Be broken, be bitter, or be better. We cannot always choose our circumstances, but we certainly can choose how we respond to them.

PRINCIPLE 11

Act and risk enmity; To remain popular, do nothing. When we take pride in our accomplishments—not in our popularity or poll numbers—we are free to forge ahead to fulfill our calling, regardless of the obstacles in our path. We must be able to challenge the status quo, instead of playing it safe.

PRINCIPLE 12

Unstring your bow. When a crisis has passed, it is essential that we know how to relax. A bow that remains perpetually strung loses its elasticity—and thus, its effectiveness. By contrast, a retreat to the sanctuary of family, friends, and faith fortifies us for the next challenge.

> *So, safe on shore the pensioned sailor lies,*
> *And all the malice of the storm defies;*
> *With ease of body blest and peace of mind*

Pities the restless crew he left behind;
Whilst, in his cell, he meditates alone
On his great voyage to the world unknown.
—WILLIAM SOMERVILLE

This book constitutes my reflections upon the remarkable power of these habits of heart, mind, and soul, which I began to discover in childhood, honed in adulthood, and tested at the center of the storm. I am still learning how to put these principles into practice in my life. As I encounter the stories and testimonies of men and women who exemplify these principles, I continue to discover how aspiring to these ideals can change my life.

> *After a storm comes a calm.*
> —MATHEW HENRY

My sincerest prayer is that you will find these principles to be as helpful in your life's journey as I have in mine—especially for the next time you find yourself in the center of the storm.

PRINCIPLE 1

Know What You Believe

*In times of crisis, we must draw upon what we believe, why
we believe it, and how we came to believe it. When adversity
strikes, we must remember our principles and why we hold
them dear. Philosophers refer to this thought process as
epistemology—the rest of us just call it common sense.*

I awoke with a start. I had been asleep for only thirty minutes.
Now, at 3:30 A.M. on November 8, 2000, the phone was ringing
insistently, and an already wildly unpredictable election night was
about to become even wilder.

Like many Americans, I had followed the arduous nip-and-tuck
battle between Governor George W. Bush and Vice President Al
Gore with rapt interest but had surrendered eventually to fatigue
upon learning of the networks' projection that Governor Bush had
been elected president. What a roller-coaster ride of emotions and
political fortunes the 2000 presidential campaigns had been! While I
had enjoyed the theater of this dramatically competitive race, along
with the rest of the nation, I yearned for the closure of Election Day.

The election had required that my duties as Florida's chief elections officer take increasing priority over my other responsibilities,
which include serving as a statewide elected member of Florida's executive cabinet, as well as managing the responsibilities for my specific

divisions under the Department of State: international affairs, culture and the arts, corporations, libraries, historic preservation, licensing, and elections. Thus, I looked forward to the return to normalcy that November 8 promised—if *normal* can describe any aspect of political life.

The election had brought the nation everything but closure, however, and my life was about to become farther removed from normalcy than I ever could have imagined.

Early the previous evening, before hundreds of polling places closed in Florida's panhandle counties that lie in the central time zone, the television networks projected Al Gore as the winner of Florida's twenty-five electoral votes. While recent polling data had deemed the race in Florida too close to call, the potential reality of a Democratic victory sent shock waves throughout both campaigns.

Along with traditional bellwether states like Ohio, Florida had joined Michigan and Pennsylvania on the watch lists of most political analysts. Together, the latter three states accounted for 66 electoral votes, nearly one-quarter of the 270 needed for victory.

In Florida, the political muscle of Governor Jeb Bush had long appeared sufficient to tip the scales in his brother's favor. In the waning days of the campaign, however, Al Gore pumped escalating resources into Florida, hoping to score an upset victory that could deliver a devastating early blow to the Republican camp, impacting the race in other states across the nation. Thanks to the hubris of television network news, this strategy almost worked.

The competitive pressures that drive network news organizations have spawned the early projections that have regrettably become a ubiquitous feature of U.S. presidential elections. These early projections may have distorted the outcome of our national elections in the information age. For example, some accounts have speculated that the networks' early projection of Ronald Reagan's 1980 victory over Jimmy Carter well before the polls closed in the Pacific time zone may have cost the Democrats several congressional seats by suppressing voter turnout.

In states like Florida that straddle two time zones, this phenomenon can impact who actually wins the state's electoral votes. Thus, election officials in these states try to restrain eager media outlets from announcing unofficial vote tallies and projections until every voter has had the opportunity to cast a ballot. For this reason, I sent each major news organization a letter several days prior to the election reminding them to hold their projections until *all* of Florida's polling places closed. One network sent me a very terse reprimand in response.

Almost immediately after the networks broadcast the Gore projection, reports of thousands of voters leaving Florida polling stations in the Republican-leaning counties of the western panhandle began to circulate throughout the rest of the state. In all the postmortem analyses of the 2000 presidential election in Florida that have fixated on butterfly ballots and other alleged difficulties experienced by voters in other parts of the state that day, this occurrence has received precious little attention. Before making the specious claim that "more people in Florida went to the polls on November 7, 2000, intending to vote for Al Gore," commentators would be wise to consider that even Democratic activist Bob Beckel estimated that the premature Gore projection cost George W. Bush eight thousand votes in Florida.

Within two hours of this announcement, the networks' confidence turned to chaos. As the actual vote tallies streamed in from across Florida, the networks' rash proclamation of a Gore victory in Florida appeared grounded upon the shifting sands of flawed data. In fact, Al Gore *never* led Florida on election night! Despite his loss of thousands of votes in the heavily Republican precincts of the western panhandle, George W. Bush continued to lead the entire evening.

Eventually, the television networks admitted their error and pulled Florida out of the Gore column. Several hours later, when

Florida's decisive role in determining the next president of the United States had become apparent, they added the state's twenty-five electoral votes to the Bush column and declared George W. Bush our forty-third president.

Al Gore telephoned his rival with his concession and prepared to address his supporters. Relieved, exhausted Republican campaign workers cheered and celebrated. I went home to sleep, naively certain that the networks could not have made another mistake. America had elected a new president—a man who had impressed me early in the campaign as the extraordinary leader the world has come to know in the aftermath of the September 11 attacks.

Then the confusion broke free of its fetters once again. It seemed that nothing was certain this evening! As reflected on the Florida Department of State's website, the vote totals in Florida had narrowed dramatically. Al Gore called George W. Bush again to retract his concession. The race for the presidency remained undecided. No one knew what to expect next.

That's when my phone rang, and I found myself at the center of a whirlwind of confusion. By Florida statute, an automatic recount must be ordered whenever a candidate wins by one-half of 1 percent or less. I hurried back to my office at 3:45 A.M. to monitor the accumulating vote totals. About two hours later, the results indeed indicated that a recount was mandated.

In accordance with state law, I immediately ordered a statewide machine recount. Despite the enormity of such an undertaking, this recount was complete within seventy-two hours of the original count on Election Night. Although there was a substantial reduction in his vote margin, George W. Bush clung to his lead by the narrowest of margins.

As the machine recount proceeded, controversy erupted at an alarming rate in south Florida. The Democratic Party hired a Texas marketing firm to place thousands of phone calls to voters in Palm Beach County to raise their level of concern regarding the so-called "butterfly ballot." The ensuing furor during those initial days merely foretold the coming storm.

Over the course of the thirty-six days that followed November 7, 2000, our nation received the civics lesson of a lifetime. Hanging, dangling, and impregnated chads joined the American lexicon, while debates about absentee ballots, undervotes, overvotes, and voter intent occurred at water coolers across the country.

Political commentators pored over every detail of the court rulings in a stupendous array of election-related lawsuits, speculating about the unprecedented brew of the law, campaign strategies, opinion polls, and administrative procedures. Late-night comedians enjoyed a heyday. It seemed that every American in every newscast, every newspaper, every classroom, every discussion, everywhere obsessed over what had happened, what would happen, what could happen, and what should happen.

IN THE MIDDLE

At hurricane central, when it appeared that the first recount would not satisfy all the parties involved, Benjamin McKay, my chief of staff, joked that we might as well just paint a target right on my back, because everyone would soon come gunning for me. Regardless of what course of action we chose, we knew we had landed in a no-win situation. Before I made my first public statement, we all knew that my office would come under fire. Yet none of us imagined the withering barrage that would ensue.

Everyone had an opinion about what I should or should not do. I was criticized for acting too hastily. I was criticized for acting too slowly. I was accused of adhering to the law too strictly. I was accused of using the law for partisan purposes. From the tabloids to the serious news outlets, I became a topic of heated discussion. Sometimes it seemed that I was *the* topic of discussion. Political cartoonists and syndicated columnists weighed in on everything from my makeup and wardrobe to my childhood and education, from my family life and political life to my love life and social life. Wild rumors were repeated with impunity. The politics of personal destruction became the default mode of many media personalities, journalists, and campaign staffers. I became the subject of many a joke (some clever and incisive, others trite and mean-spirited), the target of untold numbers of attacks, the object of unfocused ire and derision. Then came the death threats (I was informed of the first threat by the Capitol Police just moments before I opened the door to my first of only four press conferences) . . . the lawsuits (some fifty-three and counting) . . . the crushing intrusions by tabloid paparazzi (surrounding our residence, camping in their cars armed with long, telephoto lenses, and startling our friend who assists me with my chores by sneaking up to the windows to film the interior of our home). It was awful.

Who would dream that they might one day find themselves in such a situation? Certainly not me. During my eight years of political life, I had never sought the spotlight. In fact, one journalist remarked that she had observed me when I served in the Florida state senate (from 1994 until 1998) and could not remember a single bill that I had passed. Had this reporter bothered to check her facts, she would have noted that I had personally sponsored and passed more than one hundred bills during my four-year term (when, on average, senators pass ten bills per year). These bills increased funding for teachers, care for crack cocaine-addicted newborns, and child safety. They constituted landmark legislation in the areas of international affairs and insurance, created racketeering penalties for phone transit theft, and strengthened damages against white-collar crime. Further, she would have learned that during my tenure as chair of the senate's Commerce and Economic Opportunities Committee, Florida improved from forty-second to first in the nation as a state in which to start a business or to grow an existing business.

This reporter would have had to perform some research, however, because she never would have seen me grandstanding on the floor of the senate or in any committee hearing. I did not deluge newspaper editorial offices with op-ed pieces, press releases, or press conference announcements. As a state senator and then as secretary of state, I did my job, fulfilled my promises, and looked toward the future.

Prior to the recount controversy, I enjoyed a reputation as someone who did not define herself through partisanship. From my perspective, an *R* or a *D* after someone's name does not provide a road map to character. Having grown up in Florida at a time when virtually everyone, including my family, was a Democrat, I have long thought the content of one's character is the important tool for judgment, rather than a political party.

Even after the recount crisis erupted and various parties launched ferocious accusations of partisanship against me, my former Democratic colleagues in the state senate noted in media interviews that I had given more of their bills a fair hearing than any previous *Democratic* committee chair. Although they often defended me by asserting my obvious aversion to partisanship, the media rarely quoted such observations.

When I was interviewed by Diane Sawyer, she found it of interest that during the recount, when I appeared on the floor of both the Florida Senate and the Florida House of Representatives, I received a standing ovation from Democrats and Republicans alike. She wondered how I

> *If I were to try to read, much less answer, all the attacks made on me, this shop might as well be closed for any other business. I do the very best I know how—the best I can; and I mean to keep doing so until the end. If the end brings me out all right, what is said against me won't amount to anything. If the end brings me out wrong, ten angels swearing I was right would make no difference.*
>
> —ABRAHAM LINCOLN

had managed to prevent appearing overwhelmed by emotion and the drama of this event during such a historic time. "How did you not cry?" she asked. I told her the truth: I *was* overwhelmed, so I tried to think of something funny to help maintain my composure. I thought of *Austin Powers'* hilarious character "Mini Me"!

Despite the attacks I have endured since Election 2000, I still decline to engage in the politics of personal destruction. I have long focused upon policy issues rather than the cults of personality or party. I am saddened by the combative side of the political arena, in which one vicious partisan assault begets another, serving only to cheapen serious dialogue concerning the real issues that affect real people. In a perfect world, I would rather not have to comment upon the panoply of cheap shots I continue to receive. Unfortunately, such false and unfair attacks have become the perceived "truth" in the minds of many when I have declined to rebut them in the past. Thus, I now respond by striking back harder, with truth as my weapon of choice. However, I truly do not enjoy this unavoidable aspect of political life.

I wish I could say that I was prepared for the recount crisis—that I knew exactly what to do from the beginning, that I had all the moral reserves necessary to withstand the incredible pressure, that I had a firm grasp of all the technical legal issues involved, that the intense scrutiny did not throw me, that I had all the experience required to take this remarkable turn of events entirely in stride, and that I knew precisely how to stay focused on the things that really mattered. I would love to be able to say that I had thick skin and was unaffected by the outright lies stated or written or conjectured about me. I'd like to say that principled leadership in this time of crisis came as naturally to me as breathing. But none of these statements would be true.

> *As he thinketh in his heart, so is he.*
> —KING SOLOMON

I cannot say that I was prepared for this

particular crisis, which erupted as unpredictably as any sudden squall. I have been deeply gratified to find, however, that my preparation for life in general—professional and personal—served me well. I was fortunate to have an extraordinary staff surrounding me. I had access to wise and discerning counsel. My amazing husband, Anders, offered a bedrock of love and support as well as astute advice. Other family members called daily to offer encouragement and spiritual guidance. Friends sent thoughtful gifts or came to stay with me to help me attend to everyday living; and citizens across our nation sent letters, e-mails (750,000), flowers, faxes, and most importantly, prayers. But in addition to all that, I knew where to start—I knew what I believed.

WHERE TO START

The English journalist and novelist G. K. Chesterton once said, "The chief mark and element of insanity is reason used without root, reason in the void. The man who begins to think without the proper first principles goes mad; he begins to think at the wrong end."

As I looked at the task before me—applying the election laws of the state of Florida in a fair, equitable, and just fashion without regard to the maddening hue and cry all around me—at least I knew where to begin. I needed to ground myself in my basic principles as a public servant, and stand fast and firm on that foundation. I knew that this posture was the hallmark of effective leadership. It always had been, and it always will be.

Time and again during the recount crisis I recalled the stories of historical figures, some long gone, in whose trials I found sustenance and whose lives still have lessons to impart for us all. I remembered how unshakable confidence in his most cherished ideals enabled George Washington to persevere during the bitter winter at Valley Forge. Likewise, unwavering commitment to his ultimate values enabled William Wilberforce to fight untiringly for the abolition of slavery throughout the British Empire, a fight that took him fifty years to win. Undying faith in her foundational worldview enabled Sojourner Truth to connect the issues of abolition and women's rights, and to fight ardently for both. Principled leaders know what they believe. They maintain firmly established values. They know why they hold their principles dear, and they remain entirely conscious of these principles.

In the aftermath of the events surrounding the 2000 presidential election, I have had time to reflect deeply upon the many exemplars of principled leadership in whom I found inspiration. Soon I was enthusiastically researching additional role models amongst our forebears, both well known and little known, whose experience can continue to shed light as we face the inevitable crises and challenges life throws upon us. While no one escapes these inevitable storms, they can strengthen our character, skills, and wit if we survive them by drawing upon the profound lessons of the past. I hope that by sharing how I have applied these lessons to my experiences in the presidential election controversy, you, too, will delight in the wisdom and strength of these stories.

THE JUST FRUITS OF PRINCIPLED LEADERSHIP

As the smothering totalitarianism of Communism maintained its grasp on the whole of Eastern Europe after World War II, the distinctive voice of a few courageous souls dared to challenge the inhumanity and oppression of those dark regimes. Sadly, countless numbers of those voices were stilled by death at the hands of those claiming to act in the name of "the people." Yet, despite the enormous risks and ruthless consequences, some refused to be silenced or dismayed. Two of the more prominent Cold War dissidents exemplify the rewards to be gained by ardently defending our most cherished beliefs regardless of the seemingly insurmountable obstacles that arise.

One such figure is Vaclav Havel, currently serving as the President of the Czech Republic, who in less than a decade led his country out of brutal repression to become one of the brightest lights of democracy. Due to his family's prominence as business and cultural leaders prior to Communism, Havel was denied many of the educational and social opportunities afforded students who cooperated with the regime. But he persisted and grew to be a skilled writer, playwright, and literary and theater critic in the years leading up to the Prague Spring of 1968. During that time, he published some of his most famous plays.

Hopes of releasing Czechoslovakia's political and economic shackles at that time ran high, only to be dashed as Soviet troops invaded the country. The Soviets replaced the reformist government of Alexander Dubcek with a puppet government, effectively crushing the previously burgeoning spirit of liberty. Havel, however, would not be silenced. He challenged the government's policies in an open letter to the president and became one of the chief spokesmen for the Charter 77 movement in the late 1970s, which called for the end of the systematic oppression of the Czechoslovak populace.

The costs of continuing his protest activities were dear. Havel was repeatedly arrested and interrogated, and he served almost five years in prison for his trumped-up "crimes." But he remained undaunted, and the resentment of the Czech people, fueled by his example, grew into a groundswell of peaceful but powerful resistance. This outcry soon took the form of massive demonstrations for freedom that grew increasingly larger and more restless.

The mounting tensions came to a head in November 1989, when police forces violently suppressed the peaceful protests. Several weeks before, Havel had been arrested once again for his leadership of the dissident movement. The huge popular demonstrations that resulted from this government crackdown forced the country to a standstill, brought the government to its knees, and broke the Communist regime's iron grip on the nation's political machinery. Free elections were called.

Havel later related that during those few epic weeks when Czechoslovakia went from captivity to liberty, a friend suggested that he might even be elected president—this just less than a month after Havel had been arrested as a political agitator. He considered the suggestion a friendly joke. Days later, Vaclav Havel was nominated and elected the first president of a free Czechoslovakia.

Two months later, in February 1990, as the remaining Communist regimes in Eastern Europe tumbled in rapid succession, Havel traveled to the United States and delivered a stirring address before a joint session of Congress. He reflected on how quickly his country's fortunes had shifted, as swiftly as his own. He said, "We are living in very odd times. The human face of the world is changing so rapidly that none of the familiar political speedometers are adequate."

Havel and his colleagues are unlikely to have imagined such monumental changes as even a remote possibility in the early days, when their opposition was met with daily disappointments, harassment, and ever-increasing obstacles. His path from dissident playwright to international statesman was paved with hardship and struggle, and filled with opportunities to compromise his principles. But he never wavered or abandoned his beliefs, and as he stood unrelenting in the face of tyranny, the watching consciences of his fellow citizens were stirred to ensemble action that shook the world.

Havel's leadership did not end there. He reluctantly led his country through the "Velvet Divorce," which peacefully split the country in two. He was subsequently elected president of the newly formed Czech Republic, and he was reelected in 1998.

Not all stories from the Iron Curtain era are as dramatic or filled with such unexpected triumph. The Russian writer and Nobel Prize winner, Aleksandr Solzhenitsyn, endured decades of prison and exile to watch his homeland—the primary focus of his writings—elude the political reforms and freedoms his countrymen have desperately sought.

As Russia has haltingly trudged toward democracy, Solzhenitsyn has chosen to return to his country from exile in the U.S. to assist in rebuilding its intellectual and spiritual life. This task he began early in life, writing stories that were part autobiographical, part social commentary. While serving on the front lines in World War II, he was denounced for subversive writings, including making unfavorable comments about Stalin in a letter to a friend, for which he was sentenced to eight years of hard labor. In the prison camp his writings began to focus on the undisguised horrors of his captors. Truth, he decided, would be his weapon: "One word of truth shall outweigh the whole world," he would later write.

But he would have to continue to struggle under his prison sentence, which he completely served, only to be sentenced again to exile for life in Kazakhstan. In that remote land he wrote poetry, taught mathematics and physics, and grew despondent that exposing his writings to anyone might earn him a death sentence.

No longer able to tolerate the outrageous lies and increasing hostility directed toward the Russian people by the ruling regime, Solzhenitsyn lashed out in 1962 by releasing his *One Day in the Life of Ivan Denisovich*, a novel that describes the life of an inmate in a Soviet prison camp. His writings, which made him famous with the public and unpopular with the secret police, were quickly censored and put under a government ban. The swift reaction was not a surprise. "A great writer is, so to speak, a second government in his country," he said. "And for that reason no regime has ever loved great writers, only minor ones."

In defiance of the ban, his ideas continued to flourish in the Soviet underground and in the West. His next major work, *The Gulag Archipelago*, eventually won him the Nobel Prize for Literature. Once Soviet officials realized they could not contain him, they altered their strategy by expelling him from the country. Taking up residence in the U.S., Solzhenitsyn continued writing and speaking out against corruption and tyranny in government, and cautioned Americans to avoid following the road his country had taken.

In all that he has said and written, Solzhenitsyn has assumed the mantle of cultural prophet intent on throwing back the curtain of social pretense and exposing the depth of human passion in the throes of turmoil and oppression. He sees this as his calling. "Literature that is not the breath of contemporary society, that dares not transmit the pains and fears of that society, that does not warn in time against threatening moral and social dangers—such literature does not deserve the name of literature; it is only a façade."

> *The principle of principle should be at the forefront of every discussion and form the foundation of every policy. Thus, when difficulties arise—as they inevitably do— we will know where to stand and how to endure to the very end.*
> —ABRAHAM KUYPER

Like his Czech counterpart, Vaclav Havel, Aleksandr Solzhenitsyn has stood heroic in the face of great cruelty. Fortunately, their voices carried loudly above the countless others who were silenced. Holding firm to the virtues and beliefs they treasured—to their personal detriment—and shining forth through the dark cloud of oppression, they have demonstrated the requisite courage that has wrought indelible changes in their respective countries. As those changes continue to advance, these brave-hearted souls can take comfort in the fact that they have maintained their vision and emerged victorious.

THE PRINCIPLE OF *PRINCIPLE*

The most obvious lesson we can learn from inspiring role models like Vaclav Havel and Aleksandr Solzhenitsyn is disarmingly simple: principled leaders have principles. They maintain clearly articulated values that do not change with the circumstances, the political climate, the latest public opinion polls, or even in the face of repression. Coherent, deeply held beliefs guide their decisions and underlie their opinions.

I kept reminding myself of this principle when I suddenly found myself at the center of a storm. While a thousand distractions vied for my attention, I continually returned to the principle of principle, which contains the following components:

1. WE ARE WHAT WE BELIEVE

Ironically, despite our very "politically correct" world, we tend to think that what a man or woman believes is really not all that important. Sociologists pontificate on the powerful influence of climate and culture in shaping a person's behavior, but rarely do they consider the thoughts and ideas that actually drive our actions. Society aids and abets this condition by focusing on image rather than substance. This is particularly true in the realm of politics, where politicians harbor secret fears that their supporters will someday compare their rhetoric with their voting record (hence our "Promises made, promises kept" letters). The result is a paradoxical—some might say hypocritical—culture that denies the power of ideas, but fights doggedly to make certain that ideas represent the dominant cultural wisdom.

The peaks and pinnacles in the landscape of history have been formed by leaders who knew that ideas shape not only policies, but also people. These visionary leaders knew what they believed and what mindsets they confronted. William Wilberforce saw that the inhumanity of the slave trade didn't need to be regulated: it needed to be abolished. Winston Churchill saw that Nazism didn't need to be contained: it needed to be destroyed. Ronald Reagan denounced the Evil Empire; standing meters from the Brandenburg Gate in Berlin, he threw down the gauntlet on behalf of free society with the challenge,

"Mr. Gorbachev, tear down this wall." These leaders and others like them understood that political and military battles are only reflections of the life-and-death struggle between ideas. As our nation confronts the ideological prejudices and hatred that have motivated terrorists to murder thousands of innocent people on American soil, we ignore at our peril the power of ideas to shape people.

2. OUR WORLDVIEW MATTERS

In 1979, I met the American-born/Swiss-transplanted philosopher, author, and activist Dr. Francis Schaeffer and Dr. C. Everett Koop (who later became Surgeon General in Reagan's administration) at a seminar held at Georgia's World Trade Center. I was invited to study with Dr. Schaeffer at L'Abri, his international fellowship center in Chesieres, Switzerland.

My time studying and working at L'Abri was life-altering. I lived next door to the Schaeffers, with the family of their daughter and son-in-law, Debbie and Udo Middleman. While extensive study was the order of the day, I learned just as well from the chores required to maintain the fellowship—washing wooden floors to perfection on my hands and knees using a cloth; operating the ironing machine to neatly press dozens of sheets; fetching milk cans down the mountain and walking back up the hill with them heavily filled; learning to prepare the intimate Sunday evening's light meal with the Schaeffers, giving extraordinary attention to detail, beauty, and taste. Dr. Schaeffer's wife, Edith, writes of this kind of loving attention in her books, *What Makes a Family?* and *Hidden Treasures.*

I became enthralled with Dr. Schaffer's landmark historical survey, *How Should We Then Live?* As the ripple effect of the cultural rebellion of the 1960s extended well into the 1970s, Schaeffer was one of many dedicated to exploring the root causes of the societal ills that plague the modern psyche. In his extraordinary and insightful book, he offered his diagnosis of contemporary culture in the context of the rise and decline of Western civilization. He concluded that modern society's fragmentation of modern life into separate, unrelated compartments means that the treatment of the social cancers attacking the soul of America primarily address the symptoms instead of the disease. The ideas are the overarching element that inevitably matters. If we divide life into isolated categories, we aggravate our social problems—child abuse, pornography, divorce— by failing to recognize the pattern of ideas and the view of life that underlies them all.

Schaeffer asserted that the task for leaders is to challenge conventional ways of thinking, which relegate ideas to the periphery of society. He sought to restore the notion that ideas are central to behavior. Hoping to spark a recovery of sense and reason, Schaffer aimed to instill in leaders a consciousness that a society's health or illness is rooted in its worldview.

> *Man is what he believes.*
> —ANTON CHEKHOV

3. WHAT WE BELIEVE WILL ULTIMATELY DETERMINE HOW WE ACT

Every belief system has palpable, demonstrable, and visible results. We cannot divorce root from fruit. There is no task more practical, therefore, than making the effort to clearly comprehend the character and content of our own worldview. While scholars talk about "paradigm shifts" and management consultants proclaim "new pathways of thinking," we can explain the notion of a worldview much more simply. In short, a worldview constitutes the lens through which we see the world. It consists of the basic set of beliefs that colors our understanding of reality and magnifies what matters most. Whatever images meet our eyes, our worldview shapes how and what we see.

Our worldview dictates our actions as well. Each of us proceeds through life on the basis of our predispositions, which define who we are and determine what we do. Our worldview becomes the launching

> *The worst and best are both inclined*
> *To snap like vixens at the truth*
> *But, O, beware that middle mind*
> *That purrs and never shows a tooth.*
> —ELINOR WYLIE

point for our spiritual, intellectual, and social endeavors. Deep in the inner recesses of the soul, our worldview throws the switches of our lives.

This reality manifests itself most visibly in the lives of our cultural leaders. The differences between the paintings of Rembrandt, Mary Cassatt, and Picasso reflect not only divergent styles; the artists were the products of different worldviews. Likewise, the dissimilarity between the music of Bach, the Beatles, and Celine Dion, the variation between the architecture of Wren, Wright, and Pei, and the divergence between the republican politics of George Washington and the communist politics of Mao Tse-tung are all attributable to differences in worldview. While some modern observers might see these examples as merely a series of points on a vast continuum, they also represent radical conflicts of vision based on the application of distinct and competing worldviews. Whether they occur in art or politics, these widely disparate expressions illustrate the folly of trying to separate what we do from how and what we believe.

4. UNEXAMINED IDEAS CAN HAVE UNINTENDED CONSEQUENCES

Plato said, "The life which is unexamined is not worth living." That comment may overstate the case, but one truism remains: the unexamined life will invariably produce unintended results. Our ideas and principles have consequences. If we have never thought through the implications of those ideas and principles, they will surprise us with unintended outcomes, both in the short term and in the long run. If we fail to articulate or scrutinize our ideas and principles, the naturally flowing consequences of our worldview will repeatedly catch us off guard. Over the course of time, our actions generate extensive chains of causes and effects that create a future built squarely on the worldview that initiated the whole process. Ultimately, if the foundation of our ideas and principles rests upon shaky ground, anything built upon that foundation is likely to crumble.

WORLDVIEW THINKING IN A CRISIS

Reminding myself of the principle of principle was not necessarily my first instinct when the presidential election crisis landed in my lap. Everyone advised me to run for cover to find an escape from making controversial decisions, and at the beginning I was tempted. A thousand alternatives to employing the principle of principle rushed into my mind as I contemplated my circumstances. In the end, however, I realized that relying upon what I knew to be right, good, and true would not only preserve my integrity; it would also provide the most practical solution to my predicament.

Unfortunately, the subject of worldview and first principles remains largely within the purview of philosophers and academics. I see this condition as a serious problem confronting our society. Rather than being a topic of arcane intellectual debate, I hope to see an examination of worldview come to occupy everyone's focus, as it continues to be inextricably linked to all that we are and do.

We must remain perpetually aware of our presuppositions. As crises descend upon us, the temptation to forsake

> *The most practical and important thing about a man is his view of the universe. For a landlady to consider a lodger, it is important to know his income, but still more important to know his philosophy. For a general to fight an enemy, it is important to know the enemy's numbers, but still more important to know the enemy's philosophy. The question is not whether the theory of the cosmos affects matters, but whether, in the long run, anything else affects them.*
>
> —G. K. CHESTERTON

our principles for the sake of expediency grows enticingly strong. Once we take this step, however, we become constrained to live in a world of reaction. We lose the freedom to act on our own. Thus, one way we can prepare for unanticipated crises is to engage in an active program of identifying, assessing, and applying our worldview.

How might we do this? I have found several steps invaluable to me in maintaining my essential principles.

I. WRITE IT DOWN

Virtually every popular management expert, from Stephen Covey and Peter Drucker to John Maxwell and Jack Welch, has said that effective leaders must clearly articulate their basic principles—the values that define all they are and all they do. Effective leaders require more than a plan; they must also have a basis for that plan . . . a concise credo. More than a job description or a list of goals and priorities, this credo must include an unequivocal proclamation of what really matters most. A foundational statement of core beliefs must be specific, and it must be tangible. It must be in writing.

Speaker of the Florida House of Representatives Tom Feeney (2000-2002) listed the principles by which the House would consider legislation under his leadership. He distributed this information to the 120 members of the House on small laminated cards, which they could keep in their wallets for quick and easy reference, particularly as they confronted the tempests that often dominate the legislative process:

Freedom, Responsibility, and Opportunity:
Preparing Florida for the 21st Century
—SPEAKER TOM FEENEY

1. **Less Government:** Does the bill tend to reduce government regulations, size of government, or eliminate entitlements or unnecessary programs?
2. **Lower Taxes:** Does the bill promote individual responsibility in spending or reduce taxes or fees?

3. **Personal Responsibility:** Does the bill encourage responsible behavior by individuals and families and encourage them to provide for their own health, safety, education, moral fortitude, or general welfare?
4. **Individual Freedom:** Does the bill increase opportunities for individuals and families to decide, without hindrance or coercion from government, how to conduct their own lives and make personal choices?
5. **Stronger Families:** Does the bill enhance the traditional American family and its power to rear children without excessive interference from the government?

Speaker Feeney understood that in order to lead the frequently chaotic legislative process in the direction he desired, he needed to provide legislators with more than one-line platitudes. Legislators needed to know his credo so they could craft and define their proposals in light of its precepts, if they so chose.

2. READ IT REGULARLY

A written summary of your most essential principles and values will not help you very much unless you regularly review it—so do not hide it away in a journal or file drawer. You may want to put yours in the front of your daily planner. Or hang it on a plaque over your desk or on your refrigerator at home for all to see. Maybe you'd like to inscribe it on the screensaver on your computer. One of my friends input hers on the default page of her palmtop organizer. Another friend has an abbreviated version of his on the LCD screen on his cellular phone. Choose whatever place works best to remind you to regularly reaffirm what you are about and why.

3. MAKE IT THE STARTING POINT

Whenever big decisions are required, whenever courses of action must be determined, and whenever overwhelming crises strike, it is time to go back to your first principles and begin there. Your list of principles will serve as a reality check and help you set a course correction if necessary. A review of your most revered principles will help put everything in perspective and will make the path ahead a bit less uncertain. And it will enable you to do what you must, when you must.

We take this first step alone; then we communicate our ideals to others. When I found myself in the center of the storm, my first, most vital action was to begin at the beginning, by recalling why I had sought public service in the first place.

My second critical step was to reiterate for my staff and myself our duty, our responsibility, and our privilege to follow and enforce the law—and that we made certain that everyone within our sphere of influence acted with integrity. I remembered my oath of office, in which I swore to "support, protect, and defend the Constitution and government of the United States and of the state of Florida" and to "well and faithfully perform the duties of" the office of secretary of state of the state of Florida. I reminded myself of what I believed, what I knew, and what mattered most. That made all the difference.

Only a firm grasp on my own cherished principles could serve as an antidote to the media barrage that came next.

* * *

MYTH CONCEPTION:
MILITARY BALLOTS, WAR ROOMS,
AND HARD DRIVES, OH, MY!

The difference between the right word and the almost right word is like the difference between lightning and the lightning bug. Take care therefore of what you say, when you say it, and to whom.
—MARK TWAIN

Imagine you report for a major newspaper. What if you and twenty-three of your reporter colleagues spent six months and $1 million chasing a story—but found there was no story? What would you do with the 13,000-word article you and your colleagues produced, which contained no real news?

If you worked for the *New York Times*, you might cagily insert innuendo that you hope will produce something newsworthy, especially knowing other media outlets will pick up your story. You hope that these other media outlets will draw the appropriate inferences from your innuendo, thus manufacturing the story that you could not credibly create.

This scenario is exactly what happened when the *New York Times* released its long-awaited "exposé" of Florida's treatment of the absentee ballots cast in the 2000 presidential election by our men and women in uniform who were serving overseas. The 13,000-word article "broke" the news that everyone already knew—that controversy had existed throughout Florida concerning the disparate ways in which the independently elected officials in Florida's sixty-seven counties tabulated overseas absentee ballots during the recount period. A Gore operative had circulated a memo instructing Democratic observers in each county how to challenge these ballots, despite the Gore campaign's oft-repeated theme, "Count every vote."

The *New York Times* had a major problem. Their own expert indicated that any discrepancies in the counting that favored George W. Bush, if reversed, would likely not have been enough to change the results in Florida. The morning of the article's publication, buried in the middle of their news section, former Clinton strategist George Stephanopoulos stated on national television that despite twenty-four reporters, $1 million, and 13,000 words, the *New York Times* article had broken no new ground. Moreover, despite their reporters' review of more than one million documents and e-mails from my office, the *New York Times* could not find its magic memo linking me to the Bush campaign (which, of course, never existed) that it so desperately needed for its story. Hence the paper tried to manufacture news by (1) claiming that I had intentionally confused county officials concerning the Florida laws and regulations that governed the counting of overseas military ballots; (2) breathlessly reporting that I had allowed "Republican operatives" to set up a "war room" in my office (the unstated implication being, of course, that these "operatives" were Bush campaign flunkies sent to direct my decisions during the recount); and (3) suggesting that I had "possibly" violated Florida's expansive public records laws because my assistant general counsel had refused *Times* reporter David Barstow's request to fish through our computer hard drives, since our release of more than one million documents and e-mails to Mr. Barstow had been insufficient to quell his unfounded suspicion that some incriminating memo still existed that we had not provided to him.

Happily, the *Times* story died a quick death on the national media scene. *Newsweek* columnist Jonathan Alter commented, "the gigantic *New York Times* article on overseas absentee military ballots in Florida is already lining bird cages." Nevertheless, the *Times'* three carefully placed allegations about me ignited a firestorm in the Florida media.

The myth that the *Times* perpetrated about the information I conveyed to county supervisors of elections concerning the laws and regulations that governed the counting of overseas military ballots was easy to dispel. My Division of Elections had issued a news release that attempted to summarize the applicable statute and Department of State regulation, which even the division concluded was confusing. Because the division concluded that the law and regulation were too complex to be summarized without creating confusion, we issued another news release the very next day that included, verbatim, the text of the statute and the regulation. Of course, the *Times* failed to mention that the division had issued this second, clarifying news release several days before the absentee ballots were actually counted.

When we raised that fact, Mr. Barstow apparently claimed that we had never provided him with a copy of the second news release. Poppycock. The second news release was in a folder that Division of Elections Director Clay Roberts gave Mr. Barstow to inspect at his leisure.

Even given this clarification, however, the news media continued to fixate on the falsehood the *Times* planted that I had instructed the counties to use a more liberal standard for counting overseas absentee ballots than the law permitted (thereby, so they thought, confirming their notion that I had interpreted the law strictly on manual recounts during the protest phase, denying the Gore camp's demands for flexibility, while interpreting the law with flexibility when it came to military absentee ballots likely to favor George W. Bush).

Amazingly, the media had selectively forgotten that Democratic Attorney General Bob Butterworth, who had served as chair of the Gore campaign in Florida, had written the memo to the counties that encouraged a more liberal counting standard for overseas absentee ballots. This development had hardly escaped the media's attention when it happened, but they conveniently forgot about it. Mr. Butterworth did not help clarify matters when he wrote a letter addressed to me (which he also dutifully released to the media) denying that he had encouraged a more liberal counting standard.

The facts were clear, however. To be valid and counted, an overseas absentee ballot had to pass two tests, one required by the statute, the other required by the Department of State regulation. The first test required that a foreign postmark appear on all overseas absentee ballots to provide proof that a ballot was mailed from an overseas location.

The second test required proof that a ballot was cast on or before the date of the election. This proof could be satisfactorily provided in one of two ways: (1) if the voter had signed and dated the ballot by Election Day, or (2) if the postmark that enabled the ballot to pass the first test bore a date that was on or before the date of the election.

The news releases issued by the Division of Elections insisted that to be valid and counted, overseas absentee ballots had to pass *both* tests. Attorney General Butterworth, by contrast, opined that federal law had made the first test unnecessary. In other words, I stated that a ballot that was signed and dated by Election Day must also bear a foreign postmark. According to Attorney General Butterworth, a ballot that had been signed and dated by Election Day did not need a foreign postmark. The standard I announced *did not* favor the Bush campaign's desire for more liberal counting standards; the standard Mr. Butterworth proposed *did* favor those more liberal counting standards. Case closed.

Of course, I believe that the law should never make it more difficult for our military men and women to vote, particularly when they put their lives on the line every day to protect our right to vote. The law was the law, however, and I strove to uphold it, regardless of the consequences to either campaign. We made changing this law a centerpiece of our successful election reform efforts in 2001.

The "guilt by association" myth that the *Times* created with its reference to a "war room" that "Republican operatives" allegedly set up in my office was tougher to dispel. The Department of State was in between communications directors at the time the recount crisis erupted; however, I required immediate assistance in creating accurate public statements regarding the law.

Therefore, I turned to a friend of many years, Adam Goodman. My chief of staff, Benjamin McKay, acted quickly to bring Adam on board as an unpaid volunteer. While Adam had worked for Republican candidates for various offices in the past, he never acted as an emissary for the Bush campaign. In fact, Adam has never worked for *any* Bush campaign. Most, if not all, media sources assumed that "Republican operative" meant "Bush operative" and not simply "communications guru."

Meanwhile, another mutual friend, Mac Stipanovich, asked a colleague to call us on his behalf to volunteer his counsel. I appreciated the moral support that Mac's years of political experience and his knack for incisive commentary provided us. Contrary to widely published but erroneous reports, Mac did not play a decisive or even essential role in formulating the positions we took during the recount controversy. He was never present in our private briefings with our legal counsel and election division staff.

At the beginning of the recount period, I had erected a firewall between my office and any partisan activity. I informed everyone of the duty to maintain this firewall in no uncertain terms, and as far as I know, all staff members and volunteers kept their word to me that they would not conduct partisan activity in connection with their work for me.

The "war room" to which the *Times* referred actually consisted of nothing but two antiquated computers we had installed in the conference room near my office so my staff could work together on the public statements we released to the media.

The greatest media frenzy occurred over the *Times'* allegation that we had violated Florida's expansive public records laws. This allegation arose from a simple, innocent (and ultimately mistaken) statement that my assistant general counsel made in a letter to the *New York Times'* attorney, in which he addressed our reasons for not permitting the fishing expedition that the *Times'* reporters sought to conduct through the hard drives of the conference room computers (in the *Times'* words, "the war room computers").

My assistant general counsel stated that "the drives of these machines were reformatted and the software reloaded when these machines were reassigned," after the recount period ended. He made this statement because (as many computer professionals understand) the standard practice of the Department of State's technical staff is to reformat the hard drive of any computer that is transferred to a different user, to facilitate the installation of a customized package of software for that new user. Reformatting occurs *only* after all public records contained on such hard drives have been printed out or saved to another disk, so as to preserve them according to law. As all public records had been preserved as hard copies or on other disks, my assistant general counsel was simply stating that the computers in question had been subjected to the same standard procedure as any other computer within the Department of State, and that the *Times* already had in its possession all public records created on those computers during the recount period, as its reporters had requested.

Our explanation did not quench the media's thirst for controversy, however.

Later, when our investigation showed the computers in question had not yet been reformatted, we decided to quell all suspicion by taking the unprecedented step of releasing those hard drives to every media outlet that wished to inspect them—a measure that Florida law did not require us to take and that no other elected official has ever taken, to my knowledge. I doubt that any other elected official ever will.

A consortium of major media organizations throughout Florida hired a nationally renowned expert, Ontrack Data International, Inc., to inspect the drives. Ontrack found that the hard drives had not been tampered with in any way, shape, or form, and produced all documents on the hard drives for the media to view.

The results? No documents whatsoever on the hard drives indicated partisan activity in my office during the recount. The media found only two documents that the Bush campaign had e-mailed to my office—eight months *before* the recount. Did members of the media retract their innuendo that I had permitted partisan activity in my office during the recount? I regret to report they did not. Instead, they focused on the two documents they found, *which were not even created in my office.* Who has control over the e-mail one receives?

I find it truly amazing what you can accomplish if you are an embarrassed, but creative, national newspaper with an ax to grind and no real story to report.

TOP TEN LIST:
Worldview Books

When I get a little money, I buy books;
and if there is any left, I buy food and clothes.
—DESIDERIUS ERASMUS

I am a reader; I always have been. Books have been influential in shaping my thinking at every stage of my life and career. I have read dozens of books that have helped in the formulation of my worldview—classics, novels, biographies, practical philosophies, and policy analyses. But only a handful helped me fully grasp the importance of clearly articulating my first principles. Among those, some of my favorites include the following:

1. *How Should We Then Live?* by Francis Schaeffer (Crossway). This survey of the chief cultural trends throughout Western civilization is brilliant and has played an enormous role in shaping my view of the world.

2. *Thinking in Time: the Uses of History for Decision-Makers* (Free Press) and *Presidential Power: the Politics of Leadership* (Wiley), both by Richard E. Neustadt. These books are among the best published by Harvard's finest and are part of the university's most profound courses.

3. *My Utmost for His Highest* by Oswald Chambers (Barbour). I read this book daily and have written in its margins over the decades. No doubt it has been a powerful influence in my life.

4. *Exodus* and *Trinity,* both by Leon Uris (Bantam). I have read a number of Leon Uris's books, but these two have had an exceptional impact upon my worldview. *Exodus* changed my life, particularly with respect to my perceptions of Israel. *Trinity* made me weep.

5. *The Book of Virtue: A Treasury of Great Moral Stories* edited by William J. Bennett (Simon & Schuster). Through this masterful survey of some of history's great messages, Bill Bennett once again demonstrated his firm grasp upon what matters most.

6. *A Severe Mercy* by Sheldon Vanauken (Harper). An exquisite novel about life, love, giving and pain . . . and what really matters most in life. I first read this powerful book at age sixteen and have returned to it again and again.

7. *Politics of Diplomacy: Revolution, War and Peace, 1989-1992* by James A. Baker III, with Thomas M. Defrank (Putnam). My first encounter with Secretary Baker and the present United States Trade Representative Robert Zoellick from afar. Through this book and my subsequent direct personal experience with them, I have gained an understanding of the power of action when infused with integrity and purpose.

8. *Leadership Without Easy Answers* by Ronald A. Heifetz (Belknap). This is truly a fascinating book concerning systemic human behavior and how we can grow from the knowledge of those seemingly preconditioned responses; it is also used as a text for the leadership course at Harvard. I often reread portions of this book during the recount. The newest sequel with Marty Linsky promises to be even more illuminating.

9. Several children's books have influenced my worldview since early in life and have helped to shape my values and spur my creativity: *The Chronicles of Narnia* by C. S. Lewis (Harpercollins); *The Giving Tree* by Shel Silverstein (Harpercollins); *Hope for the Flowers* by Trina Paulus (Paulist Press); *The Velveteen Rabbit* by Margery Williams

(Doubleday); the *Cat in the Hat* series by Dr. Seuss (Random House); and *Lord of the Rings* by J. R. R. Tolkien (Houghton Mifflin). Okay, so that makes my top ten list longer than ten! But that's the way it is with books.

10. The Bible. How can I explain the most important book on the list to me? The only reason I possess a worldview is because of this book. It is responsible for my first principle: it provides my hope for myself and for the world.

There Is a God

Religion will come and go, but God remains.
—VICTOR HUGO

Well, I plan on being here
For a long time;
Watching you grow up;
Watching you fly away.
I plan on crying at your wedding;
Saying goodbye to my little boys;
And, hello, nice to meet you,
To the men you'll some day be;
Growing old with your mother;
Hold her hand all the way;
Falling in love with her;
Every single day.

But should I die before you wake,
There's something I would want to say:
Love life with all your might.
Love peace but be willing to fight.
Love beauty and train your sight,
Nurture your appetite,
For beauty, goodness, and truth.
Be strong and be brave.
Believe and be saved.
For there is a God.

Be men of faith and courage;
A little crazy a little bold;
Seek to find your mission;
Fear God and fear not men;
And believe me when I tell you,
Oh I wish you only joy.
And if you wish to find your life,
You must give it away.

Then when you die you will wake
In the arms of the One you pray your soul to take:
Love life with all your life.
Love peace but be willing to fight.
Love beauty and train your sight,
Nurture your appetite,
For beauty, goodness, and truth.
Be strong and be brave.
Believe and be saved.
For there is a God.

Wes King, my brother-in-law, says of this song, "I was on an airplane coming home from somewhere, and we went through the most violent turbulence I have ever experienced. I thought for a few eternal minutes that the plane might go down. I picked up the nearest paper—a sick bag—and wrote down these very words."

PRINCIPLE 2

REMEMBER YOUR RAISING

We cannot permit the biases of other persons-or our opinions of ourselves-to blind us. When push comes to shove, we need perspective. We derive our greatest understanding from our examination of our roots, our upbringing, our family, and our heritage. No matter where we go or how we get there, we would do well never to forget this fundamental axiom.

People who perform in the public eye have a choice: they may either passively permit their career to shape their life and identity or they can affirmatively decide to use their life and identity to shape their career. Unfortunately, this choice is easier to make in theory than in reality. Sir Walter Scott observed, "Very public people often forget that they ever had private lives. At that point, they lose all perspective. In particular, they lose perspective of those very qualities that enabled them to emerge from the private to the public in the first place and so they are bereft of the benefits of both."

Whether we are public or private people, we each must ask ourselves, "Who am I? What am I really like? What are my strengths and weaknesses? What are my motivations, goals, and priorities?"

The sages of the news media leap at the opportunity to supply answers to these and a thousand other questions about anyone who endures the glare of the spotlight. "Up close and personal" profiles, "in-depth" investigative reports, and "exclusive inside perspectives" purport to tell "the whole story." We are led to believe they can capture the essence of a person in a single eight-hundred-word editorial, a thirty-second sound bite, or a "profile" piece that strings together randomly collected factoids in a manner designed to match popular perceptions.

Thus, a consumer of today's twenty-four-hour cable news coverage and wall-to-wall programming can easily be convinced of the "reality" of a ubiquitous media-generated image. As we struggle to manage the pressures that the hectic pace of our society exerts, we may find little time to look behind these manufactured personae—nor do we remember that we should. But as consumers of today's "news as entertainment," we must all beware. Caricatures can quickly supplant analysis. Perception becomes reality in the eyes of too many people.

On Election Day 2000, hardly anyone outside the state of Florida had ever heard of me. One week later, hardly a soul anywhere in the nation—and perhaps in the world—who had access to the media had not heard of me. Many people formed a strong conviction about me, and about my decisions and my intentions, based solely on what they had seen, heard, and read via the news media.

Night after night, I hardly recognized myself as I watched the television coverage of the recount controversy. I was astonished by the distorted descriptions I read in newspapers and magazines of my life, my family, my work, my career, and my motivations. Many accounts had no basis in fact whatsoever.

Amidst such an environment, I found it essential to purposefully and deliberately remember who I really was (and am), and why I entered public service. Otherwise, I saw how easily I could become so consumed with those false images and misperceptions that they would begin to dominate my life and my calling. I would begin to spend more time trying to prove the news media wrong than endeavoring to do what I know is right.

Principled leaders do not permit themselves to become distracted by the temptation to be what they are not. The bright lights of fame and attention do not blind them. Neither cajolery nor applause fools them. Blistering, disingenuous attacks cannot destroy them. Remembering the trials and triumphs of their forebears, they chart their course in order to apply the lessons and share the blessings of those experiences.

Fortunately for me, I count my blessings, and I have many blessings to share.

HOME ON THE RANCH

I am a Florida girl, born at the naval base in Key West and raised in "Imperial" Polk County. Our town, Bartow, in the central part of the Sunshine State, is a wonderful world of high school football games and monumental Halloween parades, entrepreneurial businesses and no-nonsense politics, neighborhood cookouts and citrus groves, hardscrabble intellect and bootstrap simplicity. My father is an independent community banker. My grandfather was a citrus grower and a cattle rancher. I learned from both that success does not simply happen. It occurs only as a result of hard work and long hours, diligence, wisdom, persistence, and vision. I was an eyewitness to the American Dream fulfilled in the lives of ordinary people, who seized the opportunities that freedom afforded them and hammered out a legacy of prosperity and hope for their children and grandchildren.

For hours upon hours I rode through groves and cow pastures with my grandfather as he inspected trees and calves. I spent countless evenings soaking in the footed bathtub, every limb aching with the satisfied exhaustion that comes after a long day with cowboys, working cattle on horseback or at the cow pens. Such days are some of my fondest memories of Peace River Ranch in Hardee County, Florida.

I was drawn to the horses, more than any other aspect of ranch life. I remember as a small girl riding with the ranch foreman, Delbert Lowe, clinging to the back of his saddle as his quarter horse galloped through the palmettos. Delbert was tall, strong, and kind. Many years of my childhood passed before I realized that he was not the real John Wayne I so admired in the movies.

My brother, my sister, and I attended Fourth of July rodeos in Arcadia, an annual highlight of our summers. The barrel racers, calf ropers, and bronco riders were among our first heroes. When we returned to the ranch, we pretended to be them, or we would play polo (bareback!) with brooms and a basketball.

Recently I was honored to return to Arcadia and ride on a magnificent horse named "Turbo," (thank goodness he did not live up to his name amidst the sirens, horns, and firecrackers!) with Judge Don T. Hall in the Fourth of July Parade! I was flooded with memories, especially the time when, at age four or five, I rode behind Delbert, clutching the leather straps attached to leather stars on the back of his saddle as he raced around the arena. I saw the very spot where I feared I would slip off with 8,000 people watching! Fortunately, my little hands held fast. Now, decades later, people sought me out to tell me stories of my family—particularly my mother, who was a barrel-racer. They said when I was three months old she carried me on a horse in this parade, so the event was a wonderful homecoming for me.

> *To comprehend the history of a thing is to unlock the mysteries of its present, and more, to disclose the profundities of its future.*
> —**HILAIRE BELLOC**

My grandfather gave me a quarter horse for my tenth birthday. As many of my friends also rode horses, we spent magical afternoons riding, as well as evenings when a full moon could light our trail. We raced through the dunes of the nearby phosphate mines, pretending that each of us was Lawrence of Arabia! I feel profoundly fortunate to have grown up in such an idyllic place.

Academics, athletics, church, family, and friends constituted mainstays of my upbringing. As a family, we enjoyed an immense variety of sports together. Between my father's workouts and avid pursuit of tennis (he still plays at high noon in Florida's heat!) and my mother's keen devotion to white-water canoeing, kayaking, and camping, my brother, Walt, my sister, Fran, and I enjoyed many opportunities to stretch ourselves in body and spirit.

God blessed me with an immediate family, together with grandparents, first cousins, second cousins, great aunts and uncles, and other extended relations, who remained very close throughout my young adulthood. As children, we learned to celebrate life (and most holidays together) with vigor, to work hard, and to achieve so we could pass on the gifts we had received by virtue of a fortunate birth.

My father, George, is a successful banker who takes great pleasure in his work, still attending three or four meetings most weeknights and more on weekends. He bought this bank for twice its market value three decades ago, incurring a significant amount of personal debt as a result. He labored under the burden of this debt during the double-digit inflation of the 1970s, eventually earning the money to pay it off through his outstanding stewardship. As the bank's chairman and chief executive officer, he has grown the bank's assets by 11,000 percent! He works diligently within both the associations of the American Bankers and Florida Bankers, the latter of which he was president.

My father's example demonstrates that regardless of how an opportunity originally presents itself, hard work, determination, leadership and vision can enable one to enjoy tremendous success. He approaches life with a zest and joy that I have always sought to emulate. He is perhaps the most generous, wise, and kind man I have ever known.

My remarkable mother, Harriett, possesses the charm of a southern lady, the intelligence of a university professor, and the resilience and toughness of a Wall Street mogul. She exudes an infectious spirit of honest selflessness. They are perhaps the two most energetic persons I have yet to encounter, so any such positive attribute I may have came from a genetic double-dose.

My brother, sister, and I love our parents dearly, and we often talk about how amazing they are when we look back at our childhood. They focused strongly on education, but equally upon life experiences. They are creative, intelligent, adventuresome, hardworking, thoughtful . . . and fun! Both were stars in their high schools and colleges—class presidents, sports captains, or valedictorians—but they never tried to push us to follow in their footsteps. They wanted us to find our own way, the way that best suited our characters and destinies.

I remember my grandmother telling of an auto accident in which my mother was injured during her senior year in high school. One week later my grandparents dutifully took her to the train station to attend her freshman year of college with her jaw wired shut! I am awestruck by her courage and fortitude—imagine going away alone for the first time in this condition.

One of my favorite stories occurred during our parents' senior year. As student body president at Georgia Tech, my father stood up to the segregationist governor of Georgia, Marvin Griffin, by sending a telegram on behalf of the student body publicly apologizing for the governor's statement that Georgia Tech would not participate in the Sugar Bowl because the University of Pittsburgh had an African-American playing on their team. My father sent a telegram December 5, 1955 stating that "the student body of Georgia Tech sincerely apologizes for the unwarranted actions of Georgia's governor. We look forward to seeing your entire team and your student body at the Sugar Bowl" in New Orleans.

My younger brother, Walt—my over six-foot-tall brother who apparently inherited my share of height—excelled in every sport he attempted. But when he began to pursue all that college life had to offer at Georgia Tech, we heard little of sports. He surprised all of us when he managed to "walk on" the Georgia Tech football team during his senior year, as well as when he still managed to conquer the Iron Man Competition in Hawaii years later.

Walt now owns a renowned restaurant, Syzygy, in Aspen, Colorado. As a result of his residence in the Rockies, the skill and speed of his skiing have so far surpassed the rest of us, we do not even attempt to compete. He also climbs the highest peaks in exotic lands and swims in the Amazon in piranha-infested waters (with a guide watching in a dugout canoe), terrifying us all. We often encourage him to return to his golf. Walt has the biggest heart and kindest demeanor of all our family members. The velvet hammer, he acts as a special conscience for me on many occasions.

My younger sister, Fran, lives near Nashville, Tennessee, with her husband, singer and songwriter Wes King, and their darling twin boys, Harrison and Mitch. Fran excelled in sports as well, lettering in swimming and tennis on our high school teams. She continues to apply her education from Vanderbilt, Oxford, and Exeter to a writing career while passing along to her sons the unique childhood we enjoyed together. She is brilliant, constantly amazing us all with her keen wit and depth, yet retaining the ability to make me laugh until I cry with almost each encounter. She has been an extraordinary alter ego for me as I tried out ideas for this book; she has been the salve as well as instigator—whatever was necessary—for the problems I encountered with what turned out to be a huge project.

I adored my grandmothers, B and Sweetmama. I particularly spent as much time as possible during my childhood visiting B and "Papa G," my grandfather G. W. Harris, at their home in Americus, Georgia. B had two sons, and I was her first granddaughter, so I suppose I constituted somewhat of a novelty for her. B was full of love, as well as being delightfully mischievous and engaging company.

While exposing me as a child to how interesting adults could be, B suffered neither fools nor temper tantrums from children very well. She made sure I understood the consequences of my actions. On one occasion when I was a little girl, I disagreed with her directions, and I made certain I told her so. I said that I was going back to Florida. Without breaking stride, she packed my clothes in a small bandanna, put the bundle on a stick, and told me to stand on the curb to hitch a ride home. She allowed me to return only when I apologized, less than one hour later.

This memorable experience constituted just one of the many valuable lessons B taught me—to be accountable for myself, and to mean what I say or to hold my tongue. Yet she was patient and compassionate with me as well. As a child I was terrified that her smoking would harm her health. I would obsessively search out her cigarettes and give the cartons to the men who came to collect the trash. This almost became a ritual between us as her hiding places became increasingly more difficult to locate. But she never reprimanded me for those actions. Years ago, B gave me a plaque. It bore the instruction she reiterated whenever I left home to visit friends: "Remember your raising."

My husband, Anders, and I spend more time in Americus now. We celebrate Thanksgiving with my father's brother Bill and his wife Ann and family in their 1800s cabin on our family farm. During this time, I have the opportunity to refresh myself with the charm of the familiar and the warmth of memories, especially when I visit with B's sister, Josephine.

Josie tells incredible stories. She took care of my great grandfather "Papa" Easterling until he died at age 101. She ran the poignant Andersonville Prison Museum and store. Today, this site serves as a moving memorial to our United States Prisoners of War.

My uncle Bill serves on the national board for Habitat for Humanity and as a result has impacted the lives of my cousins, Bill, Lee, and David, dramatically. They have biked across the U.S. to raise money for Habitat, as well as built homes and hiked in Africa (where they bungee-cord jumped from Victoria Falls with my brother—

twice!) They started the first cooperative in Central America to directly assist the coffee growers. My uncle was also on the boards of the Hope Foundation, which provides college scholarships for Georgia students and was the model for Florida's Bright Futures Scholarships; the Sumter County Initiative that *eliminated* sub-standard housing throughout the county; and he and Ann worked diligently with many friends to ensure the preservation of the beautiful Windsor Hotel in Americus.

Thanksgiving in 2000 turned out to be particularly memorable. The farm was beautiful; we shot clay pigeons and played horseshoes. My uncle and father tease one another unmercifully about everything, including who is the better shot. Trying to gain leverage, they engaged my husband, thinking they would both better this Swede. To our utter amazement, Anders hit every single one. The holiday was a wonderful getaway, until we were relaxing—all four generations—watching the TV. The only channel with reception was airing *Inside Edition*. Who should appear on the screen—but my father! He had said he would not talk to reporters, but what father could stand by and do nothing while watching his daughter being filleted in front of his very eyes? The reporters tried hard to ruffle his feathers, but he did exceedingly well. However, I had to go outside and walk around the field awhile before I could tell him so. The next day, we went to the historic Rylander Theatre to watch *It's a Wonderful Life* and sing along with the live organ music. To my astonishment, strangers came from their seats to encourage me. My heart swelled with emotion and gratitude, just like the old-timey organ music.

As we prepared to leave Sunday to return to Tallahassee, I casually asked if perhaps they would like to caravan down to the Florida capitol for the certification. Everyone had somewhere else to go—but after a pregnant pause, they enthusiastically agreed. I gathered with my family in my Secretary of State office, and just prior to going down to the cabinet room for the presidential election certification ceremony, I asked my sister's three-year-old twins what they thought I should say. Harrison answered, "Tell the people thank-you." Minutes later, as I gazed at my beautiful family in the audience at the certification, they meant more to me than ever before.

Anders and I had made a longtime commitment to one of our best friends, Heloisa Jennings, to attend her birthday party that night. A friend who is a pilot instructor had agreed to fly us from Tallahassee to Sarasota immediately after the certification. What I did not know was that he would have me fly his plane (as I have often done, but not under these circumstances), and we would fly over the Gulf of Mexico on a moonless night using instruments, without the auto-pilot, which required my total concentration. After the unremitting crises of the recount and the culmination of the tension at the certification, the experience was utterly peaceful. While flying suspended in a starlit sky, I was able to get my feet back on the ground.

On my mother's side of the family, Sweetmama provided the glue while my grandfather Ben Hill Griffin Jr. compiled an extraordinary record of success. Granddaddy began with the ten acres that he received as a wedding gift, and he grew that asset into hundreds of thousands of acres of ranch land and citrus groves. He became a state senator, a hardworking citrus grower and cattleman, and a generous benefactor to his alma mater, the University of Florida, although he never had the opportunity to graduate. He saved a beautiful old building, Floyd Hall, and to his credit this type of historic preservation on the University of Florida campus has since become the model for preservation. My grandfather donated to the university simply because it had given him the education he needed to advance. He was grateful, and everlastingly loyal. Yet he was extremely demanding; perhaps that trait contributed in large part to his success. He is part of the last generation written about in one of my favorite Florida books, *A Land Remembered*, by Pulitzer Prize-winning author Patrick Smith. This story is truly Florida's *Gone with the Wind*. I was proud to induct

Mr. Smith into Florida's highest cultural circle, the Artists Hall of Fame, and his name now graces the marble walls at the capitol.

Besides a loving family, our greatest blessing growing up was our neighborhood in Bartow, which teemed with children. We played tag, hide and seek, Ping-Pong, basketball, "go fish," Slip 'N Slide, billiards, and tennis for endless hours. Our neighborhood attracted children who rode their bikes from miles away to join in our softball, football, and "kick the can" games. When our mother blew the whistle that signaled dinnertime, my brother, sister, and I would race the few blocks home.

In many ways, our neighborhood seemed like extended family. I believe that this environment had something to do with the array of leaders it has produced. Over the years, our neighbors became chief justice of the Florida Supreme Court (Chief Justice Steve Grimes swore me in when I became state senator from Florida's Twenty-fourth District), president of the American Bar Association, *Time*'s Man of the Year, and one of Tom Brokaw's favorite subjects in *The Greatest Generation*, (Chesterfield Smith swore me in as secretary of state), and two Florida Bar presidents (Bill Henry and John Frost lived just blocks away). U.S. Senator and Florida Governor Spessard Holland, U.S. Senator and Florida Governor Lawton Chiles, and former U.S. Rep. Andy Ireland have called Polk County their home. Senator Holland lived just a few miles away, and his granddaughter was one of my first and closest friends. A member of the United States Congress (current U.S. Representative Adam Putnam), and a renowned general (James Van Fleet) lived just blocks away.

I was a Lyndon Baines Johnson Congressional Intern for both Senator Chiles and Congressman Ireland while at college in our nation's capital. Current U.S. Senator and former Florida Governor Bob Graham was "adopted" at my parents' home in a ceremony declaring he should have been born in Imperial Polk County, but a hurricane blew the stork off course to Miami-Dade County instead.

The Girl Scouts played a formative role in my upbringing, and I have certainly learned to respect their motto, *Be prepared!* Fran and I have long been involved in Scouting, as we proudly tell anyone who will listen. My mother and her dearest friend Bobbie Henry served as Girl Scout leaders or council members for decades. They made Scouting in our area an exciting and popular endeavor. Waiting lists for their troop grew longer every year. These women were truly taskmasters, however. They made certain we worked diligently to earn many badges. They also pushed us to participate in the "Year-Round Camper" program, which entailed one camping trip per month—regardless of football season, hurricane season, holiday season, or the seasons' weather in general. Because of their encouragement and their motivating example, several of us worked very hard to attain the rank of First Class Scout, Girl Scouting's Eagle Scout equivalent.

> *A contempt of the monuments and the wisdom of the past, may be justly reckoned one of the reigning follies of these days, to which pride and idleness have equally contributed.*
> —SAMUEL JOHNSON

Summer camp also played a vital role in my personal development. While Walt went to the Y camp in Athens, Georgia, Fran and I attended Camp Greystone in Tuxedo, North Carolina. This experience helped us develop a commitment to a strong body, a sound mind, and a deeply grounded spiritual life—a foundation that continues to feed and inform my character and principles. Not only did the program provide opportunities to learn new sports (archery, riflery, sailing, fencing), it promoted close friendships and spiritual growth away from home. Fran and I still treasure the friendships forged during our summers at Greystone, and draw inspiration from lessons we learned there.

In sum, I deeply understand and appreciate the great gifts I have received in my life and the obligation—and privilege—to "give back." Even so, nothing means more to me on this earth than my faith. It is truly what matters most.

UNDERSTAND YOUR LEGACY

Principled leaders understand the concept of legacy. They purposefully stand on the shoulders of those who have gone before them while striving to pass on to future generations the blessings they have received. When they find themselves amidst a crisis, they find refuge and sanctuary in the certain knowledge of who they are and from whence they have come.

In addition to our personal legacy—the gifts we receive from our family and heritage—each of us benefits from the riches left to all of humanity by the great leaders of the past. The list of men and women whom I personally admire is long, but one favorite is an author who has managed to impart endless joy and wonder along with his poignant lessons: J. R. R. Tolkien.

One of the most popular and successful films of 2001 was Peter Jackson's adaptation of the first installment of Tolkien's *Lord of the Rings*. Even fans unfamiliar with the books from which the movie was taken cheered Frodo's bravery, Gandalf's selflessness, Sam's loyalty, and the determination of the entire fellowship to accomplish the task entrusted to them by the Council of Elrond. The timeless theme of peaceful people rousing themselves to combat a callous and determined evil resonated deeply with Americans still grieving the tragedy of September 11. Tolkien consistently presented believable portraits of moral courage in the face of hopelessness and danger that we can continue to appreciate today.

John Ronald Reuel Tolkien did not choose to lead in the arenas of politics or business. Rather, he led in the realm of the spirit. The moral force of *Lord of the Rings* reflects the moral fiber of a man who sought to carry forth the legacy of his courageous mother, Mabel. Through sheer force of will to persevere, Mabel Tolkien managed to instill her love of nature, learning, and religion in Ronald, while herself enduring tragedy, hardship, and heartache.

Mabel Tolkien and her husband, Arthur, a banker, were living in South Africa when she gave birth to their son, Ronald. When Ronald was three, Mabel moved back to England, where Ronald's brother Hilary was born. Mabel fully expected that her husband would join the family when he found a replacement for his job at the Bank of Africa. Their reunion never occurred. A bout with yellow fever weakened Arthur Tolkien, rendering him unable to travel. His condition deteriorated for a year. In February 1896, Mabel prepared to return with her sons to South Africa to care for her ailing husband. Before they could depart, she received news that Arthur had died of a brain hemorrhage.

Mabel decided to move to the country with her sons. She found a home in Sarehole, an idyllic country village that Tolkien later used as an inspiration for Hobbiton, Frodo's hometown in *Lord of the Rings*. There, Tolkien developed a deep affection for nature. While living in Sarehole, Mabel schooled her sons in history, literature, and languages. She fired their imaginations with classic adventure stories and fed Ronald's early appetite for words with lessons in French, German, Greek, and Latin. When Ronald was eight, Mabel Tolkien introduced him to one of the greatest influences in his life: the Catholic Church.

Mabel's conversion to Catholicism in the spring of 1900 brought disdain and estrangement from her family. With the sole exception of one of Ronald's uncles, who contributed school fees, they discontinued the financial assistance they had contributed since Arthur's death. Strapped for cash, Mabel and her sons moved to a low-income, industrial area near Ronald's new school. The city environment intensified Tolkien's love of nature, while the hardships his mother endured intensified his love for the Church.

When Ronald Tolkien was twelve, his mother died from complications of recently diagnosed diabetes. Believing that his mother had been a martyr for her faith, this tragedy cemented Tolkien's own religious attachment. In turn, Tolkien's fervent commitment to the Church provided the moral framework that so many readers have seen, acknowledged, and embraced in his works.

The *Lord of the Rings,* in all of its grandeur and majesty, would not exist without the influence of Mabel Tolkien. She exposed her son to fresh air and grass and trees; she instilled in him a love of stories and words; and she nourished his devotion to his faith. These values shaped him into the unique visionary who would create the world of Middle Earth. During the long years he spent writing *Lord of the Rings,* as Tolkien faced the responsibilities and distractions of raising a family and teaching college, his mother's legacy remained his wellspring of inspiration.

Mabel Tolkien purposely provided an environment for her sons that would serve as a framework for vibrant and successful lives, and she left a legacy of courage, determination, and devotion. J. R. R. Tolkien understood and applied the power of this legacy through the moral leadership his art continues to provide today.

THE FAMILIAR SOUND OF FAMILY

One of the comforting influences I enjoyed during the recount was hearing the familiar voices of my younger brother and sister on the phone; we spoke every day and night. My brother, Walt, combines a soft voice and kind nature with the strength to exercise tough love when it is necessary. His encouragement and admonitions have sustained me during some of my most difficult times. Fran and I spoke of the obvious things that sisters talked about across the nation during this time. We also discussed her children and how they were

> *It may be true that he travels farthest who travels alone; but the goal thus reached is not worth reaching.*
>
> —THEODORE ROOSEVELT

changing her life. Her husband, Wes King, often joined our conversations. Together, we tried to refocus each other's minds and hearts upon what matters most.

As they have undertaken the lifelong journey of parenthood, Wes and Fran have placed a high priority upon teaching their sons, Harrison and Mitch, a values system that can empower them and serve as a guide as challenges arise. Uniquely, Wes decided to use his skills as a recording artist to achieve this objective. While the recount crisis raged, he wrote and recorded a CD, *What Matters Most*, which sets forth the life lessons he and Fran wished to share with their sons. Many of these songs are included at the close of these chapters. Wes once told me that he designed this recording as a musical book of Proverbs. Inspired by G. K. Chesterton, George MacDonald, and his own father, Wes's lyrics stress the importance of family, the value of faith, and the true meaning of courage. During the recount, these lyrics inspired me. After the horrific tragedy of September 11, their seeming prescience brought me to tears.

They do not know it now, but one day Harrison and Mitch will look back and realize the wonderful gift their father has given them—a legacy of principles they can draw upon to thrive amidst the inevitable crises of life. When Harrison and Mitch experience their own trials, perhaps they will remember the words of the song their father wrote for them: "Inhabit the trembling, yet be brave."

KEEPING THE HOME FIRES BRIGHT

The importance of family is a frequently neglected topic among leadership materials. This topic usually appears only within the context of "how to keep family from ruining one's career," rather than "how to draw upon family as a source of inspiration." These materials teach the dubious "skills" necessary to isolate our families from our professional lives.

Unfortunately, persons who follow the advice of these guides lose one of the most powerful resources in a leader's treasury. A healthy home provides a setting in which we can examine our most intimate and empowering relationships. We have much to learn and give there, and even more to receive.

No one has taught me more about love, giving, and receiving than my incredible husband, Anders. I could not sustain my vision or energy in the political arena were it not for his unconditional love. He possesses a gift for truth and integrity unmatched by anyone I have known. Louise, his daughter, may be the best reflection of his gifts. She is bright and beautiful inside and out, and she has consistently been kind, gracious, and generous in her acceptance of me and the untold intrusions my lifestyle brings. Louise's caring and strength of character amidst her own personal difficulties inspires me daily. I deeply appreciate her endurance of the slings and arrows directed my way and her unique ways of supporting and encouraging Anders and me.

Anders' brothers, Bengt and Clas reflect the exquisite "raising" by their two wonderful parents. I had the special privilege of meeting their mother just before she died. Their families are so very precious to us, and after they visit us in Sarasota, our home seems so empty when they leave. Clas, his wife Ingrid, and their daughters Susan and Lotta, visit often, fill our lives with joy and laughter, and we miss them daily from visit to visit.

We have much to pass on. As leaders, we miss many of life's most important experiments when we grow detached from family, which ought to draw us all the more closely to our way back home. We are guided along this path when we pause to remember the following.

1. THERE IS NO PLACE LIKE HOME

The family unit remains the cornerstone of society, regardless of the many forms and definitions it can assume today. It constitutes the glue that holds cultures and nations together. When the home begins to break down, the rest of society begins to disintegrate. There is no replacement for the home, and there never will be. The government cannot substitute services for it. Social workers cannot devise programs to supplant it. Educators cannot engineer curricula that can take its place.

Among the first things we learn as children are matters of home and family—our address and phone number, our last name. At home we learn the skills of life that determine our future. Home is where we learn to love, communicate, share, and care. In the family we experience the heights of joy and the depths of sorrow that only familial bonds can evoke.

Sadly, an increasing number of homes fail to provide empowering surroundings. Many homes have become not safe havens but perilous places that endanger the lives of the children and/or spouses they were intended to nurture. Today's leaders are faced with the daunting task of reversing this devastating tide.

2. THE FAMILY CAN CONSTITUTE OUR FIRST AND BEST REFUGE

Like a snug nest, home can provide our primary source of comfort in times of trouble. It is here that we can run for an embrace, here that we can find consolation. Home can offer the love and support that guide us through the tough times. . . people who understand our emotions without hearing a word . . . a warm hug, a loving wink, a squeeze on the arm, or a kiss on the cheek that produce more confidence than any other outside expressions of reassurance.

> *Those who have no concern for their ancestors will, by simple application of the same rule, have none for their descendants.*
>
> —RICHARD WEAVER

Because love is the backbone of all virtuous deeds and the impetus for all true acts of charity, the love we can find at home calls us back again and again to discover whom we are and where we are going in life. Here, as in no other place, we might share a common vision with a group of people who firmly support us. Because it can nurture character, home often provides a perfect environment for incubating principle. Here we can learn the value of a work ethic, the nature of authority, the purpose of discipline, and the importance of sharing and community. It is often in the home that we first learn there are people who would willingly give their life for us. And thus we learn the value of our very existence.

While many institutions offer alternatives to the resources of the home, nothing else can foster the nurturing that is unique to family life. At home we can seek the answers to life's questions in an environment like none other.

3. THE FAMILY CAN COMPLETE US

According to eighteenth-century British clergyman George Whitefield, "No man is the whole of himself. His family is the rest of him." Healthy family relationships enable us to tie off the loose ends of our experience, to straighten the rumpled corners of our personalities, darn the frayed gaps in our expression, and hem the edges of our interests. Family connections make us better because they make us whole. No one is an island—or to the extent that we are, we suffer. Wise men and women have always known this truth only too well.

4. HEALTHY HOMES AND COMMUNITIES CAN CHANGE US FOREVER

Our fathers and mothers, our brothers and sisters, our children and cousins, aunts and uncles, grandparents, and all our extended relations beyond can have a lingering, lasting impact upon us. Their kindnesses remain with us long after they have departed. Their examples inspire us, and their words continue to influence our thinking.

A strong community constitutes an extension of healthy homes. Each strong family can create a web of selflessness, love, support, and concern that can bind together entire neighborhoods, towns, or even a nation. We are all members of the American family and, ultimately, the human family. As Martin Luther King Jr. wisely observed, "No man has learned to live until he can rise above the narrow confines of his individualistic concerns to the broader concerns of all humanity. Length without breadth is like a self-contained tributary having no outward flow to the ocean. Stagnant, still, and stale it lacks both life and freshness. In order to live creatively and meaningfully, our self-concern must be wedded to other concerns."

Andrew Nelson Lytle, the famed southern agrarian and longtime English professor at the University of Florida, commented, "Of a time, there comes for all of us a poignant moment—a moment when we search for our ultimate calling and destiny. It is there and then that we see ourselves in the speculum of our lives—an ethereal presence staring back at us, a reminder of our place in the world." "Nevertheless," he continued,

> it is not the reflection which confirms our purpose. If we need only see ourselves to be affirmed, we would all be bound by the ties of narcissism, needing only a house of mirrors to comfort us. It is the vision of image upon image that establishes just who we are and what we are to do—it is seeing ourselves in the context of community, of relationships, and of friendships that ultimately gives meaning to our search for meaning and purpose in life. Indeed, no man is an island.

RECOVERING AND SHARING OUR INHERITANCE

According to one of the earliest chroniclers of leadership principles, Samuel Smiles, "Great men are invariably as cognizant of the impact of the past on their thinking and doing as they are of the impact of their philosophy on their thinking and doing." Sociologist James Kullberg agrees: "Leaders are alert to all the factors of life that may influence them—both the factors within and the factors without." Thus, principled leaders are self-aware. They make much of any benefits their background has afforded them, while taking heed of the warnings to which past failures have alerted them. They undertake the various disciplines necessary to remember, and share, any blessings of their raising.

1. KNOW YOUR FAMILY TRAITS

What are your family's triumphs? What are your family's failures? Do you see multigenerational patterns emerging? What can you learn from them? How can you maximize the blessings and avoid the pitfalls? Can you find ways to break old strongholds . . . to recover neglected treasures?

Such questions are hardly trivial. They are not an exercise in pop psychology or feel-good recovery therapy. Rather, they are the sorts of questions effective leaders will regularly ask themselves. They are a healthy aspect of self-examination, personal evaluation, and assessment of one's calling.

2. PUT IT INTO CONTEXT

I once heard that novelist Tom Clancy claimed that he never read reviews of his books, and Sir Laurence Olivier always asserted that he never took notice of what the press said about his work. I confess I have a hard time identifying with this practice. While a sage U.S. senator, Connie Mack, encourages me never to read the local news, I read what people say about me. I look at the articles and check out the websites. I review as many of my e-mails as I possibly can. I even try to catch some of the news broadcasts when I actually have time for television (admittedly, a rarity). I want to know what people are saying, not because I am a masochist or a narcissist, but because I want to be able to appropriately respond to criticism. I make mistakes. I want to know how to correct them. I want to learn how to better communicate my ideas and ideals.

Nevertheless, I strive to put this process of evaluation in its proper context. I must view my clippings, my reviews, my criticisms, and my accolades within the context of who I really am and what I seek to accomplish with my life. I cannot permit unfair personal invectives and inaccurate attacks to inordinately sway me. I cannot allow the biases of others, or even my own PR, to blind me. By remembering my roots, my upbringing, and my family, I refresh my understanding of why I undertake the burdens of public life: to share the blessings I have received, to give back, to make a positive difference as a public servant (servant being the operative word). From those who are given much, much is expected.

3. SHARE THE BLESSINGS OF YOUR LEGACY

Principled leaders share the blessings of their legacy with persons who have not experienced the same good fortune. They strive to embrace their communities with the lessons, experiences, and skills their heritage has bestowed upon them. They avoid a passive acceptance or a benign neglect of our society's ills in which their legacy can become ensnared in the malevolent service of exclusion and elitism.

Whether as camp counselors, mentors, teachers, members of civic or religious organizations, or in other capacities, principled leaders sow the seeds of their harvest. They strive to multiply the blessings of their legacy.

* * *

MYTH CONCEPTION:
SINCE WHEN DID ACHIEVEMENT BECOME A VICE?

We are trying to do a futile thing if we do not know where we came from or what we have been about.
—WOODROW WILSON

When the Gore campaign began to unleash the dogs of war upon me during the difficult recount controversy, I was not inordinately surprised. When Democratic spokesman Chris Lehane called me a "crony of Jeb Bush" and a "lackey for the Bush campaign," I thought he was way off base, but I was hardly caught off guard. When Democratic strategist Paul Begala said that I looked like "Cruella de Vil coming to steal the puppies," I failed to see the relevance, but I was not shocked. When O. J. Simpson's and Klaus von Bulow's attorney Alan Dershowitz called me a "crook," I found it ignorant, but did not feel particularly outraged. Such mud-slinging caricatures, as awful as they are, seem to go with the territory these days.

But I confess that I was taken aback by the way the many media sources (news, not editorial) characterized my personal and family background. According to one widely reprinted wire report, I was little more than "a political dilettante who might be more comfortable passing finger sandwiches at an art gala than managing affairs of state." The *Sunday Telegraph* wrote me off as a "foxy, fashion-crazed, Floridian jet-setter" and a "big-haired multi-millionairess" who was "born to old money." Not surprisingly, the *New York Times* got in on the act by asserting that "in the Florida caste system," I was "a Brahmin of the highest order." My family was compared to the Rockefellers—a "baronial dynasty" according to one report, "privileged blue bloods" according to another. My sister joked that our families were hardworking "rednecks" not "blue bloods!" But the implication was clear: I was not to be taken seriously because I was a spoiled rich kid. The fate of the nation's electoral integrity had somehow fallen into the hands of a pampered incompetent. (Never mind that I had been successful in the business and government arenas and held a master's degree in public administration from Harvard.) I could not be trusted because of my heritage.

Somehow, again, it seemed to escape the notice of these publications that many of our highest-profile leaders came from backgrounds of advantage and are not excoriated for this. But hypocrisy aside, I have frankly always had a very hard time recognizing my family or myself in such descriptions. My grandfather, who labored all his life to transform a ten-acre wedding gift into a phenomenally successful business, did indeed become wealthy in his later years. My father, who owned a small-town bank and successfully built its assets, also worked hard to provide well for his family. At times, I *still* reach him at his office at midnight—hardly "banker's hours." An astute citrus farmer and rancher or a diligent, community-minded banker are hardly the images that come to mind when I think of the privileged rich, the baronial tycoons, or the detached blue blood elites the media love to disdain, albeit selectively.

How is it that a family legacy can be automatically disparaged simply because of its achievement? Since when has success become a vice in America? How did competency, ability, intellect, and accomplishment come to be political liabilities? Would I have enjoyed a better reception with the news editors in Washington, New York, Los Angeles, and London if my parents and grandparents had been woeful failures—or if they had been Democrats? (They were!)

It became painfully clear to me throughout the entire recount ordeal that certain members of the media had little interest in facts. One disturbing aspect about all of these attacks is their intentional inaccuracy. (Reporters often revealed to me that their editors insisted they create a negative story from circumstances that in no way warranted that spin; others have told me that my Harvard education, years of public service, chairmanship of key committees, passage of important bills, or other facts of accomplishment they had included in their stories were distorted or deleted by their "unbiased" editors.) Even more disturbing is the supposition that any kind of intellectual, civic, or financial attainment is fair game for ridicule . . . that the honored virtue of laying up a goodly inheritance for our children has now become a scorned peccadillo.

The genius of America has always been that our opportunities and freedoms allow men and women to achieve, to advance, and to excel. We have always celebrated and honored success. We have always encouraged families to establish legacies of every kind—material and moral, intellectual and spiritual, familial and charitable. We have always appreciated the positive contributions that accomplished men and women can make to succeeding generations. Let us hope that we can think clearly enough to do so again in the days to come.

What Matters Most

Inhabit the trembling, yet be brave.
Embrace your weakness, yet be strong.
Say what you have to say,
But always admit when you're wrong.
Accept who you are, yet keep striving,
To become that which you've been declared.
Be strong, yet bend with the wind.
Mourn, yet never despair.

Faith moves mountains.
Hope holds on.
Love has paid what is owed.
Belief is beautiful.
Trust is good.
But love is what matters the most.

Dwell in the moment, yet keep moving
Knowing you're just passing through.
Give all that you are, yet receive
All that is worthy and true.
Be at peace, but never run from the battle,
For the battle is where peace is found.
And remember if you don't have love,
You have nothing no matter how profound.

Faith moves mountains.
Hope holds on.
Love has paid what is owed.
Belief is beautiful.
Trust is good.
But love is what matters the most.

Of this remarkable song Wes writes, "A book entitled *Lillith* by [nineteenth-century Scottish author] George MacDonald sparked this song. My hope is that it speaks both of the beauty of paradox and the centrality, the weight, and the enormity of love. 1 Cor. 13 *Aequam servare mentem.*"

PRINCIPLE 3

STICK TO YOUR GUNS

We often place too high a premium on flexibility as a value unto itself. In today's relativistic climate, the person who hedges or who "splits the difference" regardless of the circumstances receives acclaim as a "moderate," while the person who adopts a strong, unyielding position gets labeled as "extreme." Effective leadership frequently requires principled compromise, yet tenacious adherence to specific principles, when accompanied by wisdom, can often provide a leader's only safe harbor in a time of crisis.

When should we compromise, and when must we hold fast? How can we distinguish between unwavering vision and blind, counterproductive rigidity? How do we master the art of *principled* compromise toward a productive end, while retaining our ability to curtail any tendency to collapse or withdraw out of weakness, boredom, or exhaustion? We can learn many lessons from a document that governs our lives today, perhaps the most striking example of a set of enduring, hallowed principles to emerge from the wedding of enlightened vision with measured compromise: the United States Constitution.

The generation that presided over the founding of the United States of America produced some of the most remarkable leaders in all of history. The era was a veritable hall of fame—filled to over-flowing with brilliant, courageous, articulate, and principled states-men, artists, journalists, merchants, and craftsmen. Think of all the heroes who emerged from that short time frame: Washington, Adams, Jefferson, Hancock, Laurens, Greene, Franklin, Henry . . . it was, by any measure, a glorious age of leaders.

Certainly, one man who must be numbered among the greats of that time was James Madison. He was a man of deep convictions who was keenly versed in literature, theology, science, and politics. But like many of his contemporaries, he was able to translate his vast learning into more than mere theory. He was a man of courageous action who put his principles into practice. As a result he left his beloved nation a lasting legacy of freedom that continues to unfold in our age.

During the Constitutional Convention in 1787, he was one of the most active debaters, and many of the wisest and most innovative provisions in the final document owe their origin to his foresight and learning. Along with Alexander Hamilton and John Jay, Madison wrote the brilliant essays published in New York newspapers that came to be known as the *Federalist Papers*. He was a trusted advisor and confidant to both George Washington and Thomas Jefferson. Later, he would serve the fledgling nation as its fourth president dur-ing the particularly difficult days of the War of 1812. He was unques-tionably a soaring comet in an age filled with shining stars.

Madison remained a humble man, however, who never lost sight of his own flaws. He knew only too well that he had a tendency to become rather overzealous during debate. His emotions often got the better of him, and he could easily deliver blasts of razor-sharp rhetoric.

Once at the Constitutional Convention he asked a fellow Virginia delegate to sit by his side and tweak his coattails if he became too obviously excited. After one impassioned speech he sat down, exhausted, and reproached his friend for not pulling at his coat. "Sir," replied the awestruck man, "I would just as soon have laid a finger upon lightning."

Similar stories abound concerning any number of our Founding Fathers. Patrick Henry was a mesmerizing orator. Samuel Adams was a firebrand of whom it was often said that he spoke with the voice of the Divine. Normally a quiet and reserved man, when George Washington addressed his fellow patriots, the force of his character held his audience in thrall. And when the venerable Peyton Randolph arose to speak, an admiring silence reportedly enveloped his listeners.

History affords ample evidence that in any age or era, unswerving conviction carries a peculiar power that inevitably arrests the attention of individuals and nations. Uncompromising vision and principled passion command an almost indescribable appeal.

An effective leader, however, must leaven his or her passion with judgment. Based on the circumstances at hand, does the advancement of the leader's principles require rigidity or compromise? Madison, whose central role in the drafting and adoption of the Constitution earned him the moniker "Father of the Constitution," presided over a stunning array of compromises in the framing of that document. Having endured the searing tests of time for more than two centuries, however, the Constitution now embodies the result of this shared vision: the greatest principles of self-government ever written.

STANDING FAST

As they debated how the Constitution should reflect the relative merits of representative government, federalism, and the separation of powers, Madison and his fellow framers confronted the real threat that the great American experiment could dissolve in political and economic chaos. The governing Articles of Confederation had created an ineffective central government that possessed no real authority to mediate the competing interests of the former British colonies. The fact that these individuals managed to forge our enduring system of checks and balances amidst such a crisis is a testament to their extraordinary leadership. With amazing skill, the framers artic-

> *Courage is not having the strength to go on; it is going on when you don't have the strength. Industry and determination can do anything that genius and advantage can do and many things that they cannot.*
>
> —THEODORE ROOSEVELT

ulated a fundamental set of principles and used the broad authority they had received from the Congress of the Confederation to make the compromises necessary to enact these principles.

Unlike the predicament the framers faced, the Election 2000 recount controversy more than two centuries later posed no constitutional crisis or threat to democracy. We simply experienced a historically close election, with the leadership of the world's only superpower at stake. In contrast to the hysterics of some commentators at the time (and since), the laws of Florida—and our nation—proved equal to the task of resolving this unprecedented convergence of electoral circumstances.

Also unlike the framers, who possessed the broad power to remake the government of our nation, I had no authority to reconstitute the intricate framework the Florida legislature devised for resolving challenges to an election. As secretary of state, I had plainly sworn to uphold the law.

Contrary to popular accounts, my decisions did *not* "cut off" all recounts. Indeed, had the Gore campaign not challenged my decision to certify the election according to the statutory schedule, Al Gore might well have obtained the statewide manual recount he sought.

By statute, the Florida legislature created two distinct phases of an election challenge: a "protest" and a "contest." The protest phase, which would occur before Florida's Elections Canvassing Commission certified the statewide results, permitted candidates and political parties to obtain county-specific manual recounts under *particular* and *limited* circumstances. The law did not permit me, or anyone for that matter, to declare a statewide recount during the protest phase.

The contest phase—which could not begin until after the election had been certified at the close of the protest phase—allowed *any* taxpayer to obtain *any* relief a circuit judge deemed necessary to remedy a "rejection of a number of legal votes sufficient to change or place in doubt the result of the election." Thus, a circuit judge could have declared a statewide recount during the contest phase, together with uniform standards for determining a legal vote. (A seldom reported fact, we requested the Florida Supreme Court to declare uniform counting standards less than one week after the election; however, the court denied our motion. By a 7-2 vote in *Bush* v. *Gore*, the United States Supreme Court declared the absence of such uniform standards to be unconstitutional.)

The Florida legislature set a strict deadline for the end of the protest phase. The law required all counties to submit certified totals to my Division of Elections by 5:00 P.M. on November 14, 2000, which was seven days after Election Day. My decision to enforce this deadline, however, did *not* mean the end of all recounts. In fact, had Al Gore not fought my enforcement of that deadline (thereby enabling me to certify the election on November 17, 2000, the deadline for our receipt of overseas military ballots), he could have filed his contest more than one week earlier.

Even if the circuit judge hearing the contest had refused to order a recount (as Leon County Circuit Court Judge Sander Sauls did in Gore's contest two weeks later), the Florida Supreme Court would have issued its ruling ordering a statewide recount much earlier. (As it was, the Florida Supreme Court issued that order on December 8, 2000, just four days prior to the December 12, 2000, "safe harbor" deadline under federal law that the five-justice majority of the U.S. Supreme Court invoked in refusing to permit further recounts in Florida.")

In other words, had former Vice President Gore's contest commenced according to the schedule that the legislature intended for election challenges to follow, Gore's recount efforts may well have survived the U.S. Supreme Court's ruling in *Bush v. Gore*. The Florida Supreme Court might have had more than one week, instead of just over one hour, to devise and implement a statewide recount using the uniform counting standards the U.S. Supreme Court mandated.

> *Courage is the price that Life exacts for granting peace, The soul that knows it not, knows no release From little things.*
>
> —AMELIA EARHART

With such a clear path to the fair and orderly resolution of the post-election storm in place, how did we manage to take the express lane to chaos instead? Politics.

As the *Washington Post* reported in *Deadlock,* its book about the recount controversy, Al Gore chose the advice of his political advisors over the counsel of his lead Florida attorney, Dexter Douglass, in deciding to challenge my enforcement of the law:

> Gore's gamble was to stretch the first, "protest," phase by seeking a later deadline for counting, thus shortening the time available for phase two, which was a lawsuit contesting the results. Some lawyers for Gore thought this strategy was a mistake. Dexter Douglass, Gore's old Tallahassee hand, believed that they should let Katherine Harris certify the results and go straight to the lawsuit . . . Better, Douglass felt, to get the whole election in front of one judge with the power to order a recount and set the standard.

> *Understanding is knowing what to do; wisdom is knowing what to do next; virtue is actually doing it.*
>
> —TRISTAN GYLBERD

As the *Post* duly points out, Al Gore failed to take his Florida lawyer's advice because his political advisors feared the repercussions of a certified Bush victory. Gore might lose support for his challenge in Washington, in the media, and with the public. While I do not question the legitimacy of this political calculation, it did not compel me to ignore the law. Had I agreed to the former vice president's demands, I would have had to disregard the law to protect his short-term political viability at the expense of his long-term legal interests.

After the automatic machine recount mandated by statute was complete (which occurred due to the less than one-half of 1 percent margin between the candidates), the Gore campaign filed a protest by petitioning for manual recounts in four heavily Democratic counties only: Palm Beach, Miami-Dade, Broward, and Volusia. By statute, the canvassing boards could grant such a request by ordering a sample recount that had to "include at least three precincts and at least 1 percent of the total votes cast" for the candidate who had petitioned for the recount, or on whose account a political party had made such a request. If the sample recount indicated "an error in the vote tabulation which could affect the outcome of the election," the canvassing boards were required to choose from three options, one of which was a manual recount of all ballots cast in that county.

As these four cherry-picked counties completed their sample recounts, questions arose concerning whether the results of those sample recounts showed "an error in the vote tabulation which could affect the outcome of the election," so as to require these counties to choose one of the three courses of action. Two counties, Broward and Palm Beach, requested advisory opinions from my Division of Elections on this matter.

Section 106.23(2) of the Florida Statutes authorizes the Division of Elections to issue opinions upon such requests and states that "the opinion, until amended or revoked, shall be binding on any person or organization who sought the opinion or with reference to whom the opinion was sought." The division's opinion was crystal-clear, based on the language of the protest statute. "An error in the vote tabulation" occurred when a vote counting machine failed to count a *properly marked* ballot. "An error in the vote tabulation" did not refer to circumstances involving voter error, in which a vote counting machine had refused to tabulate an *incorrectly marked ballot*.

The division's opinion *did not* state that manual recounts designed to correct voter error could not occur at all. The opinion did not preclude the possibility that a court could properly order such manual recounts as part of a contest proceeding. The opinion merely indicated that manual recounts to correct voter error were not permissible during the *protest* phase.

U.S. Court of Appeals Judge and University of Chicago Law School Senior Lecturer Richard A. Posner, in his book on the recount controversy, *Breaking the Deadlock,* agrees with the Division of Elections' rationale in this matter. He reasons, "Voter error is not tabulator error; the voter is not the tabulator of the vote." He argues that the Florida Supreme Court's "mistaken interpretation of 'error in the vote tabulation'" drove its decision extending the deadline for counties to certify their final results from November 14 to November 26.

While the Florida Supreme Court held that an irreconcilable conflict existed between the protest statute's November 14 deadline and its provision for manual recounts (which, presumably, would take longer), Judge Posner states,

If, as the election officials ruled, ["error in the vote tabulation"] refers only to a breakdown of the tabulating process-[meaning that] unspoiled ballots have not been counted-the hand recount should not take much time at all. It will be obvious at a glance which candidate received the vote on those ballots. Judgment, interpretation, disagreement, objection, challenge, and resulting delay come into play only when, because the ballot was spoiled, the voter's intention is an enigma.

Judge Posner continues,

> The only thing that could make the seven-day period for the submission of a county's votes unreasonably short (other than extraordinary circumstances such as fraud or some natural disaster) would be a desire to recover spoiled ballots as votes, a process that is time-consuming because of its subjectivity. In the exercise of her discretion to interpret and apply the statute, the secretary of state was entitled to conclude that wanting to recover votes from ballots spoiled by the voter was not a proper reason for the extension of the statutory deadline-especially in a Presidential election, in which delay in certifying the results of the election could cause chaos.

Ultimately, our opinion regarding the type of recounts Florida law permitted diverges from Judge Posner's thesis; we disagree with his argument that the Florida Supreme Court did not have the authority to order a statewide recount to remedy voter error, even in the contest proceeding. Nevertheless, his thorough, incisive reasoning provides welcome support for the Division of Elections' advisory opinion, which we have always known to be correct, but which has been the subject of misplaced and misinformed scorn and ridicule.

When the four-justice majority of the Florida Supreme Court ordered a belated statewide recount on December 8 (without declaring uniform counting standards, which we had requested the court to declare weeks earlier in a motion that the court denied), they capped a stunning month-long display of judicial gymnastics. Our system of governance is based upon a balance of power amongst our three branches of government: the executive, the legislative, and the judicial. By law these branches are mandated to perform separate duties. The executive branch administers the law; the legislative branch writes the law; and the judicial branch interprets the law. When the four-justice majority of the Supreme Court joined their three dissenting colleagues to issue the court's first ruling, which extended the deadline for submission of county returns and delayed certification until November 26 (thereby writing new law, not interpreting the law), they abandoned traditional judicial decorum, chiding me for being too much of a stickler about the law—as if this trait somehow constituted a defect in character. They said, "The will of the people, not a hyper-technical reliance on statutory provisions, should be our guiding principle in election cases." They ruled that certification constituted such a significant event, with such momentous implications for Al Gore's ability to obtain a "full and fair" (for only four Democratic-majority counties) manual recount, that they had no choice but to legislate from the bench and change the law.

Once this ruling had transformed the legislature's orderly process for settling election disputes into a chaotic free-for-all, this four-justice majority of the Florida Supreme Court reversed themselves, deciding in their December 8 decision that certification meant nothing. They added uncertified recount totals that Palm Beach County submitted *after* the new deadline the court had created to the totals the Elections Canvassing Commission certified on November 26. They added partial recount returns to the certified total that Miami-Dade County never even submitted.

When the damage had already been done to the cause of an orderly, fair statewide recount, the four-justice majority finally agreed with what my office had told them just before they eviscerated the November 14 deadline: that certification operated merely as a procedural milepost between the protest and contest phases of a cohesive legislative plan to settle election disputes. Certification had no impact on any person's right to pursue a manual recount of any sort or scope.

To their everlasting credit, the dissenters to the December 8 decision, Chief Justice Charles Wells, Justice Leander Shaw, and Justice Major Harding, remained consistent. I did not agree with their prior decision to move the November 14 deadline to November 26, but I immensely respected their courage as they stood fast in their convictions while the other four justices flip-flopped.

Justice Shaw issued a statement that echoes my feelings about this controversy. In his concurring opinion to the court's order dismissing Al Gore's contest pursuant to the directions of the U.S. Supreme Court, Justice Shaw stated as follows:

> Both the search for the truth and the right to vote are of paramount importance, but they are circumscribed by a higher, overarching concern—the general welfare of our democracy. The general welfare is informed by our law. The law infuses the fabric of our society and breathes life into all our legal principles. Inherent in the law are the basic concepts of fairness, reliability and predictability, and the constitutional safeguards of due process and equal protection were designed to promote these interests. Although the pursuit of the truth and the preservation of the right to vote are worthy goals, they cannot be achieved in a manner that contravenes these principles.

I was determined throughout the entire recount controversy to stand fast and firm on an immutable principle of American justice: the rule of law. I could not allow circumstances to alter this conviction, even though I knew I confronted a no-win situation. When I was assailed in the press, when I was besieged with lawsuits, when I was hammered by special-interest groups, and when I was mocked by pundits and late night comedians, I felt that my first and foremost duty was to cling to my convictions, do my job, follow the law, and stick to my guns. The rule of law, after all, is an essential aspect of American liberty.

UNBOWED PERSISTENCE

Throughout history, the greatest achievements have usually been propelled by an against-all-odds tenacity. The unshakable conviction of the rightness of the cause, of its destined and providential place in the overall scheme of things, has kept adventurers, discoverers, and creators going despite overwhelming adversity and fierce opposition.

A study of leadership in America by anyone in my generation would be wholly incomplete without a discussion of Ronald Reagan, who met every challenge with his unbowed determination to stick to his guns. No other single person can be said to have had a greater impact and presence on the American political stage since Franklin D. Roosevelt, one of President Reagan's heroes.

As one of the rare personalities of our era who literally defined a decade, President Reagan reintroduced a no-nonsense approach to political action with his informed, forceful style, an infectious sense of humor, and an overarching charisma. Adhering closely to his simple yet comprehensive and elegant political philosophy, he encouraged a new generation of conservative activists to become politically active, prompting me and a number of my peers to enter the political arena and even to switch our partisan allegiance.

Reagan energized the Republican Party on every level, which resulted in the GOP's capture of many state legislatures and governorships in the 1980s and 1990s, as well as in the party's 1994 landslide victory in which it won a majority in both houses of Congress for the first time in four decades. That same year I was elected to the Florida Senate, defeating the Democrat incumbent; this was the first time since Reconstruction that a Republican majority controlled the Florida Senate.

Reagan's path to power was marked with the dominant traits of leadership. His story is a powerful testimonial to the man from Dixon, Illinois, who was born into poverty and who graduated from the virtually unknown Eureka College. Rising from his first job after college as a radio announcer in Davenport, Iowa, to his stature as a contracted actor for the Warner Brothers movie studio, he eventually became the president of the Screen Actors Guild, where he began to challenge the liberal orthodoxy that had already thoroughly infected Hollywood. In a letter to a supporter in the early 1960s, Reagan detailed a conflict he had with a director and studio executives who wanted to remove a film scene that included a child praying. He won that argument (as he almost always did) after getting them to admit that they were devoted atheists who were intent on using the film industry to foist their ideology onto an unsuspecting public. Seldom were his opponents so forthright.

Reagan's televised speech in support of Barry Goldwater in 1964 turned the national political spotlight in his direction. In his stirring remarks, titled "A Time for Choosing," he clearly articulated that the battle for America's soul was a battle for ideas, with enormous stakes at risk. He said, "You and I have a rendezvous with destiny. We will preserve for our children this, the last best hope of man on earth, or we will sentence them to take the first step into a thousand years of darkness. If we fail, at least let our children and our children's children say of us we justified our brief moment here. We did all that could be done."

Though Goldwater lost the presidential election, Reagan identified himself as a man of courageous, countercultural ideas who would be a force to be reckoned with in the future. Only two years later he won a landslide election for governor of California, a job to which he would be reelected in 1970.

From the outset of his political career, Reagan believed that persistence in doing what he believed to be right constituted the only methodology of leadership. In fact, he personified this principle. Speaking to students at Cambridge University in 1990, he urged them to doggedly adhere to their first principles, whatever the cost. "A leader, once convinced a particular course of action is the right one, must have the determination to stick with it and be undaunted when the going gets rough," Reagan said.

Leadership is about stability, holding our ground, not being blown about by every wind of ideological fluctuation. We need to stick with the principles we believe are right and true, no matter how pragmatic other alternatives appear.[3]

Reagan put that lesson to good use immediately upon being elected president in 1980. Inheriting a shattered American economy from Jimmy Carter, an economy wracked with double-digit inflation, 20 percent interest rates, and stagnant productivity, Reagan turned the intelligentsia's conventional economic wisdom on its head.

The so-called "experts" had come to accept high rates of inflation as a necessary evil of a growing economy. Reagan believed that bringing what he called the "cruelest tax of all" under control must constitute the first step of any responsible economic recovery strategy. Lower rates of inflation would reduce interest rates, while generating a climate of increased stability and predictability for businesses and investors alike, leading to long-term economic growth. Thus, Reagan threw his support behind Federal Reserve policies designed to swiftly kill the nation's inflationary albatross.

This decision initially threw the American economy into a deepening recession. Factories closed. Double-digit unemployment ensued. Republicans suffered massive losses at the polls in 1982. How did Reagan respond when his popularity plummeted and the pressure to abandon his economic policies intensified? He told the nation: "Stay the course." Reagan understood that this short-term pain was necessary to reverse years of economic policies that had favored high taxes and even higher government spending, much as a doctor opts to excise an infection that other doctors have unsuccessfully treated with conventional antibiotics.

*A pound of pluck is worth
a ton of luck.*
—JAMES A. GARFIELD

The death of double-digit inflation cleared the way for the dramatic tax cuts Reagan had pushed through Congress in 1981 to work their magic upon the American economy. The combination of low inflation and lower taxes, which enabled working men and women to keep more of what they earned, launched the largest peacetime economic expansion in American history up to that time. The American people rewarded President Reagan with a stunning forty-nine state reelection landslide in 1984.

Naysayers contend that the historically high federal budget deficits of those years discredit Reagan's economic policies. While enormous budget deficits unquestionably plagued the Reagan years, the notion that such deficits resulted from the 1981 tax cuts is erroneous. The federal government's tax revenues increased following the 1981 tax cuts. The intransigence of a Democratic Congress on domestic spending, however, combined with the increased military spending necessary to win the Cold War, ensured that spending increased at a rate that far outpaced these higher tax revenues.

Reagan always contended that tax cuts would produce an expanding economy, which would generate sufficient increases in tax revenue to balance the federal budget. Ironically, despite the media's constant ridicule of this assertion, Reagan was proven right by events that occurred under President Bill Clinton. Analysts have concluded that the budget surpluses of the late 1990s *did not* result from the Clinton tax increase of 1993; rather, these surpluses were the product of accelerating economic growth and the resulting increases in federal tax revenue, combined with reductions in spending, made possible in part by the end of the Cold War.

President Reagan demonstrated the same determination and tenacity throughout his two terms as president as he stared down the looming forces of international communism embodied in the monolithic Soviet Union. Knowing that the battle was one primarily of ideas, not military might, and that the Communist system was unwieldy and unworkable, Reagan loudly proclaimed its demise at a time when constant Cold War tensions were assumed to be a permanent fixture of international relations.

Speaking at the commencement ceremonies at the University of Notre Dame in 1981, he prophetically declared, "The West will not contain Communism, it will transcend Communism. We will not bother to denounce it, we'll dismiss it as a sad, bizarre chapter in human history whose last pages are even now being written." At the time, his statement seemed to many to be pure fantasy. In June 1982, he delivered a speech before the British House of Commons, where he announced that "Marxism-Leninism will be left on the ash heap of history." He reiterated this concept often, including in his famous Evil Empire speech to a rapt audience in Orlando, Florida, in March 1983.

While liberals on both sides of the Atlantic howled that President Reagan was driving the world to the brink of nuclear war, his first principles told him that the Communist aggression was unsustainable and that citizens under that system yearned for the very freedoms their political masters sought to destroy. The seeds of its destruction were already sown, and it would be only a matter of time before they bore fruit.

Reagan did not fight the ideological battle with words alone; he initiated a defense policy built off his fundamental beliefs. He strengthened the military and committed the necessary resources to answer the Communist threat, making our nation's armed services the most technologically advanced in the world. He refused to capitulate any of the West's strategic advantages to the Soviets, who were surprised when, in his second summit with Soviet Premier Mikhail Gorbachev in Reykjavik, Iceland, in 1986, he refused to budge on the development of the Strategic Defense Initiative (derisively called "Star Wars" by its critics).

Reagan transcended communism in our hemisphere as well, through the "Reagan Doctrine," which prevented the Soviet Union and Cuba from pursuing their goal of establishing Marxist-Leninist client states throughout Latin America and the Caribbean. He also strengthened diplomatic and military ties with our allies in NATO, particularly with his like-minded colleagues British Prime Minister Margaret Thatcher and German Chancellor Helmut Kohl, who contributed greatly to heading off the Soviet military threat.

> *Brethren, stand fast.*
> —PAUL OF TARSUS

Of all of America's political leaders during the 1980s, none were as vocal about the inevitable demise of the Soviet Union as Ronald Reagan. Only a man so daringly confident in his convictions could have traveled to Berlin in 1987 and boldly called for the dismantling of the Berlin Wall that had divided not only Germany, but the East and the West, free society and the enslaved, for more than a quarter of a century—with no indications that the situation was soon to change.

Yet slightly more than two years later, the wall would literally come crashing down, freeing hundreds of millions of people who had lived in political and economic bondage since the end of World War II. Ronald Reagan envisioned this dream, then formed a strategy to break the back of the Communist empire that he executed flawlessly. It is a fitting tribute that a section of that wall, now completely dismantled, stands in the garden of the Ronald Reagan Presidential Library in Simi Valley, California.

It takes a figure like President Reagan, with such dramatic and history-creating accomplishments, for us to see the intimate connection between the concept of vision and the application of a world-view. After two decades of tumult and declining confidence, Ronald Reagan gave the American people a renewed sense of confidence regarding our unique shared identity as Americans. As only the Great Communicator could, he reminded us of what the American experiment was all about in his farewell address to the American people: "I've spoken of the shining city all my political life. In my mind it was a tall, proud city built on rocks stronger than oceans, windswept, God-blessed, and teeming with people of all kinds living in harmony and peace, a city with free ports that hummed with commerce and creativity. And if there had to be city walls, the walls had doors and the doors were open to anyone with the will and heart to get here."

President Reagan enabled us to remember the thrill and responsibility of living in a City on the Hill. And as only a great leader can, he helped us to believe it and to live it. He modeled one of the most valuable contributions a leader can make to an organization or effort: helping followers turn theories into practice and inspiring them to join in the hard work and sacrifice. But this can never happen if we abandon our principles in midstream. We must not only arrive at the right ideas; we must develop the capacity to stick to them. In order to accomplish this feat, we must become the reference point for all those persons who come under our guidance and direction.

Reagan never failed to squarely confront a challenge. He knew that a leader, particularly the leader of the free world, must act decisively. An excellent example is his approach to the escalating terrorist threat. As terrorist states grew bolder in targeting American citizens around the globe, Reagan understood that the challenge was to raise the stakes beyond what the terrorists could bear. When he ordered a bombing of Tripoli, including the home of Libyan General Miramar Gadhafi, a primary sponsor of terrorist activities, he took the battle to the opponents and raised the stakes. The net result was to reverse the initiative and to temporarily stand down terrorism directed at Americans.

Many lesser leaders would rather have tried to negotiate "peace" with America's enemies, regardless of the price, but Reagan understood that the conflict with America's enemies was over more than just government policies—it was over a conflict of visions and ideology. To countenance compromise on that basis would have meant an embrace of inevitable defeat. When the opportunity for genuine nuclear arms reduction agreements with the Soviet Union arose towards the end of his second term, however, Reagan did engage in compromise—principled compromise that set the stage for the end of the Cold War.

Reagan's leadership abilities were not reserved for the stage of national and international politics. They formed an integral part of his personality. His subordinates could testify to the many ways he empowered them to be able to get the job done. His recipe for organizational success was simple: "Surround yourself with the best people you can find, delegate authority, and don't interfere." He took the time to cultivate the next generation of up-and-coming leaders. As president, he spent an inordinate amount of time with young people, and he encouraged them to be active in the political process—at the polls, in campaigns, and in their careers. In a fitting tribute, the Young America's Foundation purchased the Reagans' beloved home of twenty-four years, Rancho del Cielo, to use as a center to continue to communicate President Reagan's legacy to future generations.

Nurturing the next generation of leadership inevitably means getting out of their way. It requires special grace to move on and out of the scene to allow new leaders to assume the mantle on their own. And Reagan, as only he could, moved from the center stage of politics with style and grace. He allowed his presidential successors to forge their own plans and make their own mistakes without his interference. He understood one of the best-guarded secrets of leadership—in the end, no matter the choice of the leader, it must not be about feeding the ego; a leader's role is to empower and enable others. That principle defines servant leadership—a quality we desperately need to cultivate in the leaders of our time.

The Reagan presidency was not perfect. Reagan made mistakes, to which he attested and made amends. Thus, in the final analysis, he was able to overcome these errors. History will bear witness to the greatness of Ronald Reagan because he was courageous and undaunted. He taught us as a country to embrace the truth of our role in the world, to understand the ideas behind it, and to never relinquish them. In his struggles, whether as head of the Screen Actors Guild, as governor of California, or as president of the United States, he never shrank from a battle. He believed in the power of his ideas, so he anticipated victory. He learned that lesson from one of his role models, Winston Churchill, who said, "When you feel you cannot continue in your position for another minute, and all that is in human power has been done, that is the moment when the enemy is most exhausted, and when one step forward will give you the fruits of the struggle you have borne."

As I was preparing to do the research for this book, Ronald Reagan immediately came to mind as I thought of examples of leaders who stuck to their guns. On further study, I found that Reagan's life constitutes a veritable primer on tenacity as an essential trait of greatness in a leader.

INCULCATING TENACITY

The moral endurance necessary to stand on principle, regardless of the cost, is not a natural inclination for most of us. Our protective instincts incline us toward ill-advised compromise. We may hedge or fudge at times, even when we face the inconsequential. When push comes to shove, most of us prefer to waffle, wiggle, and waver rather than risk the wrath and ire triggered by uncompromising conviction. Steadfastness in the face of adversity, opposition, or persecution must be nurtured, developed, supported, and encouraged every step along the way.

1. ESTABLISH YOUR CONVICTIONS ON THE FOUNDATION OF CLEAR-EYED VISION

Vision is the ability to see beyond the constraints of present circumstances to the possibilities of the future. It is the talent to view what exists in terms of what ought to be. Vision is the passion to live life beyond the limits imposed by the tyranny of the urgent. We live under the thumb of expediency. As a result, the ideal of the visionary is all too often seen as little more than a lost cause. Throughout the ages, wise men and women have recognized vision for what it is: the hope of the future, the mainspring of progress, and the provocation for success. Vision has always provided the basis for genuine persistence and passion.

It is difficult to be indifferent while maintaining a steady vision. Samuel Johnson said, "Indifference in questions of importance is no amiable quality." Neither is it an enduring quality. In order to take a stand, we have to stand for something. In order to hold on, we have to hold on to something tangible, substantive, and palpable.

2. DIFFERENTIATE TRUE PRINCIPLE FROM MERE PREFERENCE

A principle upon which we are willing to stake all that we are and all that we do cannot simply be a matter of penchant, prejudice, or preference; even less can it simply be a matter of fashion or social currency. A principle must be rooted in unchanging ideas and unchangeable ideals. It must take the form of an absolute. It must be a unified aspect of our personal sense of calling, of duty, of responsibility, and of destiny.

To quote Samuel Johnson again, "The future is purchased at the price of vision in the present." Thus, we need to make certain that the things we stand for are really worth standing for—much is at stake.

3. PICK YOUR BATTLES

Not every issue is worth a fight. Not every cause is equally worthy of our involvement. We should not feel compelled to stake our life, honor, and fortune on every struggle that confronts us. Once we decide that a particular foe, human or situational, is worth battling, we also need to sense the most appropriate time and place to engage it. We must be as wise as serpents and as innocent as doves. We must be good strategists.

Sometimes, of course, our battles pick us. We do not always have the luxury of scheduling sickness or adversity. But even when the crises come unbidden, we have a host of choices. Our ability to persevere in the midst of the raging storm often depends upon our judgment concerning what matters most—and when it matters most.

> *Without belittling the courage with which men have died, we should not forget those acts of courage with which men have lived. The courage of life is often a less dramatic spectacle than the courage of a final moment; but it is no less a magnificent mixture of triumph and tragedy.*
>
> —JOHN KENNEDY

4. KNOW THAT YOU MAY LOSE

To lose a battle is not to say that we were necessarily wrong to undertake it in the first place. Sometimes lost causes are precisely the right causes. If we measure principle by pragmatism, then our principles are more than a little hollow. "Any coward can fight a battle when he's sure of winning," George Eliot once said, "but give me the man who has the pluck to fight when he's sure of losing. That's my way, sir; and there are many victories worse than a defeat."

Standing by our principles proves to be reward enough in and of itself. If a turn of events justifies our confidence and confirms our conviction with success, then all the better. But it is far more preferable to take a stand for what is right, even in defeat, than to compromise the things that matter most, even in triumph.

Top Ten List:
Profiles in Persistence

I found my heroes in books. I observed how it was that they were able to overcome adversity, stand fast in trials, and persist in their convictions heedless of the cost. Thus over time, I came to comprehend the vast difference between being a politician and being a statesman.
—CALVIN COOLIDGE

According to the English pundit and critic Samuel Johnson, a leader is "a man who bears in his life both the most tangible and intangible qualities of heart and mind and flesh. Best we study these well." So, what is it exactly that makes a leader? Which character traits are necessary to steer people and nations in the right direction? How are we to "study well" what is "the most tangible and intangible" simultaneously?

Perhaps the very best way to wrestle with these relevant questions is to read biographies of great leaders of the past. Many of the stories I tell in this book were gleaned from my library of biographies of the best and brightest women and men ever to grace history. These are among my favorites:

1. *John Adams* by David McCullough (Simon & Schuster). This marvelous work by a Pulitzer Prize-winning historian is rich in original historical research yet reads like a well-paced adventure novel. One of America's greatest patriots finally emerges from the shadows of his contemporaries George Washington and Thomas Jefferson.

2. *When Character Was King* by Peggy Noonan (Viking). Peggy Noonan is perhaps one of the most talented writers alive today. Her profile of Ronald Reagan is politically insightful, spiritually provocative, and intellectually rousing.

3. *Washington* by Douglas Southall Freeman (Touchstone Books). Even the single-volume abridgement of this magisterial seven-volume work is perhaps the best book available on the father of our country. Once you read this you are certain to want to read several more about this remarkable man.

4. *A Worthy Company* by M. E. Bradford (Plymouth Rock). This collection of brief lives of each of the signers of the U.S. Constitution is a delight to read and offers a new perspective of the founding era.

5. *Then Darkness Fled* by Stephen Mansfield (Cumberland House). I was awed as I read of Booker T. Washington's heroism, courage, and tenacity in this lucid and invigorating biography.

6. *Theodore Rex* by Edmund Morris (Random House). This is just one of several biographies of Teddy Roosevelt that I have appreciated. The fact is, I never tire of reading about this remarkable man of action, vision, and conviction.

7. *Truman* by David McCullough (Simon & Schuster). The author provides a revealing glimpse into this extraordinary leader's thoroughly American story. This book left perhaps the biggest impression upon me of any biography I have read.

8. *Eric Liddell* by David McCasland (Discovery House). This fascinating account of the life of Scotland's beloved Olympic champion goes far beyond the plot of the film *Chariots of Fire*.

9. *The Last Lion* by William Manchester (Little Brown). This is undoubtedly a powerful depiction of unwavering conviction. That Winston Churchill was able to emerge from his season of political exile and isolation to save the

free world from the Nazi terror is a stunning tale—far stranger than fiction.

10. *Lincoln* by David Herbert Donald (Simon & Schuster). This outstanding account by a Pulitzer Prize-winning author provides an incisive view of the Great Emancipator, from his early boyhood to the raging battles of the Civil War.

Excavate

When they excavate these ruins,
Thousands of years from now,
Will they wonder what I was doing,
Who I was and what my life was about?

When my riches lie in ruin,
On the landscape of my past,
Will they uncover that I was pursuing,
The things in life that really last?

Where your treasure is
The things you love own a part of you
And there will be your heart
So live in light of the future.
Learn from yesterday
Because what we do now will echo forever
We are only promised today.
Where your treasure is
The things you love own a part of you and
There will be your heart.

Should you dig for the Son of Heaven,
Some holy grail you hope to exhume,
All that's left are the people who love Him.
The greatest treasure is an empty tomb.

Where your treasure is
The things you love own a part of you
And there will be your heart
So live in light of the future.
Learn from yesterday
Because what we do now will echo forever
We are only promised today.
Where your treasure is.
The things you love own a part of you and
Where will be your heart?

Wes notes, "I will never forget my trip to Israel with my wife and our dear friend Jim Martin. This trip changed our lives. As we stood before the ruins of civilizations just like ours, we were struck with the speed of life and the truth of Jesus' command, 'Do not lay up for yourselves treasures upon earth, where moth and rust destroy and thieves break in and steal.' (Matthew 6:20)"

PRINCIPLE 4

FINISH WHAT YOU START

*Leaders finish what they start. They do their job, no matter
how difficult the task. Where others might choose a
well-worn path, leaders blaze a new course through the
wilderness. In fact, leaders will often walk steadfastly
toward the roar of danger. That is not raw courage; it is
responsible accountability, down-to-earth practicality, and
levelheaded sensibility.*

No sooner had I learned that I had won election as secretary of
state than I learned that I would serve as Florida's last *elected*
secretary of state. I announced I would neither seek nor accept an
appointment from Governor Jeb Bush to continue as the appointed
secretary of state.

That same election, Florida voters had approved a constitutional
amendment that reorganized Florida's executive cabinet, reducing its
membership from seven elected officials to four, beginning in January
2003. The reorganization effort stemmed from the philosophy that
the governor and a six-member statewide elected cabinet created a
lack of accountability and was a difficult manner of governance in a
state that is now our nation's fourth largest and the sixteenth largest
economy in the world. In so doing, the amendment had the effect of
transforming the cabinet-level elective offices of secretary of state

and commissioner of education into gubernatorial appointments while consolidating the cabinet-level offices of comptroller and treasurer/insurance commissioner into an elected chief financial officer. (This officer will remain a member of the cabinet, together with the governor, the attorney general, and the commissioner of agriculture.)

In their mad rush to portray me during the Election 2000 recount as a "partisan hack," numerous media accounts misreported the nature of this constitutional amendment. They inaccurately stated that the voters had "eliminated" what they called my "inconsequential" or "largely ceremonial" office, breathlessly speculating that as a result I would be likely to skew my decisions in order to secure an appointment from an incoming Bush administration.[4] My response? Perhaps they could make me ambassador to Chad. (The media have derisively repeated this joke often, without giving me proper credit as its source!)

> *It is natural to mean well, when only abstracted ideas of virtue are proposed to the mind, and no particular passion turns us aside from rectitude; and so willing is every man to flatter himself, that the difference between approving laws, and obeying them is frequently forgotten.*
>
> —SAMUEL JOHNSON

All kidding aside, in order to remove any question concerning the impartiality of my decisions, I stated within the week that followed Election Day 2000 that I would neither seek nor accept an appointment within the administration that resulted from that election. The media refused to report this statement, even though it was consistent with the position I have articulated since immediately following my 1998 election, when I announced that I would neither seek nor accept appointment in 2003 to another term as secretary of state. I simply prefer elective office.

Despite my best efforts to rebut the false reports about the fate of my office in every speech I deliver and distribute to the press, media sources persist in representing that the office of secretary of state has no real substantive duties, and that it will be "eliminated."

In response, I describe my duties, which rank as the most expansive of any secretary of state in America. While Florida's next secretary of state will no longer share executive power with the governor and the other elected officials who comprise the executive cabinet, the secretary of state will still be responsible for the Florida Department of State and its almost 700 full-time employees, whose many departmental programs impact the lives of hundreds of thousands of real people. In 1999, the Florida legislature voted to preserve the secretary of state's authority over these programs based upon the recommendations of an interim committee appointed by the governor of Florida, the president of the Florida Senate, and speaker of the Florida House, which resulted from the interim committee's extensive ten-month review of this reorganization.

While some media sources engaged in idle speculation about my future (and spread the opinion that I had no future in politics), I went back to work. I had a job to finish. I began to study the factors that had contributed to the election storm in the first place, and how we could ensure smoother sailing in the future. The answer seemed clear: we needed to pass a revolutionary election reform package.

The 2000 presidential election in Florida revealed concerns that had festered in the elections systems of many states across our nation for decades, but which no one had summoned the political will to address. As Florida's chief elections officer, I felt duty-bound, as well as inspired, to lead an effort to capitalize upon the heightened focus on election laws and procedures that arose in the aftermath of Election 2000.

When I spoke about our election reform goals in the early days after the end of the recount, I was publicly accused of merely paying lip service to this objective. When I testified before Congress, both Democrats and Republicans praised the election reform bill I had proposed, but media sources further avowed that we would never pass it through the Florida legislature, and that I was just grandstanding. Again, we proved them wrong. In a marvelous display of courage and bipartisanship, the Florida legislature passed, and Governor Jeb Bush signed into law, virtually every aspect of the bill I proposed as part of the landmark Election Reform Act of 2001 that has garnered national acclaim.

The Election Reform Act outlawed the "punch card" voting system and its controversial hanging, dangling, and impregnated chads. It appropriated $24 million over two years to assist Florida's sixty-seven counties in the purchase of touchscreen and marksense, or "optical scan," voting systems with "precinct-based" tabulation capabilities. The act also appropriated $6 million for intensified voter education efforts. It divided this amount equitably among Florida's counties, so that each county could customize an effective voter education program for its citizenry. These reforms struck at the root causes of the undervotes and overvotes that have plagued elections across our country for many years.

Professor Larry Sabato of the University of Virginia, whom the *Wall Street Journal* has called "the most quoted professor in the land," said, "What Florida is doing is leading the way for the nation."

After the intensely negative publicity punch cards received during the recount, Florida's replacement of these systems was necessary to restore public faith in the elections process. Standing alone, that measure would not have reduced the undervotes and overvotes attributable to voter error, however, because marksense systems actually experienced a *higher* rate of rejected ballots than punch card systems. In order to reduce the opportunites for voter error, the Election Reform Act requires each county to employ "precinct level counters," which must be programmed to instantaneously inform a voter when he or she overvotes a race or fails to cast a vote in any race at all, so we can correct such mistakes before an affected voter leaves the polling place.[5]

The Election Reform Act also requires each county to use

"provisional ballots" so that no qualified voter will ever again be turned away at the polls on Election Day due to questions concerning eligibility to vote. The act also makes certain that our men and women in uniform abroad will never again suffer the indignity of challenges at home to their right to vote. To date, Florida is the only state that has not only passed extensive, thoroughgoing election reforms but also has provided the funding for them.

While other states and Congress debated basic election reform proposals, Florida did not rest on its laurels. On June 20, 2001, I announced the formation of my Select Task Force on Voter Accessibility in Florida, whose goal was to develop proposals that would forcefully address the exclusion of persons with disabilities from full and equal participation in our elections process. This task force drafted legislation that embodied its recommendations, which we shepherded through the Florida legislature, achieving final passage in the final hours of the final day of its 2002 regular session. Florida is the first and only state to pass this particular legislation to date.

I am particularly proud of this civil rights legislation. It empowers many persons with disabilities to vote in private without assistance for the first time, finally vindicating their right under the Florida Constitution to vote in secret, regardless of ability or disability. This legislation also mandates accessibility standards for all polling places. Florida State Senator Richard Mitchell, a Democrat from Jasper who co-chaired my task force, had indicated at the beginning of the 2002 regular session that the passage of this bill would mark the brightest moment in an otherwise difficult legislative session dominated by contentious debate. He was absolutely correct.

IN IT FOR THE LONG HAUL

However long it takes, whatever the costs involved, however difficult the task, and whatever the risks, principled leaders are dedicated to finishing what they start. They fulfill their responsibilities and remain true to their duties.

Examples of the ability to work faithfully toward an ultimate goal despite the obstacles encountered along the way abound throughout history. But perhaps no one in all of history better exemplifies this virtue than one of my favorite historical figures, William Wilberforce. As a member of the British Parliament, Wilberforce introduced antislavery measures year after year for almost fifty years. In 1833, as he lay dying, he received word that his bill to outlaw slavery throughout the British Empire would finally pass. His life's work finally complete, he died less than sixty hours later.

> *All that is necessary for evil to triumph is for good men to do nothing.*
> —EDMUND BURKE

No issue has inspired the passionate outrage of principled leaders throughout history like the wretched practice of slaveholding. Ardent abolitionists included those who had experienced this evil first-hand—Harriet Tubman, Sojourner Truth, Frederick Douglass—and those courageous individuals who found it so reprehensible that they were emboldened to fight for its eradication.

After a decade fraught with political strife and stained with intermittent bloodshed over the future of slavery in America, the United States in 1860 had become a powder keg of sectional tension, ready to explode with the slightest provocation. With the election to the presidency that year of a self-educated lawyer from Springfield, Illinois on a platform opposing the further extension of slavery, the nation reached the point of no return on the path to civil war.

As he led the country through the dark days that followed, Lincoln's skills as a statesman enabled him to save the Union from a determined effort to destroy it. All the while, he overcame incompetent generals, political predators, and personal tragedy. On many occasions he could have surrendered to despondency, yet he never gave in to despair. Rather, through his ironclad determination he persevered, at times single-handedly willing the Union to victory.

Lincoln's potent resolve did not arise upon his inauguration as president. It was the product of years of suffering trials and heartbreak, while continually forging ahead regardless of the obstacles he faced. Lincoln overcame the death of his mother during his early childhood, the death of two sons, the mental instability of his wife, and his own bouts with depression, in each of these rooting himself in the following axiom: "I planted myself upon the truth, and the truth only, so far as I knew it, or could be brought to know it," he said.

Writing to his junior law partner, William Herndon, in 1848, he urged him to maintain a keen focus on the goal ahead. "You can not fail in any laudable object, unless you allow your mind to be improperly directed," he wrote. On another occasion, he replied to an inquirer, "I know not how to aid you, save in the assurance of one of mature age, and much severe experience, that you can not fail, if you resolutely determine, that you will not." History records his many similar encouragements to persevere.

Political failure and personal disappointment did not deter Lincoln from pursuing his destiny. Upon the occasion of his defeat in one of his unsuccessful bids for the United States Senate, he said, "The path was worn and slippery. My foot slipped from under me, knocking the other out of the way, but I recovered and said to myself: 'It's a slip and not a fall'." Every time he slipped, Lincoln managed to recover and learn from his defeats. He would need this dogged tenacity when he assumed the presidency of a nation that was soon to be violently torn in two.

> *We should remember that it is no honor or profit merely to appear in the arena, but the wreath is for those who contend aright.*
>
> —JAMES A. GARFIELD

One reason that Lincoln was able to

persevere through the searing trauma of the Civil War was his understanding of the enormity of the crisis before him. Nothing less than the freedom of millions hung in the balance. He weighed the practical stakes inherent in the looming conflict in 1858, when he prophesied, "I believe this government cannot endure, permanently half *slave* and half *free*. I do not expect the Union to be *dissolved*—I do not expect the house to *fall*—but I *do* expect it will cease to be divided." He continued to reiterate this message as the struggle with the South dragged on. Speaking to an Ohio regiment late in the war, he emphasized, "In this great struggle, this form of Government and every form of human right is endangered if our enemies succeed. There is more involved in this contest than is realized by every one."

Writing to one political ally in the midst of the abolition battles prior to becoming president, he identified the level of fortitude required to prevail in such a struggle: "The fight must go on. The cause of civil liberty must not be surrendered at the end of one, or even one hundred defeats." This bold vision was vital to sustaining the Union cause throughout the war, especially when the Confederacy's strategy of attrition had begun to show signs of success.

Upon assuming the presidency, Lincoln was consistently forced to choose between determination and disappointment, as repeated opportunities to resolve the military and political crisis proved elusive. He was also subjected to scathing criticism and faint praise from those outside, and sometimes, inside, the government. "I have endured a great deal of ridicule without much malice; and have received a great deal of kindness, not quite free from ridicule. I am used to it," he replied to one correspondent. But this was nothing new, for he had already learned to disregard the fickle attitudes of critics and the constant flux of public opinion.

Once the battle with the South had been engaged, Lincoln rose to the occasion. Writing to his secretary of state in the early days of the war, he said, "I expect to maintain this contest until successful, or till I die, or am conquered, or my term expires, or Congress or the country forsakes me."

Determined to succeed, Lincoln saw that the only way to secure victory was to match and surpass the resolve of the enemy, which required new methods of thought and action—what today we would call "thinking outside of the box." In his 1862 Message to Congress, he said, "The dogmas of the quiet past are inadequate to the stormy present. The occasion is piled high with difficulty, and we must rise with the occasion. As our case is new, so must we think anew and act anew. We must disenthrall ourselves, and then we shall save our country." His message was clear—the heightened level of hostility necessitated a proportionate increase in the Union's resolve.

> *Those who are quick to promise are generally slow to perform. They promise mountains and perform molehills. He who gives you fair words and nothing more feeds you with an empty spoon. People don't think much of a man's piety when his promises are like pie-crust: made to be broken.*
>
> —**CHARLES HADDON SPURGEON**

As history has shown, many of the Northern generals early in the war did not share this attitude. General George McClellan consistently refused to press his military advantage against the Confederate forces in the Peninsula Campaign. In the days after the stunning victory at Gettysburg, Lincoln repeatedly urged General George Meade to finish off Robert E. Lee's army before they crossed the Potomac River back in the South. His pleas went unheeded, and the war dragged on unmercifully.

But in General Ulysses S. Grant, Lincoln found a kindred spirit. Grant knew how to force his way through defeat to victory. In one telegram to Grant, who was engaged in a pitched battle with the Confederate forces, Lincoln urged him, "I have seen your dispatch expressing your unwillingness to break your hold where you are.

Neither am I willing. Hold on with a bull-dog grip, and chew and choke, as much as possible."

Abraham Lincoln's example has guided many presidents in the dark hours of our country's history. An ordinary man who possessed extraordinarily resolve, Lincoln was able to rise up in America's hour of need and lead the country into a new era.

The primary ingredient for his eventual success was his persistence—a character trait to which we all might aspire. Reflecting on that possibility, Lincoln said, "The sense of obligation to continue is present in all of us. A duty to strive is the duty of all of us. I felt a call to that duty." Happily for America, it was a duty he saw through to its successful completion.

WITH ALL ENDURANCE

This lesson constitutes one of the most important messages we can learn. It comprises the ideas and values we must instill in our children: that patience, commitment, diligence, constancy, wisdom, and discipline will ultimately pay off if we defer gratification long enough for the seeds we have sown to sprout and bear fruit. As I have learned through the trials of the past few years, often we have no idea what sacrifices we will be asked to make or griefs we will be asked to bear when we endeavor to serve our ideals. We uphold our principles in good faith, accepting that we are unable to see around the corner.

Striving to lead a principled life is a serious business! A flippant, shallow, and imprecise approach to anything—be it sports or academics, profession or pleasure, friendship or marriage—is unlikely to satisfy any appetite over the long term, and is ultimately self-defeating.

The world is indeed full of seemingly harmless distractions—humorous and silly, banal and trivial. We face the perpetual temptation to take the path of least resistance and to value that which we can obtain cheaply and easily. According to the poet Edward Lear, we ought to "beware of all such things."

This admonition does not mean that we cannot have fun; that we cannot ever let down our guard; that we are compelled to maintain constant intellectual vigilance; or that we must pursue every cause with bulldog tenacity. But, as Lear continues, "It is all a matter of proportion." He explains that while there is nothing intrinsically wrong with the transitory, lightweight, or comic, we invite trouble when we permit the shallow to overwhelm the serious. "When what people want now replaces what people need always, then the truth is obscured."

In our culture of e-mail, microwavable meals, and predigested formula entertainment, we can easily neglect this profound lesson, as temporary expediencies tend to supersede permanent exigencies.

Our pragmatism is no longer particularly pragmatic. Our practicality is no longer very practical. We cannot wait for anything. We lack the kind of determination that enabled Abraham Lincoln to keep going despite the obstacles he faced and William Wilberforce to endure through years of defeats and ultimately to prevail in their great causes.

I particularly love Wilberforce's story, because it shows that the race is truly won by the tortoise and not the hare. Perseverance—not riches, not connections, and not even knowledge—ultimately fulfills the responsibility and wins the prize.

So, how do we train ourselves to finish what we start? How do we cut across the grain of our one-step ready-in-minutes culture? How do we sub-

> *Nothing can take the place of persistence. Talent will not. Nothing is more common than unsuccessful men with talent. Genius will not. Unrewarded genius is almost a proverb. Education will not. The world is full of educated derelicts. Persistence and determination alone are overwhelmingly powerful.*
>
> —CALVIN COOLIDGE

due our got-to-have-it-now appetites so we can undertake our tasks with forbearance and resolve? First, we must come to the realization that such a virtue is hardly easy to maintain.

I. TO SEE THINGS THROUGH TO THE END DEMANDS COURAGE

Though we tend to admire courage, we often have to admit that the virtue contains an inexplicable combination of boldness and madness. Concerned with our health, welfare, and reputation, we find it more than a little extraordinary when anyone risks life and limb for the sake of others—much less for the sake of principle. Indeed, prior to September 11, 2001, we had seemingly moved into an age with a dearth of heroes. Our primary interest in the athletes and celebrities we had once adulated had devolved into a voyeuristic fascination with their foibles. But on September 11 we witnessed the extraordinary heroism of ordinary people. Just when we thought bravery had practically become a forgotten virtue—a lost cause—we saw that its potential rests in each and every one of us.

> *Courage is not simply one of the virtues, but the form of every virtue at the testing point, which means, at the point of highest reality. A chastity or honesty or mercy, which yields to danger, will be chaste or honest or merciful only on conditions. Pilate was merciful until it became risky.*
>
> —C. S. LEWIS

While we earnestly pray that another September 11 will never happen, we all must prepare ourselves for whatever trials we might face. Doubtless, however, we will be asked to meet unexpected challenges that require genuine valor to finish what we start and to fulfill our responsibilities. Each of us will have to confront tremendous obstacles, fierce opposition, jeering criticism, and perhaps even physical danger.

To finish well will cost us something. It may cost us everything.

Just ask anyone who has ever run a marathon or competed in a triathlon. Ask our veterans, our firefighters, our paramedics, our police. Starting is easy, but finishing is hard. Finishing requires blood, sweat, and tears. Finishing requires courage.

2. TO SEE THINGS THROUGH TO THE END DEMANDS WISDOM

We admire knowledge. We covet understanding. But we tend to be rather suspicious of wisdom. In today's fast-paced world, we seem to have little time to look beyond our snap judgments and quick assumptions. Wisdom seems like an outdated concept, as its nurture requires us to reject the easy answers society places before us. To exercise wisdom, we must proceed cautiously, suspending judgment until we have researched and analyzed all of the relevant facts.

Throughout ages past, individuals and nations have cherished wisdom as more than mere wishful thinking or hopeful yearning. We have acknowledged its vital role in sustaining stable societies and healthy cultures. And we have recognized its essential role in enabling us to finish what we start.

English essayist Samuel Johnson declared,

There are, indeed, many truths which time necessarily and certainly teaches, and which might, by those who have learned them from experience, be communicated to their successors at a cheaper rate: but dictates, though liberally enough bestowed, are generally without effect, the teacher gains few proselytes by instruction which his own behavior contradicts; and young men miss the benefit of counsel, because they are not very ready to believe that those who fall below them in practice, can much excel them in theory. Thus the progress of knowledge is retarded, the world is kept long in the same state, and every new race is to gain the prudence of their predecessors by committing and redressing the same miscarriages.

In other words, one of the characteristics of wisdom is the ability to practice what we preach! If we are going to finish the race set before us, then we will not only need to run with endurance; we will need to run with discernment, informed by our vision, bolstered by our courage, and inspired by the experience we absorb from our wise forebears. One of the greatest ways to practice efficiency and time management, better than any of the instant meals and short-cut appliances we can buy, is to take our time and avoid repeating the errors of the past.

3. TO SEE THINGS THROUGH TO THE END DEMANDS WORK

The callow side of our nature does not much care for work. We complain about it. We chafe against it. We will do just about anything to get out of it. Nevertheless, we probably would reluctantly admit that nearly everything in life worth anything at all demands of us a certain measure of labor and intensity. And though this might appear at first glance to be a plight of woe and hardship, it is a part of the glory of the human experience. The good news is that work is good. Work is the means by which we achieve, at long last, our destiny. It is the means by which we attain our calling.

The remarkable Helen Keller once

> *I wish to preach not the doctrine of ignoble ease but the doctrine of the strenuous life; the life of toil and effort; of labor and strife; to preach that highest form of success which comes not to the man who desires mere easy peace but to the man who does not shrink from danger, hardship, or from the bitter toil, and who out of these wins the splendid ultimate triumph.*
>
> —THEODORE ROOSEVELT

said, "I long to accomplish a great and noble task, but it is my chief duty to accomplish humble tasks as though they were great and noble. The world is moved along not by the mighty shoves of its heroes, but by the aggregate of the tiny pushes of each honest worker." Every time you simply put your nose to the grindstone to accomplish your work, every time you put your shoulder to the plow to undertake your labor, every time you push through your exhaustion to the end of the day, you move the world along with tiny pushes.

ALL THE WAY

Since courage, wisdom, and hard work are difficult virtues to achieve and maintain, how do we begin to build them into our lives so we will be able to stand fast during the storms that inevitably and invariably rage around us?

1. FOCUS ON THE SOLUTIONS, NOT THE PROBLEMS

Often we get so caught up in the problems that we neglect the most important responsibility of a principled leader in a crisis: solving the problems and ending the crisis. We focus on the fact that we have been unfairly treated, that we have been blindsided, that our words have been misquoted, that our ideas have been misrepresented, and that our goals have been subverted. While such injustices may have occurred, dwelling upon them accomplishes nothing. Instead of wallowing in self-pity, we must address the root of the problems and train our attentions on solutions. We must provide answers. General George Patton had a basic rule for all his commanders: "Never bring me problems without at least three possible solutions." While such an approach seems best suited for a work environment (we have certainly endeavored to follow its precepts in my office), it can apply to almost any aspect of life, professional or personal, public or private.

2. KEEP YOUR EYE ON THE RIM, NOT ON THE SCOREBOARD

Legendary UCLA basketball coach John Wooden constantly exhorted his players to focus on their game, their intentions, their skills, their fundamentals, and their strategy. If they followed this teaching, the score would take care of itself. All too often, particularly when the storms of life strike, we tend to obsess over the scoreboard rather than attend to our shot. We're looking over our shoulder, paying more attention to the next person than we are to what actually matters—why we are there and what we are trying to accomplish. When we allow ourselves to be drawn off track, we will have a very hard time finishing well—if we are able to finish at all.

During the recount, I have said that our focus upon following the law was simple; however, disallowing the personal attacks from becoming major distractions was more difficult. The morning after the news media broadcast aerial views of Ryder trucks being escorted by law enforcement on their way to deliver ballots to Tallahassee— reminiscent of O. J. Simpson's SUV being followed by police cars— I recall reading an online news report that took my breath away. The article quoted an evening TV commentator's statement that "America was watching in hope that O.J. Simpson had murdered Katherine Harris." At the time, I knew neither the commentator, Bill Maher of the former *Politically Incorrect* program, nor that he was attempting humor. In light of the serious threats I had received, I was more than a little distracted! Nonetheless, we continued to focus "on the rim" and exercise the oath of office . . . to follow the law.

3. BALANCE URGENCY WITH PATIENCE

In a crisis, things are urgent. Something has to be done, and it has to be done immediately. A principled leader never hesitates when action is needed, when decisions must be made, or when duty calls. But an effective leader also will always look before leaping. A sense of urgency is a virtue when lives are at stake, when justice is threatened, or when truth is jeopardized; however, urgency must be balanced by patience. All actions must be considered, and all decisions must be weighed. The consequences of our moves and directives must be kept in view. Before we pull the trigger, it is always a good idea to take a deep breath and exhale. It is always appropriate to season urgency with discretion. In the midst of a crisis, there is nothing worse than someone who has suddenly become a loose cannon.

The terror, sacrifices, and hardship that so many people endured as a result of the events of September 11 put the average pressures and minor emergencies of our lives in perspective. But at some time, each of us is likely to face a challenge that will require courage that seems beyond our grasp. On such an occasion, we can draw strength from the memory of that day, those heroes, and others like them. Suddenly, we may discover that summoning the inner reserves to face our trials—to finish what we start—is not so difficult after all.

* * *

MYTH CONCEPTION:
WINNERS AND LOSERS

As a man thinketh in his heart so is he.
—KING SOLOMON

Everyone loves a winner. The sweet smell of success draws nearly all of us like moths to a candle flame. Prior to the tragedy of September 11, popularity, celebrity, prominence, and fame had served not only as the hallmarks of our age, but also as the only credentials we required for adulation or leadership.

In the radically altered environment that followed the horrific attacks upon our nation, Americans experienced a profound rebirth of unity, spirit, and resolve. Churches, synagogues, mosques, museums, and historic sites experienced record attendance. All of us searched for the meaning beyond the mundane. We replaced our normal fixation upon celebrities and athletes with our veneration of the ordinary men and women who, on that awful day, proved themselves capable of the extraordinary.

For quite some time prior to this extreme test of our national mettle, our society had exalted sum over substance. We had valued lip service to popularly accepted notions over true adherence to genuinely held convictions. As a result, we tended to be not particularly fond of the peculiar, the obscure, or the unpopular. In fact, we viewed with skepticism anyone who failed to garner kudos from the world at large. If someone fell prey to vilification, defamation, or humiliation, we simply assumed that she or he was somehow at fault.

I dearly hope that our nation can maintain the dramatically different set of values it appeared to adopt in the immediate aftermath of September 11. We must do so, however, while retaining our ability to question our assumptions and to challenge easy platitudes. Just as President Bush counseled us to expect a long, difficult road to victory in our nation's war against terrorism, we must also steel ourselves for the long battle to restore civility, charity, and compassion to our society.

In sum, we must retain our courage to express unpopular and unconventional viewpoints. We must redouble our determination to do what we believe is right, even if the popular "wisdom" tells us that we are on the "losing" side of an issue.

I do not know how many times I was told that even though I was right in strictly upholding the law and seeing the election through to the bitter end, I was ruining my career and destroying any chance I once had of a future in elective office. I was washed up, they said.

Quite frankly, I worried about that a bit—in those very rare moments when I had time to breathe, when I had time to think through the implications of everything that was transpiring. But while I knew it ought to be the goal of every principled leader to prevail in the end, I also knew that whatever happened during the post-election storm, whether in the courts, in the press, or in the late night monologues, my responsibility was not to win at any cost; it was to do what was right . . . to make certain the rule of law prevailed.

Throughout the recount crisis my husband, Anders—who had only been a U. S. citizen for five months—offered me the *best* advice. He said I must protect my staff from the strategic maneuvering of either party. Most importantly, within two days after the election his was the only voice in the wilderness that reminded me of this simple truth—that I had to act with the utmost integrity, because, he said, "regardless of who becomes the next president of the United States, you will have to live with the consequences of your actions for the rest of your life." His words set the tone for the next thirty-six days.

My standard for measuring what it meant to win or lose simply had to rise above immediate expectations and short-term pragmatism. I realized that the lowest common denominator should not be my guide, regardless of how much it was urged upon me by friends and foes alike. I had much to accomplish, then and still, and over the course of a lifetime, I still desire to finish what I have started.

Connie, Come to Georgia

Connie, come to Georgia.
Drive down Highway 85.
Meet me at Grandma's graveside.
We'll speak of when she was alive.
In the silence of the day,
We'll place flowers on her grave,
And we'll ask the question, "Why"
Did we let her slip away,
Just before we got to say,
How much she means, and just goodbye?

Connie, tell me about Papa.
I was so young when he passed on.
Tell me, did he love Grandma?
Was she the same when he was gone?
In the silence of the day,
We'll place flowers on his grave,
And we'll ask the question, "Why"
Did we let him slip away,
Just before we got to say,
How much he means, and just goodbye?

Seems the older that we get
The need to not forget
Is so much stronger 'cause we know.
Time waits for no one. Let us say

All we need to say,
While today is still today.
Connie, sure do miss you.
More than a sister, you're a friend.
Distance can't separate us
From these memories deep within
Remember towards the end,
Where Grandma might cry at any time.
Could she have been remembering,
All those sad unsaid goodbyes?
She had her share of lonely days,
When she placed flowers on a grave,
And she asked the question, "Why"
Did she let them slip away, just before she got to say,
How much they mean, and just goodbye?

Connie, come to Georgia.

"If it were not for my daddy buying me a guitar for my fourteenth birthday,"
says Wes, "and my brother Mitch being such a fine writer and musician, I would
not be making records. Mitch usually dreams his best work. He called me one
night after having dreamed the idea for this song. He asked me to help him finish it, and I am glad he did."

PRINCIPLE 5

DO WHAT IS RIGHT—AND THE FUTURE WILL TAKE CARE OF ITSELF

It is not enough to know what is right. It is not even always enough to do what is right. To do the right thing in the wrong way can easily result in disaster. It is vital that we do what is right and that we do it in the proper manner. Principled leaders realize that if they focus on doing the right thing in the right way, the future will take care of itself.

What enables someone to exercise principled leadership? What character traits must we possess in order to endure the tumults and storms of life? How must we rise to an occasion, meet a challenge, and face down adversity in order to be truly effective?

Good intentions and fine rhetoric are not enough. If we are going to lead— whether at home, on the job, or before the entire nation—we cannot just "talk the talk"; we must "walk the walk." We must adhere to that adage in the context of our everyday lives, not just when the eyes of the world are upon us. Integrity is about

> *There is only one form of political strategy in which I have any confidence, and that is to try to do the right thing—and sometimes be able to succeed.*
>
> —CALVIN COOLIDGE

who we are and what we do when no one is looking. We win or lose the great battles of our lives before we take the field, through how we prepare for the onslaught.

Throughout history, real stories of heroism and leadership have not relied upon extraordinary ability, uncommon giftedness, exalted genius, or even incisive vision. Rather, the constants we see are unwavering character, moral resolve, and determined, practical ethics.

DO THE RIGHT THING

Contrary to every reasoned expectation, the heroes of history ultimately triumphed not because they had superior armies, better strategies, greater resources, wiser counsel, or more support. They might not have initially prevailed at all. Eventually, however, they won the long-term battle because they were willing to do what was right—no matter what.

One such leader emerged as Germany, still wrestling with the effects of its World War I defeat and struggling to find definition as a nation, confronted the rise of the National Socialist Party. Hitler's Nazi movement promised the German populace the illusion of economic stability, national recognition, and European dominance, as well as offering perverted theories that wickedly manipulated the German people's woes. Few people recognized the evil undercurrents that flowed below the tide of Hitler's nationalist rhetoric, and few fought the surge. But Hitler did not fool Dietrich Bonhoeffer.

Born in 1906 in Breslau, Germany, Bonhoeffer exemplified dignity, action, and vitality as a leader throughout his adult life. At a time when silence and compliance provided the only hope of security, and when principled resistance served as an invitation to persecution and death, Bonhoeffer chose to do what was right, regardless of the consequences. His courageous life and heroic death during World War II have inspired secular and religious leaders alike.

The political evils that Bonhoeffer confronted were not ambivalent moral issues. His government sanctioned the military occupation of peaceful neighbor states, as well as the deportation and murder of millions of innocent people. In a series of lectures and radio broadcasts in 1933, before Hitler usurped power in Germany, Bonhoeffer publicly exhorted his fellow citizens to resist the depredations of the Nazi party. While he did not then foresee the specific evil and magnitude of the Holocaust, he presciently outlined the consequences of Nazism.

> *There is little extraordinary about the achievements of a genius, a prodigy, or a savant. Inevitably, a great leader is someone who overcomes tremendous obstacles and still succeeds. That is the essence of courage. It is the ability to maintain, in the face of grave perils, a kind of incognizance of the consequences of doing right. It is the ability to maintain great strength without any impulsive compulsion to use it—that strength is to be held in reserve until and unless it becomes necessary to use it for the cause of right.*
>
> **—TRISTAN GYLBERD**

During the 1930s, Bonhoeffer searched for the proper way to check the evils of his age. He spoke to college students in America, taught congregations in London, and ran an underground seminary in Berlin that attempted to produce church leaders with the backbone to resist Nazi rule. In each action, he roused people to moral consciousness instead of falling in with the prevalent passiveness of the time.

Bonhoeffer strove to do what was right in spite of the danger it posed. While abroad in America and England, he realized that he belonged in Germany, fighting Nazism from within. His return to Germany, given his vocal opposition to the ruling government, did not serve his personal best interest; but Bonhoeffer's primary concern was the good of his nation and its people. This same principle guided his decision to collaborate with high-ranking German military officers in a plot to assassinate Hitler. The plot, which was to plant a bomb in a meeting room where Hitler was seated, nearly succeeded. Bonhoeffer struggled with his conscience over the commission of murder, but he concluded that the prevention of many more murders was possible only through Hitler's death.

Bonhoeffer's complicity in the plot led to his arrest and imprisonment in a concentration camp, where he continued to exhort his fellow prisoners daily, as well as urging his nation to action in letters smuggled from prison that chronicled the evil workings of the Nazi regime. Bonhoeffer held to his moral compass despite the most extreme persecution. He even refused to escape from prison in order to safeguard his family from possible reprisals.

Dietrich Bonhoeffer died on April 9, 1945, only three weeks before the American liberation of his prison camp. He was hanged as a traitor, an ironic sentence for the man who refused to betray his moral convictions or the best interests of his country. While Bonhoeffer did not emerge victorious to guide Germany in postwar healing, his steadfast courage and his resistance of evil continue to inspire the triumphs of freedom.

Remaining true to our beliefs is difficult. Doing so when it is not popular constitutes the mark of true fortitude. But truth be told, when we offer ourselves only the option of doing what is right, the future will take care of itself.

THE MAKING OF A VISIONARY

We may embrace the practices of standing by our ideals, sticking to our guns, and doing what is right. But to accomplish our goals, we must take the latter principle one step farther. In addition to doing what is right, it helps to do the right thing the right way. As we hold to our vision, we must cultivate opportunities to act effectively. Like speechmakers who take the time to "soften up the audience" before delivering a difficult message, we do well to create a receptive atmosphere rather than impose our will or further antagonize a hostile opponent. We need to do our homework, discover what is called for, rally our friends, and know our enemy—especially when that enemy is our own impatience, anger, arrogance, or weariness.

The more clarity we can bring to our first principles, the more likely we will be guided to right action—the right way—in times of crisis. Our principles complement and support one another. When we do the right thing, we can have faith that the future

> *The streets of hell are paved with good intentions.*
> —MARK TWAIN

will take care of itself because we have acted according to *all* of our principles.

What about those times when we have done what we believed to be right, only to have our actions backfire? Many of us have experienced the unforeseen and sometimes harmful repercussions of well-meaning, poorly timed, or badly conceived attempts to help others. For example, I recall a story about villagers in a developing nation who were taught to garden to alleviate their food shortage. Unfortunately, the erstwhile aid workers planted an unfamiliar vegetable none of the villagers would eat, and the project failed. The aid workers were dedicated, altruistic people who genuinely wanted to help, but their "we know best" assumptions overcame the fundamental respect due others; they forgot to ask, "What do you like to eat?" They did the right thing in the wrong way.

One powerful example of someone who did the right thing the right way—and therefore lived to profoundly influence the course of history—began as an obscure sixteenth-century Augustinian monk at an unknown university in the backwaters of Germany—Martin Luther. Luther never dreamed that he would light the fire of the Protestant Reformation. Circumstances unexpectedly thrust him onto the international stage, making him the primary target for both the religious and the imperial authorities who held Europe under their monolithic control.

Not born to a particularly wealthy family, young Martin was fortunate to receive an education, beginning with Latin school in Mansfeld in 1492. He later attended schools in Magdeburg and Eisenach, and graduated from the University of Erfurt with a Master of Arts degree. In May 1505 he began his preparation for a career in law. An unexpected encounter with a thunderstorm interrupted his studies, however. On his way back to the university during a severe storm, Martin's fear of being struck by lightning spurred him to vow that he would enter the priesthood if he were spared. He survived the storm, and thereafter reluctantly left the university to join the Augustinian order, fulfilling his vow.

Luther quickly climbed the ecclesiastical ladder, achieving ordination as a priest. He then began teaching moral philosophy and biblical theology at the University in Wittenberg, where he quietly conducted his classes until October 1517.

> *Most people aren't appreciated enough, and the bravest things we do in our lives are usually known only to ourselves. No one throws a ticker tape on the man who chose to be faithful to his wife, or the lawyer who chose not to take the drug money, or the daughter who held her tongue again and again. All this is anonymous heroism.*
>
> —PEGGY NOONAN

Meanwhile in Rome, Pope Leo X had authorized Prince Albert of Germany to sell indulgences (essentially certificates purchased for the forgiveness of sins), and summoned a monk named Johann Tetzel to sell indulgences in Prince Albert's realm.

Over the years Luther had developed theological beliefs that prompted him to question the Church's practice regarding indulgences. Not fond of Tetzel's character or his salesmanship, Luther challenged the monk to an academic debate on indulgences by posting a set of points for discussion on the community bulletin board of the day—the local church door. The date was October 31, 1517, and the list of debate points was his now famous Ninety-five Theses.

Anticipating only local interest in his challenge, Luther, along with the rest of Europe, was astonished when copies of his Ninety-five Theses were translated into several languages and circulated as far as England in a period of less than a month. This unprecedented challenge of the prevailing orthodoxy propelled Luther into the forefront of both church and state politics.

Almost immediately, Luther's new theological ideas became the target of numerous works of rebuttal. The barrage of invective steeled Luther's soul, and he responded to it in depth with his vast erudition and keen use of logic. His ferocity infuriated his opponents, who had intended to marginalize the upstart. He refused to be frightened into silence or compliance, however, despite threats of imprisonment and possible execution. Luther was not looking for trouble, but he was not running from trouble, either.

Having frustrated church authorities at the Diet of Augsburg in August 1518, Luther was later summoned to Rome by Pope Leo X. But Luther's political protector, Frederick the Wise of Saxony, prince of the domain in which he lived, refused to send him to Rome, knowing that certain death awaited him there. The attacks against Luther grew, only because his ideas had sparked religious debates across the whole of Europe.

Luther's failure to appear in Rome prompted Pope Leo X to issue a bull of excommunication against Luther, effective January 1521. Once a copy of the order reached Wittenberg, Luther's university friends threw a party at which Luther burned a copy of the bull. In response, Pope Leo X asked the political authorities to become involved. The emperor of the Holy Roman Empire, Charles V, declared Luther an outlaw and forbade anyone within his domain to protect him.

Luther was summoned to appear before the emperor at the Diet of Worms in April 1521, a meeting characterized as a hearing. Everyone on

> *Courage is a character trait most oft attributable to men. In fact, it is the universal virtue of all those who choose to do the right thing over the expedient thing. It is the common currency of all those who do what they are supposed to do in a time of conflict, crisis, and confusion.*
>
> —FLORENCE NIGHTINGALE

both sides knew what was going to happen; they had seen it all before. Several decades earlier the Bohemian reformer, Jan Hus, had been awarded safe conduct to appear before the church authorities at the Council of Constance, but once he arrived his safe conduct was stripped, and he was tried in a proceeding at which he was forbidden to defend himself. Hus was immediately convicted and burned at the stake, and no one doubted that the same fate awaited Luther at Worms. Both the church and the political authorities were looking to crush the escalating religious revolt.

As expected, after his arrival Luther was informed that he would not be given an opportunity to defend himself. On a table piled high were Luther's books, and seated around the room according to their stations were powerful secular and religious officials. Before the crowd, Luther was asked if the books were his and if there was anything in the books he would recant.

Luther, overcome with his change of circumstances, asked for time to consider his answer. This was granted, and he was summoned back the next evening. Gathering his nerve, Luther gave a summary defense that his examiner ignored. He was directed to answer "yes" or "no" as to whether he would retract his inflammatory views. Resigning himself to a likely death sentence, Luther replied, "Unless I can be instructed and convinced with evidence from the Holy Scriptures or with open, clear, and distinct grounds and reasoning— and my conscience is captive to the Word of God—then I cannot and will not recant, because it is neither safe nor wise to act against conscience. Here I stand. I can do no other. God help me! Amen."

Luther refused to buckle, but he also declined to give his opponents any ammunition they could use to execute him. He kept his cool and did not directly insult Emperor Charles V or Pope Leo X. He did what he believed was right, and he did it the right way.

The dazed bureaucrats were speechless as Luther was permitted to leave the city unharmed. The emperor did issue a general pardon for anyone who killed Luther, but Luther's friends staged a "kidnapping" and took him to Frederick's Wartburg Castle, where he remained for the next eight months. During that time, he translated the New Testament into German, another turning point in the Reformation.

Luther continued to challenge religious authorities for the rest of his life. Remarkably, having lived a full life, he died of natural causes in 1546, leaving a host of writings and sermons behind him. His self-defense at the Diet of Worms proved to be one of the defining cultural moments of the last millennium. Untrained as an orator and professionally called as a professor, not a politician, Luther stood firm against the most powerful figures of his day and survived to unintentionally lead Europe into a new era. When circumstances demanded it, he held firm at the risk of his life. Through it all, he refused to take any action that would have led him to abandon his moral compass.

From his beginnings as a modest teacher of strong principle, when called, Luther proved to be a visionary leader whose firm convictions and unwavering fortitude forever changed the monolithic spiritual worldview of a continent.

> *Error lives but a day.*
> *Truth is eternal.*
> —JAMES LONGSTREET

THE TRUTH WILL OUT

The truth will prevail. Right will endure. Integrity will triumph in the end. Justice and virtue are able to withstand every charge. Such ideals are sufficient unto themselves; in due course, they will prove their own value and veracity. As Shakespeare once quipped, "In the end the truth will out."

I clung to this maxim throughout the post-election storm. My greatest solace in that difficult time was my conviction that I had acted consistently and fairly at all junctures. In particular, I had taken special care to ensure that this description applied not only to the decisions I made, but also to how I made them.

The Bible's book of Esther has long meant a great deal to me. As with the other heroes and leaders I discuss in this book, I do not seek to equate myself to her status, her experiences, or her courage. Rather, I merely aspire to her model of selfless determination to do what is right, regardless of the cost or consequences. Esther, a Jewish woman, became queen to King Xerxes (or Ahasuerus), whose vast reign extended from India to the upper Nile in southern Egypt. No one knew of Esther's heritage except her uncle, Mordecai, but the truth would prove crucial. When Mordecai discovered a plot to annihilate the Jewish people, he asked Esther to go before the king to plead for their salvation. He said, "And who knows but that you have come to royal position for such a time as this?" (Esther 4:14, NIV.) At peril to her own life, Esther approached her king to intervene with the truth. The Jewish people were saved, and today this celebrated event is commemorated annually as Purim.

Esther faced greater danger than I could comprehend in my wildest imagination. Nevertheless, she provided me with a vital example that I drew upon as the recount controversy peaked in intensity. If this incredibly brave woman could have faith in the future when her life was at stake, how could I *not* have faith in the future when only my political career was in jeopardy?

Soon after the massive media consortium that conducted its own recount of the 2000 presidential election in Florida released its findings (one year later, in November 2001), a *Sarasota Herald-Tribune* columnist waxed as follows in a commentary he titled "Katherine Harris could have been a hero to her party and country":

> Not-yet-elected congresswoman Katherine Harris will probably claim, if she hasn't yet, that an exhaustive presidential ballot review confirms she was right. It doesn't. What the just-released study of Florida's machine-rejected presidential ballots really shows is that the hand-count Harris helped derail in the fall of 2000 would have elected her man anyway.

Aside from his misinformed assertion that I "derailed" manual recounts[6] and his false implication that I made "electing my man" the objective of my decisions during the recount controversy, this columnist missed the mark entirely when he advised me as to how I could have been "a hero."

I never set out to be a hero to anyone. Not to President Bush. Not to Governor Jeb Bush. Not to former Vice President Gore. Not to the Republican Party. Not to the Democratic Party. And not to the media. I simply performed my duties in a manner faithful to the rule of law, to my oath of office, and to the people of Florida.

In time, I have faith that this truth will become more apparent to more people. As commentators begin to examine the events of the recount controversy through the more objective vantage point of history, I hope that their analysis of *how* I followed the law will inform their opinion of *why* I followed the law.

The controversy that surrounded my decision to deny Palm Beach County's request for an extension beyond the Florida Supreme Court's expressed deadline for the submission of recount returns provides an instructive example. When the Florida Supreme Court rewrote the law to move the deadline for counties to certify final vote returns to my Division of Elections from November 14 to November 26, it included the following curious directive:

> In order to *allow maximum time for contests* . . . amended certifications must be filed with the Elections Canvassing Commission by *5 P.M. on Sunday, November 26, 2000,* and the secretary of state and the Elections Canvassing Commission *shall* accept any such amended certifications received by 5 P.M. on Sunday, November 26, 2000, provided that the office of the secretary of state, Division of Elections is open in order to allow receipt thereof. If the office *is not open* for this special purpose on Sunday, November 26, 2000, *then* any amended certifications shall be accepted until 9 A.M. on Monday, November 27, 2000. (My italics.)

This order did not instruct me to announce whether my office would be open that following Sunday. Had I wished to assist the Bush campaign, I would have waited to ascertain the progress and direction of the recounts before I made that decision. Then, if the recount totals indicated that Al Gore was moving ahead in the vote count, I could have decided to keep my office closed on Sunday in order to give the Bush campaign until Monday morning to find votes before the Elections Canvassing Commission certified Al Gore as the winner. By contrast, if it appeared on Sunday afternoon that George W. Bush would retain his lead, I could have walked into the Capitol without any notice whatsoever, opened for business, and demanded all amended certifications by 5:00 P.M. that day.

Instead of embarking on such a disingenuous course of action, we announced on Wednesday, November 22 (the morning immediately following the Florida Supreme Court's order), that we would be open on Sunday (Thanksgiving weekend) in order to accept amended certifications so as to permit either candidate the maximum amount of time to conduct a postcertification contest. At that time, we did not know that Palm Beach County would choose to take Thanksgiving Day off, which prevented that county's manual recount from finishing by Sunday's 5:00 P.M. deadline, as did the other counties.

The Florida Supreme Court's unambiguous order gave us no choice but to deny Palm Beach County's eleventh-hour request for an extension. By its own express terms, the court's order set hard-and-fast deadlines "in order to allow maximum time for contests."

Imagine the hue and cry if I had violated the court's order, thereby delaying the commencement of contest proceedings by one day or more. Imagine if that loss of time had been why Florida could not complete a recount ordered by a court in the contest phase before the federal deadline. I can envision the headlines: "Setup! Harris Knew Palm Beach Extension Would Cut Off Statewide Recount in Contest"; "What Did Harris Know, and When Did She Know It?"; and "Harris Helps Bush Campaign by Violating Supreme Court's Order."

Of course, many people have accepted the often-repeated myth that Palm Beach County finished its recount in the two hours it requested after the 5:00 P.M. deadline. Palm Beach County did *not* finish in two hours. It did not finish in two days. In fact, it *never* finished. The county canvassing board simply could not produce reliable numbers. Today, Palm Beach County's still untotaled results are on display in the Museum of Governance and Political History, which is located in Tallahassee at Florida's old Capitol.

On Sunday just after 7:00 P.M., Al Gore had gained 215 votes, according to reports. After days of audits, Palm Beach County submitted an unsigned, uncertified spreadsheet to the Division of Elections, which showed Al Gore with a net gain of 188 votes. Then again, some sources reported this number as 174. The Florida Supreme Court's order of December 8 stated this number as being 176 or 215.

Perhaps this time Joseph Goebbels' adage, "[If you] tell a lie that is big enough, and repeat it often enough, the whole world will believe it," will be defied. To date, however, numbers of widely disseminated distortions about the recount have been accepted as "truth" in our country's political lexicon. While the media are fully aware of the above-cited facts, they have yet to report them accurately. I continue to have faith, however, that the truth will eventually be reported, thereby vindicating my motives. In the meantime, my task has been to continue doing the right thing. Nothing more and nothing less.

Not surprisingly, I have found this task to be easier said than done. To summon the fortitude and clarity to carry through, I have found it helpful to reaffirm a number of presuppositions in my own heart and mind:

I. DOING RIGHT DEMANDS A PASSION FOR TRUTH

Truth is not an abstract notion. It is not a projection of some artificial ethical system. Truth is a manifestation of the way things actually are—a part of the warp and woof of the real world. A passion for truth, then, is a passion for clear-eyed, sane and sensible, rubber-meets-the-road reality. Truth is believable—because it squares with the world as it actually is and with us as we actually are. It is objective, consistent, and balanced. It is accessible, knowable, and comprehensible. . .dependable, predictable, and unchangeable.

> *He that is warm for truth, and fearless in its defense, performs one of the duties of a good man; he strengthens his own conviction, and guards others from delusion; but steadiness of belief, and boldness of profession, are yet only part of the form of godliness.*
>
> —SAMUEL JOHNSON

When we live in accordance with the truth, not only is the right thing easier to discern, but it is easier to do. Truth is not only sensible and sane; it proves to be remarkably fruitful and productive. We are able to make progress, serve justice, satisfy hope, confirm love, establish trust, and safeguard freedom.

The principled leader will always have a passion for truth—to know its dimensions, to secure its affirmations, and to stand upon its foundations. The principled leader will always seek to live in the light of truth.

2. CHARACTER REALLY IS THE ISSUE

If we are going to do what is right, we will have to root our lives in substantive character. We will have to inculcate virtue. We will have to build a strong moral foundation. Philosopher and Oxford scholar Os Guinness has said, "In the end, who we are when no one sees will determine what we can do when everyone is looking."

When the storm strikes, it is not the Dow Jones Industrial Average that matters most to us. It is not the international balance of trade that captures our imagination. What we really want to know— *all* we really want to know—is whether our leaders are willing to do what is right. When push comes to shove, what matters most to us is not so much what we do as who we are. Character is the issue that supersedes all other issues.

3. LEAVE THE RESULTS TO PROVIDENCE

If we do the right thing in the right way, the future will take care of itself. Why? Because the future is in the domain of Providence. We can't worry ourselves over outcomes we cannot control. Especially in times of crisis, when we need all of our inner resources available, we only spin our wheels and waste critical energy when we fret over potentialities beyond our purview.

If we attempt to make decisions with an eye toward history, if we attempt to fulfill our calling in light of how we will be remembered, or if we strive to control the outcome of events by manipulation or exploitation, we are likely to be undone by the consequences of our self-aggrandizement or shortsightedness. It would be far better, in the end, to leave the end alone and focus instead on the choices that are actually within our control. . .to do what is right in the here and now and leave the future to sort itself out.

And who is there to harm you if you prove zealous for what is good?

But even if you should suffer for the sake of righteousness, you are blessed. And do not fear their intimidation, and do not be troubled,

but sanctify Christ as Lord in your hearts, always being ready to make a defense to everyone who asks you to give an account for the hope that is in you, yet with gentleness and reverence;

and keep a good conscience so that in the thing in which you are slandered, those who revile your good behavior in Christ may be put to shame.

For it is better, if God should will it so, that you suffer for doing what is right rather than for doing what is wrong.

1 PETER 3:13-17 (NASB)

When the recount controversy erupted, thankfully, I was able to remember that I did not need to *be* perfect in order to *do* right. Character is not the absence of faults but the willingness to deal with faults with transparency and integrity. I was able to remember that I did not need to understand all the long-term implications of everything before me—that character is not prescience but steadfastness in what we believe is right. I was granted the grace to be reminded that if I would just do my job, the future would take care of itself.

* * *

MYTH CONCEPTION:
CHARACTER *DOES* MATTER

Character is the only secure foundation of the state.
—CALVIN COOLIDGE

During the post-Cold War, economic boom years of the 1990s, our nation engaged in a lively debate concerning whether character mattered in our leaders. In times of relative security, prosperity, and ease, we may find it easy to think that our leaders' character is not an essential concern for the health and welfare of humanity and nations . . . as proven by our relative sense of comfort. When a crisis strikes, however, we immediately know otherwise. The extraordinary character that ordinary Americans displayed in the hours, days, weeks, and months following the September 11 terrorist attack on Washington and New York should forever quell that debate. The tireless courage of police officers, firefighters, rescue workers, and ordinary citizens like Lisa Beamer buoyed the spirit of America. The compassion, tenacity, forthrightness, and resolve of local, state, and national leaders reinvigorated our sense of purpose as a people and as a nation.

It was not merely adversity that united the nation in those days. Rather, leaders like Rudy Giuliani and George W. Bush showed us their mettle. They showed us their moral resolve. And in so doing, they fostered a spirit of unity.

Leadership expert John C. Maxwell has said, "Crisis doesn't make character, but it certainly reveals it. Adversity is a crossroad that makes a person choose one of two paths: character or compromise. Every time he chooses character, he becomes stronger, even if that choice brings negative consequences."

Almost one year after the terrorist attacks, public opinion polls indicated that President Bush had continued to maintain an astonishingly high job approval rating—in the seventieth percentile range. According to the *Los Angeles Times,* he had "the highest and longest sustained job approval rating ever recorded." President Bush gained his mandate to govern not by simply running an effective campaign and garnering vote totals; he earned it by doing the right thing the right way in a time of terrible difficulty.

She Stands

When the night seems to say
All hope is lost, gone away,
But I know I'm not alone,
By the light, she stands.

There she waves, faithful friend,
Shimmering stars, westward wind,
Show the way, carry me,
To the place, she stands.

Just when you think it might be over,
Just when you think the fight is gone,
Someone will risk his life to raise her,
There she stands.

There she flies, clear blue sky,
Reminds us with red, of those who died.
Washed in white, by the brave,
In their strength, she stands.

When evil calls itself a martyr,
When all your hopes come crashing down,
Someone will pull her from the rubble,
There she stands.

We've seen her flying torn and tattered,
We've seen her stand the test of time,
And through it all the fools have fallen,
There she stands.

By the dawn's early light
Through the perilous fight,
She stands.

"I thought I was patriotic before 9/11," Wes writes. "I thought I loved my country and was thankful for the sacrifice of my forefathers. I was wrong. I suppose it is a part of the human condition to be complacent when given the chance. We default to taking things for granted. It often takes tragedy to awaken us from our daydreams and remind us that freedom comes with a price that we pray our children never have to pay. The flag is always flying to remind us of that inescapable fact. She flies from one generation to the next and far too quickly becomes decoration, at best, for many. Then one day a tyrant tries to tear her down, and it is then that those fortunate enough to be born in the greatest nation on the face of the earth will risk their lives to raise her. And there She Stands."

PRINCIPLE 6

FEED YOUR MIND

Winston Churchill once said, "In order to lead, one must read." The best preparation for times of difficulty is a well-rounded, well-trained mind. Undisciplined thinking creates a terrible impediment on the day of testing—whether that day of testing is a September 11, the loss of a job, the birth of a child, the beginning of a new semester, or the resolution of an election conflict.

In the hours immediately following the first recount in Florida, when lawyers acting on behalf of the Gore campaign requested selective hand recounts in four of Florida's most heavily Democratic counties, even the most seasoned experts in election law were unprepared for the unprecedented situation that had arisen—so I knew I had a lot to learn. Together, my office, the state of Florida, and our nation careened toward the unexplored realms of election law—a body of law singularly beset with nuances, complexities, technicalities, and subtleties.

Thankfully, my parents always encouraged me to develop my capacity to read, study, and grow, and as a result, I have long been an inveterate learner. They persuaded me to attend a small liberal arts college, despite our family's close and historic ties to both the University of Florida and Florida State University. They encouraged my study in

Spain during my junior year so I could pursue my interests in language, literature, music, history, and art. They supported my decision to go to Switzerland after I received my undergraduate degree to study philosophy and theology at L'Abri with Dr. Francis Schaeffer. They also served as my chief cheerleaders when I decided to study at Harvard for a master's degree in public administration, concentrating in international affairs and negotiations, while I was serving in the Florida state senate.

> *A broad interest in books usually means a broad interest in life.*
> —LYMAN ABBOTT

As an avid reader for as long as I can remember, I have read everything from thick historic novels to the backs of cereal boxes, from enduring masterworks to temporal policy papers, and from soulful spiritual exhortations to brief e-mail transmissions. To my delight, my grandmother gave me her collection of dozens of leatherbound classics; one of my lifetime projects is to read each one at least once. My parents read to us for hours as children, and one of our favorite collections included dozens of classics, from *Little Women* and *Black Beauty* to tales of King Arthur and Robin Hood to *Arabian Nights* and *Call of the Wild*.

Our home runs perpetually short of bookshelf space-despite the fact that books lay everywhere throughout. I always have a stack of books by my bedside, a paperback tucked into the side pocket of my briefcase, and another protruding from my purse. I usually find myself attempting to read three or four books at one time. I tend to find authors I adore, then I try to devour every morsel they have created.

I have always harbored a hunger to grow and learn, not because intense study has come easily for me, but because I know that it will be good for me. I have tried to stretch myself intellectually because I know that effective leaders perpetually add to their store of knowledge, understanding, and wisdom. In every culture throughout history, from King Alfred the Great and Charlemagne to our own

Thomas Jefferson and John Adams, the most noted leaders have been the most dedicated readers.

This is not to imply that leaders must be intellectual snobs or ivory tower elitists. On the contrary, effective leaders are often the most down-to-earth people in any given community at any given time. But over the course of their lives, the greatest leaders have developed the habit of private reflection as the basis for their public service. They have acquired the habits of inquisitiveness and thoughtfulness. They appreciate rip-roaring yarns as much as harmonious nuances of narration; they relish well-drawn characters as much as graceful and temperate prose; they celebrate evocative imagination as much as clear articulation. They love words, ideas, and stories. They love to laugh and cry. They yearn for grace and consolation. They care passionately about beauty, goodness, and truth. They are humble enough to know that they do not know everything they need to know. They appreciate the gift of participating in the great conversation about ideas across the ages. They are necessarily a breed apart because they have intimately connected themselves to the human experience through knowledge.

> *The man who does not read good books has no advantage over the man who can't read them.*
>
> —MARK TWAIN

IN THE COMPANY OF THE WISE

One such individual was the spiritual leader, Aiden Wilson (A. W.) Tozer. Born in rural Pennsylvania in 1897 to a family of meager means, Tozer never enjoyed the benefits of attending college, but in the early years of his adult life, he read voraciously and grew in erudition well beyond his years and formal education. He absorbed life's lessons from those who had plowed the intellectual ground before him, and encouraged others to appropriate the lessons of history.

"To think without a proper amount of good reading is to limit our thinking to our own tiny plot of ground," he wrote in his book *Man—The Dwelling Place of God.* "The crop cannot be large. To observe only and neglect reading is to deny ourselves the immense value of other people's observations; and since the better books are written by trained observers the loss is sure to be enormous."

From the works of writers on faith, he mined nuggets of wisdom and insight from generations past with which to enrich the members of his congregation, and later the innumerable readers of his books. He encouraged others to maintain a vigorous intellectual life and take a proactive approach to learning. For him, books were to be experienced interactively as a cooperative exchange between the reader and the writer, thereby bringing out the richness of the text.

"The best book is not one that informs merely, but one that stirs the reader up to inform himself," Tozer said. "The best writer is one that goes with us through the world of ideas like a friendly guide who walks beside us through the forest pointing out to us a hundred natural wonders we had not noticed before . . . If he has done his work well we can go on alone and miss little as we go."

> *I really believe you can't build a self without books. You get an inner voice by listening to someone else's words in your ear.*
>
> —JANE HAMILTON

Tozer's quest for learning was not a purely academic pursuit, but a crusade for the truth. By delving into his books, he interacted with the great thinkers and visionaries of history. His studies fed his unquenchable fire for knowledge; each new volume raised questions for further inquiry and understanding. He saw this process as the "midwife to assist at the birth of ideas that had been gestating long within our souls." The result was almost a half-century of ministry to his congregations, and more than forty books, some of which remain spiritual classics to this day.

Tozer's intellectual endeavors mirrored those of his nineteenth-century spiritual predecessor, Charles Spurgeon, who also lacked a formal academic education, but who quickly became the spiritual hub for the social and political leaders of Victorian London. His tireless efforts in preaching and writing resulted in over forty-one thousand pages of printed sermons, and his combined writings fill one hundred twenty-three volumes. But such productivity reflected not merely his uncanny genius, but also his aggressive love of learning.

"The man who never reads will never be read," Spurgeon said. "He who never quotes will never be quoted. He who will not use the thoughts of other men's brains, proves that he has no brains of his own. Brethren, what is true of ministers is true of all our people. You need to read." He practiced what he preached. By the time of his death, Spurgeon's private library exceeded twelve thousand volumes.

"My books are my tools," he explained about the sources of his inspiration. "They also serve as my counsel, my consolation, and my comfort. They are my source of wisdom and the font of my education. They are my friends and my delights. They are my surety, when all else is awry, that I have set my confidence in the substantial things of truth and right."

In their own time, both Tozer and Spurgeon were men of influence because they were men of learning. We continue to feel their impact today. By devoting themselves to a vigorous intellectual life, their lives overflowed with the fruit of their hard work. While their natural gifts made learning easier, they had to apply their studies in order for their knowledge to ripen into wisdom. This process required their significant investment of time and effort. But the return is felt in the many lives they have touched.

THE LEADER'S LEARNING LIFE

The poet and historian François Fénelon once said, "If the crowns of all the kingdoms of Europe were laid down at my feet in exchange for my books and my love of learning, I would spurn them all." He reasoned, "I would soon be bereft of the crowns anyway, because to rule long and rule well, one must continue to grow in knowledge and understanding." Like Tozer and Spurgeon, he realized that leaders could not afford the luxury of intellectual stagnation.

Principled leaders have always compre-hended this very basic truth. Thus, for a leader, all talk of education must serve as a reminder that we have only just begun to learn. Our magnificent heritage has introduced us to the splendors of literature, art, and music; history and science and ideas. A lifetime of adventure and riches awaits us in these vast arenas.

> *The end of reading is not more books but more life.*
> —HOLBROOK JACKSON

Indeed, the most valuable lessons education can convey are invariably the lessons that never end.

I. LEADERS ARE READERS

Our electronic age has spawned a host of distractions to keep us from the intellectual life. Meaningless sitcoms, the Xbox, and end-less hours of surfing the Web soak up much of the time we might otherwise devote to more challenging pursuits. Despite the rise in literacy in America, most people don't read because they feel it is unnecessary. C. S. Lewis found this trend to be true several decades ago:

> The majority, though they are sometimes frequent readers, do not set much store by reading. They turn to it as a last resource. They abandon it with alacrity as soon as any alternative pastime turns up. It is kept for railway journeys, illnesses, odd moments of enforced solitude, or for the process called reading oneself to sleep. They sometimes combine it with desultory conversation; often, with listening to the radio. But literary people are always looking for leisure and silence in which to read and do so with

their whole attention. When they are denied such attentive and undisturbed reading even for a few days they feel impoverished.

Many people do not read today because, with so many diversions and demands on our time, we must work to read. Reading requires discipline and initiative—learning traits that go hand in hand with effective leadership. Reading helps us understand the world. When a leader successfully navigates through the postmodern maze of image over substance, the route to what matters grows much shorter, and people wish to follow. People who are unwilling or unable to read find themselves buffeted by a world that quickly changes direction.

The ability to sense these shifts increases our opportunities to succeed in life. Thus, a gulf can open between those who read and those who do not. Reading and learning should never become the province of the elite. Seeing the disparity that can be created and the relative ease by which it can be remedied, I have made innovative adult literacy programs administered through our libraries a cornerstone of my tenure as Secretary of State.

2. LEADERS READ DEEPLY

> *You may perhaps be brought to acknowledge that it is very well worthwhile to be tormented for two or three years of one's life, for the sake of being able to read all the rest of it.*
>
> —JANE AUSTEN

According to Joseph Addison, "Reading is to the mind what exercise is to the body." Those who diligently strive to learn must develop disciplined habits. People who want to read must make the time to read, or the distractions of life will simply crowd out even the best intentions. Amidst the tyranny of the urgent, which seems the natural accompaniment to modern life, readers must find ways to catch moments of quiet, snatches of solitude, and brief interludes of attentiveness to the ideas and ideals of literature.

Invariably, the relentless prioritizing of time leads to a necessary prioritizing of content. At some point serious readers must come to the realization that they will never be able to read everything on their wish list, so they begin to read selectively, substantively, and deeply. They read important books. They read the classics. George MacDonald asserted, "There is a great deal of difference between the eager man who wants to read a book and the tired man who wants a book to read. A man reading a Le Quex mystery wants to get to the end of it. A man reading a Dickens novel wishes that it might never end."

3. LEADERS READ OUT OF THEIR TIME

G. K. Chesterton stated that "you can find all the new ideas in the old books; only there you will find them balanced, kept in their place, and sometimes contradicted and overcome by other and better ideas. The great writers did not neglect a fad because they had not thought of it, but because they had thought of it and of all the answers to it as well." Books from earlier ages provide us with a perspective that books from our own day simply cannot. Even our philosophical adversaries share a vast number of assumptions with us because they are our contemporaries. But writers from the past can often help us think outside the box. They help awaken us from the spell of contemporaneity.

The famed literary critic William Hazlitt stated,

I hate to read new books. There are twenty or thirty volumes that I have read over and over again, and these are the only ones that I have any desire ever to read at all. Some judge books as they do fashions or complexions, which are admired only in their newest gloss. That is not my way. I do not think altogether the worse of a book for having survived the author a generation or two. I have more confidence in the dead than the living. Contemporary writers may generally be divided into two classes—one's friends or one's foes. Of the first we are compelled to think too well, and of the last we are disposed to think too ill, to receive much genuine pleasure from the perusal, or to judge fairly of the merits of either.

> *The reading of all good books is like a conversation with the finest men of past centuries.*
> —RENÉ DESCARTES

If the mark of a good leader is that she or he will seek the best, the most experienced, and the wisest counsel, then inviting the counsel of the past is a foregone conclusion. William Ellery Channing said, "It is chiefly through books that we enjoy intercourse with superior minds. In the best books, great men talk to us, give us their most precious thoughts, and pour their souls into ours."

LEARNING TO LEARN

Francis Bacon wrote, "Some books are meant to be tasted, others to be swallowed, and some few to be chewed and digested; that is, some books are to be read only in parts; others to be read but not curiously; and some few to be read wholly, and with diligence and attention." A significant aspect of learning how to learn is honing the ability to assess and distinguish between our sources of information. When we can discern what is and what is not important, who is reliable, what his or her agenda or bias or cultural conditioning might be, we really begin to grow and mature. This process involves the development of a number of disciplines, habits, and appetites:

1. PRACTICE THE ART OF BROWSING

Browsing is but one of the many time-honored traditions that have been heedlessly cast aside amidst the hustle and bustle of modernity. Nevertheless, it is a habit that seems almost as natural as breathing in a bookstore. Whether visiting a fine old antiquarian dealer with dusty shelves, dark labyrinthine rooms, and hidden treasures amidst every stack, or a familiar neighborhood shop featuring fresh coffee, warm conversations, and the latest bestsellers, readers cherish these comfortable haunts nearly as much as they love the books they ultimately find there. (My favorites are in Aspen, Georgetown, Coral Gables, and yes, I have a favorite in Sarasota that no matter the time constraints, I visit every day when I awaken.)

It is amazing what we can learn simply by keeping our eyes open in such a place. In any bookstore or library, I love to look around, notice the displays and what people are reading, and soak in the atmosphere. I am consistently amazed by what I learn about myself and my community—as I am sure you will be. Merely by experiencing these moments and granting ourselves the time to think and process these observations, we can experience quiet epiphanies.

> *A well-read people are easy to lead, but difficult to drive; easy to govern but difficult to enslave.*
>
> —BARON HENRY BROUGHAM

2. READ ABOVE YOUR HEAD

Learning costs us something. To make it really pay off in the long run, we must invest in the process and defer immediate gratification. The whole point of learning, after all, is to stretch and grow—to broaden our horizons, sharpen our skills, and mature our perspective. We're not likely to widen our experience if we read "the same old same old." We need to intentionally break the mold, challenge ourselves. Norman Cousins wisely observed, "The way a book is read—which is to say, the qualities a reader brings to a book—can have as much to do with its worth as anything the author puts into it." Leaders are interested in the world and its wonders, and are unafraid to approach topics of which they know little. Leaders always reach higher and expect the most from themselves; that trait ultimately makes them effective leaders.

3. HAVE A PLAN

Oliver Wendell Holmes offered this advice: "It is a good plan to have a book with you in all places and at all times." While that axiom may be true, it constitutes only partial advice. It is not sufficient that a leader reads. It is not even sufficient that a leader reads a great deal. We must read wisely with an overall strategy in mind. The purpose of learning is not the mere accumulation of knowledge. Though reading is, in and of itself, a delightful pastime, it does not constitute an end in itself. The hope is that the process of learning results in enhanced judgment, understanding, and wisdom. Thus, it is vital that we develop a systematic plan of reading. I recommend keeping a list of books you want to tackle. (Mine is ever-growing.) You may wish to keep notes on your progress and your insights along the way. Then apply what you learn and use what you discover. As an only slightly less-than-obsessive collector of quotes, one of my favorite gadgets is my new scanner pen that downloads highlighted text to my computer or handheld organizer. Many of the passages and sayings I have saved have made their way into this book, and I truly hope you are enjoying them as much as I do!

> *Reading maketh a full man, conference a ready man, and writing an exact man.*
> —FRANCIS BACON

4. FOLLOW THE FOOTNOTE TRAIL

According to Clarence Cook, "For lovers of books, a house without books is no house at all; and in a family where books make a great part of the pleasure of living, they must be where they can be got at without trouble, and what is of more importance, where they can share in the life about them and receive some touches of humanity they supply and feed."

How can we create a useful and dynamic learning environment

rather than a mere collection? The answer is to follow the footnote trail. Who are the favorite authors of your favorite authors? Love the biography you just read? Has the author written others? Did the author rely on certain sources? When we follow these lines of influences, sources, and references, whole worlds open up. We need not acquire a costly personal library to enjoy the extraordinary world of books, of course. Make certain that you and every member of your family has a card at your local public library—and *use it*.

> *A little library, growing every year, is an honorable part of a man's history. It is a man's duty to have books. A library is not a luxury, but one of the necessaries of life. Be certain that your house is adequately and properly furnished—with books rather than with furniture. Both if you can, but books at any rate.*
>
> —HENRY WARD BEECHER

5. TURN OFF THE TUBE

Television has become America's drug of choice—a kind of electronic Valium that virtually everyone across this vast land uses. More than 98 percent of all households have at least one television set. While it is probably not wise for leaders or anyone to be entirely unaware of what broadcasters are sending into American homes, it is equally unwise to squander too much of our time watching it. Wonder how you will ever find the time to actually read everything you know you should? Turn off the television—and the kids' Playstations while you're at it. Watch less and read more.

> *Of all the diversions of life, there is none so proper to fill up its empty spaces as the reading of useful and entertaining authors.*
>
> —JOSEPH ADDISON

6. TAKE JOY IN THE JOURNEY

We enter a world of sensual and intellectual delights in a library. And so it ought to be. Thus, Winston Churchill said, "If you cannot

> *When you sell a man a book you don't sell him just twelve ounces of paper and ink and glue—you sell him a whole new life. Love and friendship and humor and ships at sea by night—there's all heaven and earth in a book.*
>
> **—CHRISTOPHER MORLEY**

read all your books, at any rate handle, or as it were, fondle them—peer into them, let them fall open where they will, read from the first sentence that arrests the eye, set them back on the shelves with your own hands, arrange them on your own plan so that you at least know where they are. Let them be your friends; let them be your acquaintances." Learning ought to be a joy. Reading is not simply a pragmatic exercise. Reading should be a delight.

Oswald Chambers expressed this sentiment well when he wrote, "My books! I cannot tell you what they are to me—silent, wealthy, loyal, lovers. I do thank God for my books with every fiber of my being. I see them all just at my elbow now—Plato, Wordsworth, Myers, Bradley, Halburton, St. Augustine, Browning, Tennyson, Amiel, and the others."

Likewise, C. S. Lewis described the joyous atmosphere that ultimately shaped his view of the world:

I am the product of long corridors, empty sunlit rooms, upstairs indoor silences, attics explored in solitude, distant noises of gurgling cisterns and pipes, and the noise of wind under the tiles. Also, of endless books. My father bought all the books he read and never got rid of any of them. There were books in the study, books in the drawing room, books in the cloakroom, books—two deep—in the great bookcase on the landing, books piled as high as my shoulder in the cistern attic, books of all kinds reflecting every transient stage of my parents' interest, books readable and unreadable, books suitable for a child and books most emphatically not.

When I found myself at the center of the storm, when the election recount controversy seemed to rage out of control, I had the marvelous advantage of a firm foundation afforded by a lifetime of learning. I did not have all the answers, but I knew how to get them. I was not the ultimate expert concerning the law or the media, but I had the tools with which to think and decide and act, and so I never felt entirely overwhelmed.

> *You can't get a cup of tea large enough or a book long enough to suit me.*
> —C. S. LEWIS

Top Ten List:
Favorite Classics

When you reread a classic you do not see more in the book than you did before; you see more in you than was there before.
—CLIFTON FADIMAN

When I was a child, my parents filled our home with thick, substantive, and enduring books, and they communicated their hearty, enthusiastic appetite for reading. Dozens of great works have given me a rich perspective of the times in which we live and the problems that we face—a perspective that policy analysis alone can never adequately provide. Great leaders have always wrestled with the great ideas. John Ruskin said, "A life being very short, and the quiet hours of it few, we ought to waste none of them in reading valueless books." These are some of my personal favorites, for their intrinsic value and for the sheer wisdom and delight of them.

1. *The Federalist Papers* by James Madison, Alexander Hamilton, and John Jay. This collection of newspaper editorials that supported the new American Constitution is brilliantly written and provides a rare glimpse into the original intentions of the Founding Fathers.

2. *The Prince* by Machiavelli. One of the most influential works of political commentary ever written. By turns disturbing, brilliant, and insidious, it is essential reading for anyone who wishes to understand modern political ideologies and methodologies.

3. *Pride and Prejudice* by Jane Austen. While I was working toward my graduate degree in public policy at Harvard, I would often curl up in front of a fireplace with one or another of the novels of Austen or the Brontë sisters, and

marvel at their literary prowess and their profound ability to see so clearly into the dilemmas of human relationships, social inequities, and cultural changes.

4. *The Count of Monte Cristo* by Alexandre Dumas. A powerful book that transcends time and place, this morality play offers today's readers a reflection of their own soul.

5. *The City of God* by Saint Augustine. This masterwork served as a kind of intellectual manifesto for Western civilization. It is arguably the most influential book ever written.

6. *Hard Times* by Charles Dickens. Any work by Dickens is worth reading again and again. In his ability to create memorable characters, page-turning plots, and sublime themes of justice, mercy, and humility, Dickens is unsurpassed.

7. *Pilgrim's Progress* by John Bunyan. Out of the turmoil of the English civil war and the struggle for religious liberty emerged one of the most remarkable classics of all time. If you've ever been in a fight for your life where issues of principle are at stake, you'll appreciate the value of this work.

8. *The Lord of the Rings* by J. R. R. Tolkien. This trilogy, written only a few decades ago, has grown steadily in popularity as it has found its way into the hearts of successive generations of readers. The books are not only a sumptuous feast; their insights into the character of modern life and human psychology are nourishing beyond measure.

9. *Democracy in America* by Alexis de Tocqueville. This glimpse of the youthful and energetic American republic is not only a fascinating historical chronicle, it is also a reminder of what made America so distinctive among the nations of the earth.

10. *Kidnapped* by Robert Louis Stevenson. The adventure stories of this Scottish writer defy convention or even description. They have all the blood and thunder you might expect but are liberally seasoned with all the big themes of psychology, sociology, philosophy, and theology. And one more . . .

11. *The Yearling* by Marjorie Kinnan Rawlings. (I just could not limit my list of favorite classics to ten.) Jody and his pet deer, Flag, traverse old Florida. The eloquence and detail of this Pulitzer Prize-winning novel provide a stark contrast to its description of a difficult life during unsettled times. Yet this classic shows steadfast principles and values that never change. I cry every time I read it.

It's Amazing What You Can Accomplish If You Do Not Care Who Receives the Credit

Effective leaders are much more concerned with getting their work done, accomplishing their priorities, and fulfilling their calling than they are with getting credit for doing so. They remain focused on the tasks at hand. They are driven by principles and goals, not by power or glory.

No man or woman is an island. There are no successful Lone Rangers—not in business, not in politics, and not in life. Loose cannons foil the best strategies. Wild cards trump the best intentions. Rogue agents jeopardize the securest operations. Even the archetypal "Lone" Ranger had Tonto as a mirror, valued consultant, and support—not to mention Silver as his vehicle and facilitator.

Our effectiveness depends upon the presence of people who know us, and to whom we ultimately answer. If we are to be successful, we must be accountable. We must serve as team players and team builders.

John C. Maxwell memorably stated, "Collaboration is multiplication." If we are willing to work with others, to yield to someone else's expertise in an area, to put cooperation above our individual interests, and to allow others to succeed in their own areas of proficiency, then we will accomplish much more than we ever could alone—more than we ever dreamed possible. I have learned from countless examples that the best solutions to a problem often come from the most unlikely sources.

Henry Ford once said, "Success in any enterprise begins when we acknowledge what it is that we do not know, not when we trumpet what it is that we do know." He lived and worked in light of the old adage: "A humble man who builds a team to compensate for his weaknesses will always go farther than the prideful man who builds a team to complement his strengths." Ford often admitted that he had no idea how to solve every mechanical or technical problem that might arise in the manufacture of automobiles. "I don't need to have the answer to everything in my head," he said, "as long as I know how to hire smart guys who do."

In any enterprise, team building maximizes effort, encourages diversity of opinion, utilizes a wise division of labor, and provides critical checks and balances. Common sense tells us to always welcome the input of others, to seek to build bridges of cooperation, to try to complement others' talents and permit them to complement ours, and to embrace the opportunities to coordinate our resources, perspectives, and efforts. Unfortunately, team building does not come naturally to most of us.

In actuality, we often do not like to admit that we need help. Remaining true to the great American tradition (or myth) of rugged individualism, we insist on our right to "do it my way" and our ability to stand alone against the tide. We cherish our self-reliance and our independence. (In fact, inhabitants of my birthplace, Key West, Florida, are known for their feisty desire to secede from the United States in order to form an independent "Conch Republic.") Besides, working with others can be complicated and messy. Team players must share glory and share blame, and we may be reluctant to do either.

Accountability to a larger team also exposes us to more intense scrutiny. Our mistakes ultimately come to light, and we don't like to admit when we are wrong. We all have defense mechanisms that spring into place whenever anyone ventures too close to the restricted zones of our lives. Our guard immediately goes up whenever someone even hints at our faults or foibles. The process of admission, confession, correction, and repentance wounds our pride. Taking responsibility constitutes one of the most difficult challenges we ever have to address.

Early in life we learn to look out for number one, to pamper ourselves, and to encourage self-actualization, self-awareness, and self-esteem. But this process has swung out of balance, tempting us to succumb to an epidemic of selfishness. Instead of using these qualities to become wise and effective, we have been inclined to become self-absorbed, self-concerned, and self-consumed.

The whole of history contradicts the modern cult of self-service and self-satisfaction. Throughout the past, wise men and women have demonstrated the immense value of unselfish team building. They have shown us the true significance of humble reliance on others. They have willingly shared credit and glory and prosperity with others, knowing full well that they have sacrificed little, if anything, as a consequence. On the contrary, they have known that cooperation, accountability, and collaboration offered them substantially greater benefits.

ALL HANDS ON DECK

During the post-election storm, I was blessed and honored to have an extraordinary team with whom to work. From the first moment of the automatic machine recount, through the myriad of controversies (including over fifty-three court cases) that ensued, we worked harder and longer than we ever thought we could. I was also grateful to have extraordinary friends upon whom I could rely, particularly when the storm grew exceptionally intense and the waves of controversy and criticism broke ever higher over our bow.

BENJAMIN MCKAY

Throughout my eight years of public service, Ben McKay has been one of my closest advisors and confidants. Ben became my chief of staff just six months before the recount controversy erupted, but I cannot imagine how anyone could have handled this unprecedented crisis more skillfully, professionally, or honorably.

My association with Ben began with my election to the Florida Senate in 1994. As my senate chief of staff, Ben quickly distinguished himself as a creative problem-solver. His thorough understanding of the legislative process and his exemplary organizational and administrative skills enabled us to achieve the passage of more than one hundred bills that I sponsored, including groundbreaking legislation in the areas of commerce, international affairs, insurance, education, and child safety.

> *A prudent question is one-half of wisdom.*
> —FRANCIS BACON

When I became Florida's secretary of state in 1999, I entrusted Ben with implementing the international affairs agenda we had championed in the legislature. During his tenure as my first undersecretary for international and legislative affairs, Ben's remarkable versatility shined. He articulated my vision, established a workable legislative and administrative framework, and at the same time successfully managed the daily operations of more than thirty programs.

Operating under the world's microscope during the recount controversy, Ben assembled a quality team and effectively enforced our objective of following the law, regardless of the consequences. Ben deserves credit for the fact that no one ever questioned the competence of my staff during this period, despite the partisan rancor and media distortions that attended our actions.

I am particularly proud of the fact that starting with the beginning of the 2002 fall semester, Ben will pursue his master's degree in public administration from Harvard University's John F. Kennedy School of Government, an extraordinary opportunity that I enjoyed and dearly appreciate today. I hope the same for him.

DAVE MANN

At the same time that Ben McKay became my chief of staff, I promoted Dave Mann to be my assistant secretary of state. Dave had served the Department of State for almost three decades, most recently as the director of our Division of Corporations. In that capacity, he had presided over the digitization of Florida's registration system for corporate and business filings. Since our Division of Corporations processes more filings than any other state in the nation, this innovation has saved a tremendous amount of time and taxpayer money while enabling public internet access to images of millions of filings.

As my assistant secretary of state, Dave manages the operations of the Department of State's seven diverse divisions. During the recount crisis, he made certain that the critical services we provide to the public remained uninterrupted, despite the intense media attention every department employee endured. Dave's character, discernment, professionalism, and superior administrative skills exemplify the ultimate career public servant.

CLAY ROBERTS

As director of the Department of State's Division of Elections and a fellow member of Florida's Elections Canvassing Commission, Clay also came under the media's fire. A West Point graduate, Clay has combined military precision with integrity, commitment, and exemplary judgment in his management of the Division of Elections.

Of all the members of my team, Clay has borne the most unfair

> *Knowledge is proud that he has learned so much; wisdom is humble that he knows no more.*
>
> —WILLIAM COWPER

attacks. For example, in its partisan, biased, and wholly misinformed diatribe of a "report" on the 2000 presidential election in Florida,[7] a majority of the U.S. Commission on Civil Rights attacked the manner in which the Division of Elections handled the list of potentially ineligible voters, compiled pursuant to the orders of the Florida legislature.

Aside from its gross exaggerations concerning the impact of errors contained in this list,[8] the commission's majority failed to acknowledge

> *Never be ashamed to own you have been in the wrong; 'tis but saying you are wiser today than yesterday.*
>
> —JONATHAN SWIFT

that the Division of Elections, under Clay's leadership, continued the same cautious approach to the list for which the majority praised Clay's predecessor, Ethel Baxter. Further, in their eagerness to attack Clay's leadership, the majority failed to mention that Ms. Baxter continued to assist the supervisors with the list as Clay's assistant director until her retirement just five months before Election 2000.

Additionally, in contrast to media accounts, Clay provided legally correct advisory opinions to the supervisors during the recount controversy. As I described in more detail in Principle 3, the advisory opinions regarding the legality of manual recounts during the "protest" phase of the recount period that the Division of Elections issued under Clay's guidance have finally received the vindication they deserve in U.S. Court of Appeals Judge and Chicago Law School Senior Lecturer Richard A. Posner's book, *Breaking the Deadlock.*

In mid-2002, I promoted Clay to the position of general counsel for the Department of State. As we continued to confront a myriad of election-related lawsuits that threatened Florida's ability to implement its groundbreaking election reforms effectively in time for the 2002 elections, Clay's expertise in this area made him the logical choice for this new challenge.

DEBBY KEARNEY

Debby contributed her outstanding skill and professionalism as our general counsel from 1999 to mid-2002, when she left for an excellent opportunity to serve as general counsel for the Office of the [Florida] State Courts Administrator. Debby served as deputy general counsel to Florida's Constitutional Revision Commission (which drafted a series of major amendments to the Florida Constitution that the voters adopted in 1998), as well as deputy general counsel to Democratic Governor Lawton Chiles. In both capacities, she worked directly under the leadership of Dexter Douglass, a Tallahassee attorney who became Al Gore's lead Florida attorney during the recount controversy.

Aside from her outstanding ability to ascertain and apply the law, Debby served as a voice of calm and reason amidst the tumult we endured. When I made it clear to my staff that I would adhere strictly to the law during the recount controversy no matter the pressure, I could not have had a more perfect person in place to make sure this principle became practice.

I was particularly proud when Debby received the Florida Bar's Claude Pepper Outstanding Government Lawyer award in 2001. Honored on the heels of the Election 2000 recount controversy, this award demonstrated the high esteem in which attorneys across Florida held Debby's even-handed, thorough approach to this controversy as well as to her duties in general.

> *The art of being wise is the art of knowing what to overlook.*
> —WILLIAM JAMES

JOE KLOCK

Joe's extraordinary contributions as our lead outside counsel throughout all of the recount cases have been well documented in the media and in a panoply of post-recount books. Joe and the law firm he leads as managing partner, Steel Hector & Davis, brought inestimable integrity and expertise to our efforts to follow the law, regardless of the consequences. Known as a principally Democratic law firm that claims Janet Reno as a former associate, Joe's firm helped us maintain the firewall necessary to sustain our department's integrity in the process. His team worked countless hours in our office, my home, and their offices. I was especially pleased to work with Donna Blanton, a former newspaper reporter, whose mother Libby Blanton and my mother had sustained a deep friendship during decades of working together in Girl Scouting.

ADAM GOODMAN

Adam has been my friend and close personal advisor since my first senate campaign in 1994. Several eminent leaders across our nation reflect Adam's tremendous skills as a professional media consultant, including former New York Mayor Rudy Giuliani, Environmental Protection Agency Administrator (and former New Jersey Governor) Christie Todd Whitman, and Congresswoman Jennifer Dunn.

When the recount crisis erupted, I was between communications directors. Adam volunteered to help me. At his own expense, Adam flew to Tallahassee for what he thought would be a few days. Throughout the recount period and its immediate aftermath, Adam dealt with the media on my behalf while helping me draft accurate public statements concerning the law.

Courage is what it takes to stand up and speak; courage is also what it takes to sit down and listen.

—WINSTON CHURCHILL

In addition to the "war room" myth,[9] the most absurd controversy the media tried to create about Adam was that the state of Florida *did not* pay him a salary for the work he performed for me. After some discussions about this issue, Adam and I concluded that he should remain an unpaid volunteer. How scandalous! Since when did saving taxpayer money and avoiding potential conflicts of interest become a negative issue that the press feels a need to "expose"?

JOAN JONES AND MAUREEN GARRARD

I have known these women since before my days of public service. While I work closely with them professionally, I count them as dear friends and confidantes. For my entire career in public service, particularly during the recount controversy, they offered advice, counsel, and support regarding every aspect of my life. I could not have made it through the storm without their encouragement, sound judgment, and quirky senses of humor.

SUELLEN CONE AND BONNIE KIDD

Suellen began as my administrative assistant in 1999. Like Debby Kearney, she served under Governor Lawton Chiles and Al Gore's lead Florida attorney, Dexter Douglass, prior to joining our office.

Suellen demonstrated extraordinary commitment and skill (as well as patience!) in handling the tremendous demands of the recount controversy. She managed the flood of phone calls, letters, and e-mails with professionalism and courtesy. She also kept me on track with her kind, but honest, appraisals of my approach to this intense situation.

Bonnie is one of the most thoroughly decent and dedicated individuals with whom I have ever been associated. As my scheduler since early 2000, she has endured the rigors of managing the enormous demands for my time (especially since the recount) with grace and professionalism. I receive amazing compliments concerning her demeanor and skill as I work throughout Florida.

Any discussion of the extraordinary group of people who sustained me through this trying period would be incomplete without a mention of the dedicated professionals of the Florida Department of Law Enforcement (FDLE) Security team who protected my husband and me round-the-clock when the FDLE determined that credible threats had been made against me. Working with these stellar men and women was perhaps the nicest experience of the recount. Each agent had such a unique personality and attributes—some very funny, some deeply kind, some with whom we shared a great deal in common—that a special place was created in our hearts for them. We felt extremely secure in their care. Each night we jointly experienced the jibes of the late-night comedians, viewing them into the wee hours. Rarely could I eke out more than three or four hours of sleep each night. On the evening the U.S. Supreme Court made their final decision, one agent said he watched me simply slide down on the sofa, sound asleep.

Throughout the recount crisis, it was obvious to us all that we would likely have succumbed to the fierce waves if we had not had all hands on deck. A remarkable commitment to team building, a spirit of cooperation and selflessness, and an unwavering intention to uphold the law ultimately enabled us to weather the storm.

THE LAST SHALL BE FIRST

During the early days of Rome, a hero emerged who defied the assumptions that we in the modern age hold toward our leaders—namely, that their egos are invested in being leaders. In a fight with a neighboring tribe, several Roman generals had allowed themselves and their army to become surrounded and cut off by the enemy. The situation seemed hopeless. Several riders were able to break away, and news of the impending military disaster reached Rome. A hurried council was held, and it was decided that a former commander named Cincinnatus should be called upon.

Again riders were dispatched, this time to an outlying farm. There the riders found Cincinnatus, working his fields. Hearing of the situation, he quickly set his affairs in order, changed from his farming clothes into his military uniform and armor, and set out at the head of a hastily assembled army to assist his trapped countrymen. Soon the already gloating enemy found themselves surrounded by Roman forces. The Roman victory was complete. Cincinnatus became an overnight celebrity, and the Roman army triumphantly returned to the city. Honors, awards, positions in government, and even kingship were offered to Cincinnatus. He did the unthinkable. He went home to work his fields.

Roughly two thousand years later, another Cincinnatus arose. With his country on the verge of war, not with a neighboring tribe but with the greatest power in the world, a planter named George Washington left his farm to draw the sword against England. Writing to his brother on the day he took command, he commented, "I am embarked on a wide ocean, boundless in its prospect, and from whence perhaps no safe harbor is to be found." Yet he faced the task ahead with the determination not to achieve honor for himself, but to get the job done. He wanted to see his country free. When the war ended nearly ten years after he had taken command, Washington, too, did the unthinkable. He went home to his farm.

Like Cincinnatus, Washington's country adored him. He had seemingly accomplished the impossible. Many Americans, indeed much of the world, had thought it absurd to pick a fight with the biggest kid on the political block, Great Britian. The idea that such a fight could actually be won seemed a proposition not worth consideration to most. Yet, with the help of the French, the thirteen former British colonies won their independence. At Yorktown a very humiliated Cornwallis surrendered to a ragtag group of colonists under the command of General Washington.

George Washington's image became the face of this victory. Naturally, his fellow patriots wished to heap honor upon him. Calls rang out from every corner of the new, vibrant nation that Washington

A wise old owl sat on an oak,
The more he saw the less he spoke;
The less he spoke the more he heard;
Why aren't we like that wise old bird?

—EDWARD RICHARDS

should become its leader, perhaps even its king. With his leadership of the stunning victory having earned him the adamant support of the people and the army, any position he desired would have been within his easy reach. Instead, Washington went to the president of Congress and laid his sword at his feet. The war was over. His task accomplished, Washington was ready to return to his cherished home, Mount Vernon.

On December 23, 1783, General Washington gave the following speech:

Mr. President, the great events on which my resignation depended having at length taken place, I have now the honor of offering my sincere congratulations to Congress, and of presenting myself before them, to surrender into their hands the trust committed to me and to claim the indulgence of retiring from the service of my country. Happy in the confirmation of our independence and sovereignty, and pleased with the opportunity afforded the United States of becoming a respectable nation, I resign with satisfaction the appointment I accepted with diffidence. The successful termination of the war has verified the most sanguine expectations, and my gratitude for the interposition of Providence and the assistance I have received from my countrymen increases with every review of the momentous contest. I consider it an indispensable duty to close this last solemn act of my official life by commending the interests of our dearest country to the protection of Almighty God, and those who have the superintendence of them to his holy keeping. Having now finished the work assigned me, I retire from the great theater of action, and, bidding an affectionate farewell to this august body, under whose orders I have so long acted, I here offer my commission and take my leave of all the employments of public life.

In the famous Saint Crispin's Day speech in Shakespeare's *Henry V*, the young and ambitious Henry boasts that "if it be a sin to covet honour/I am the most offending soul alive." Not so with George Washington. When unlimited power was likely within his grasp, General Washington knelt to the task of selfless service. He obeyed orders. He yielded to the authorities placed over him. Perhaps most important, he set aside personal ambition, personal preference, personal security, and personal opinion in order to serve his country. He subordinated himself to a higher cause, and in the end his greatest concern was not that he receive credit, but that his job was done.

> *The heart of a fool is in his mouth, but the mouth of a wise man is in his heart.*
> —BENJAMIN FRANKLIN

THE GENIUS OF ACCOUNTABILITY

According to the famed English critic G. K. Chesterton, "America is the only nation in the world that is founded on a creed." He recognized that other nations are generally accidents of history. They forge their identities on such things as common ethnicity, geography, or social tradition. America, by contrast, was founded on specific principles, virtues, and ideas. The values Americans espouse—freedom, human dignity, and social responsibility—define our communities and commitments in ways that altogether transcend ethnicity, geography, and tradition.

Ultimately, these values did indeed take the form of a creed, which is codified in a sovereign standard of law: the U. S. Constitution.

This deliberate codification of our great experiment in liberty has always struck visitors to America as something quite extraordinary. Alexis de Tocqueville called it "American exceptionalism" when he came for his famous tour of our fledgling nation at the beginning of the nineteenth century. Another European visitor, the renowned historian Sir Henry Maine, described the same sense of awe at "the evident genius of the American Constitution."

Though our ever-expansive vision has demanded the occasional amendment of the Constitution; though our creed has often been tried and tested; and though the character and scope of the nation has changed substantially from the days of the thirteen colonies, the primary elements of this remarkable document have remained unchanged—they have not only endured, they have flourished.

This durable creed was originally rooted in a clear understanding of the need for accountability, cooperation, and reconciliation among varying interests. The Founding Fathers made checks and balances and the separation of powers the hallmarks of the new system of government they devised. Called "federalism," their design placed a premium upon an effectively functioning national government possessing enumerated, limited powers, with the diverse band of states that comprised the new union retaining powers that preserved their essential distinctiveness.

The Constitution enshrines the idea of teamwork, as applied to the task of building a nation. The same checks and balances notions that inspired federalism formed such concepts as the bicameral legislature, the Bill of Rights, the separation of legislative, executive, and judicial powers, and the indirect presidential tallying of the Electoral College.

> *Wisdom is oft times nearer when we stoop than when we soar.*
> —WILLIAM WORDSWORTH

The principles enunciated in the Constitution have driven the eventual realization of the framers' dream of government by, of, and for the people. As a living, evolving document, the Constitution has continued to animate our government and the society over which it presides with the aspirations of every American for freedom and self-determination. When our society has fallen short of the justice and equality to which our Constitution aspires, the elegant prose and philosophical poetry of this simple charter has implored and inspired us to change.

The true genius of the Constitution rests in its respect for the fundamental common sense and decency of the American people. As de Tocqueville reportedly observed, "America is great because she is good, and if America ever ceases to be good, she will cease to be great."

Washington reflected the values of the new nation and its people when he surrendered his sword, his commission, and his authority to Congress. He demonstrated his commitment to these principles when he walked away from the soldiers who wished to make him king, instead returning to the life of the land at Mount Vernon.

Indeed, it is amazing what we can accomplish when we do not care who gets the credit.

BUILDING A TEAM SPIRIT

We cannot build any team upon the shifting sands of detachment, absence of commitment, or undefined freedom. Rather, we unleash the great promise of united effort only when individuals share an established identity, a vision for the future, and a commitment to sacrifice for a cause greater than any individual achievement. Whether we are called to lead in those rare times, places, and circumstances that require heroic action or in the relatively mundane but still vitally important spheres of daily life—home, workplace, church or organization—how do we create an effective, positive team, one built on a firm foundation that can rise to any occasion and weather any storm?

1. REMEMBER THE GOAL

What are you actually trying to accomplish? What is your goal? How do you measure success? Any group of individuals will encounter difficulties if they forget why they banded together in the first place, whether that group consists of a family, a company, a political party, or a charitable institution. If the members of the team cannot clearly articulate their shared objectives, the team will soon disintegrate into competing factions.

Coaches, generals, and entrepreneurs instinctively know that getting their team members to understand their mission, to embrace and to own it, constitute the most critical components of a successful game plan, project, or enterprise. Industrial pioneer Josiah Wedgwood asserted, "Camaraderie may be more important even than competency in preparing for a prosperous endeavor."

Of course, we cannot neglect technical precision and excellence just because everybody in the office gets along so well. An excess of familiarity can breed complacency as people start to depend too much on each other while failing to perform their own work. If your team remains focused on the central goals you have articulated together, you will more likely remain sufficiently adaptable, flexible, collaborative, communicative, competent, dependable, disciplined, selfless, inspirational, and motivated. As a team, you will undertake any necessary measures to reinforce each team member in their dedication to doing the right thing, staying on course, and fulfilling the team's calling. As British Prime Minister Benjamin Disraeli said, "The secret of success is constancy to purpose."

2. SURROUND YOURSELF WITH STRONG PEOPLE

Principled leaders do not permit strong, bright, and gifted subordinates to intimidate them into jealously guarding power and prerogative. Instead, they delegate increasing amounts of responsibility to team members, motivating them to achieve greater and greater levels of excellence.

Effective leaders remain well aware of their own shortcomings and weaknesses. Instead of hiding or ignoring such deficiencies, however, they purposefully surround themselves with competent men and women who can fill the gaps in their competency. Peter Drucker noted that "effective managers hire to their weaknesses rather than to their strengths."

Visionaries should hire administrators. Managers should hire thinkers. Motivators should hire implementers. Leaders must remain focused on "the big picture" and hire experts to manage the detailed particulars.

If a leader's aim is to get the job done, to do it well, and to have maximum impact, then leaders must refrain from designing a team around the objective of making themselves look good. A team should be balanced, goal-oriented, and crackling with energy. Henry Ford summed up this idea: "The men on my workforce cannot outshine me. If they are smarter, work harder, and are more innovative than me, that is all to my credit. I hired them, after all. Their success is my success. I am not trying to build up my reputation; I am trying to build up my company. I don't want to sell myself; I want to sell cars."

3. LEARN TO DELEGATE

Effective leaders do not set out to prove they can accomplish everything. They know they cannot do all things effectively, so they do not even try. Instead, they delegate responsibility to others. They make clear assignments, provide precise instructions, and offer helpful evaluations. Next, they turn their team members loose and let them do their jobs without constantly interfering in their work. Then, if and when the team succeeds, the leader is the first to celebrate.

Delegation is one of the most difficult managerial disciplines to learn. It is not so much that we do not want to let go of certain things; it is that we do not let go well. We continue to micromanage, thereby smothering our team, or we become so "hands off" in our approach that the team has no idea that it actually is a team. Either extreme will quash the team's competency, efficiency, creativity, and motivation.

4. SEEK WISE COUNSEL

Principled leaders know that they do not know it all. As secretary of state, I have responsibility for a wide range of departments, agencies, programs, projects, and initiatives touching on policy concerns as divergent as international trade, the arts, historic preservation, elections, libraries, corporate and business registrations, and the licensing of private security officers. Further, as a member of Florida's statewide-elected executive cabinet, I work with others to address critical areas for our state such as sovereign submerged lands, power plant sitings, education issues, law enforcement, veterans, and even clemency. Before Election 2000, did I have every provision of the more than one hundred pages of Florida election laws memorized? Of course not. Was I intimately familiar with the uniquely differing aspects of polling procedures in each of Florida's sixty-seven counties? No. But when the post-election storm hit, I needed to become an expert in every nuance of the law—and quickly.

What did I do? I sought wise counsel. I called on experts to give me a crash course. I posed every hypothetical situation that I could imagine. I pondered every conceivable question. I explored all possible alternatives. Both within my office and outside it, I called on the best and the brightest to show me what I needed to study, provide me with the material they suggested I read, and offer interpretations where the data seemed foggy or imprecise. I was not about to go it alone.

Effective leaders always question their own expertise in a crisis—

which becomes a provocation for them to seek help. Overweening self-confidence can prove disastrous. But humility can pave the way to an extraordinary new level of communication, creativity, and proactive engagement.

> *The wisest man is the one with the largest circle of counselors.*
> —C. S. LEWIS

I refuse to surround myself with "yes-people." None of us can do all we are called to do if we try to go it alone. Working together with others affords us a host of advantages. If we do not care who gets the credit, it is amazing what we can accomplish.

5. LEARN FROM YOUR CRITICS

Who likes to be told that they are wrong? Not I. I would prefer to be infallible and unassailable! I find people who agree with me agreeable. Thus, criticism can rub me the wrong way. If it is fallacious, I am annoyed by it. If it is accurate, I am stung by it. Either way, I would rather not be wrong, and never have to deal with the consequences.

But I also know that failure is often the back door to success. Each of us makes mistakes. Each of us has failed. Try as we might, it is simply not possible to hide our shortcomings from everyone, everywhere, all of the time. We stumble, and our critics are usually well poised to see the results that ensue.

As if that fact were not difficult enough to accept, we must also admit our mistakes to learn from them. Our critics can actually help us with this task. Ralph Waldo Emerson admitted, "I do not wish my critic well when he identifies my most obvious weakness, yet he has wished me well in doing so if I have the courage to hear and heed."

Of course, we must separate the legitimate from the illegitimate, the constructive from the destructive, the helpful from the debilitating, and the accurate from the exaggerated and the downright false. Once we have successfully completed this task, we have learned vital lessons

> *There is glory in a*
> *great mistake.*
> —NATHALIA CRANE

that we probably could not have learned any other way. We must face the notion that those who always support us are not likely to tell us some of the truths we really need to hear.

During the recount crisis, did I learn anything from accurate criticisms? Absolutely. Did I also learn from the distortions and stinging attacks my critics aimed at me during the post-election storm? Certainly. I learned some serious lessons; and I also learned to treat absurd and misinformed attacks with a sense of humor.

For example, even as I finish this book, a few male commentators who have apparently remained locked in a hermetically sealed vault since the end of the recount continue to make comments about my makeup. Fortunately, I have seen these newscasters in person addressing the camera, and I can tell you, quite frankly, that they had applied far more makeup than I have ever consider wearing! Just for the record: I haven't owned blue eye shadow since my early teenage years, and the rainbow colors I saw "enhancing" my face in newspaper photos made me wonder whether a creative retoucher had been at work.

On one of the nights I could not sleep during the recount period, I ventured out to my neighborhood Target to purchase additional holiday decorations. Due to the lateness of the hour, I hoped I could slip in, buy what I needed, and slip out without any notice. Even late at night, however, I faced a long line at the checkout counter. When the clerk glanced at my credit card, she loudly asked if I was *the* Katherine Harris, to which I responded, "Yes, but I only have one layer of makeup on tonight. I am traveling incognito." I think I shocked both my security agent and myself. The entire group of people in the vicinity broke out in laughter. After that moment, I no longer worried about what anyone said about my appearance.

* * *

MYTH CONCEPTION:
THE POPULAR VERSUS THE ELECTORAL VOTE

Much of the genius of a nation of liberty is its protection of the freedoms and prerogatives of the few against the freedoms and prerogatives of the many.
—JAMES MADISON

Critics of our federal system of checks and balances had a heyday with the 2000 presidential election—a very bitterly fought, close race, though by no means the bitterest or the closest. Both candidates, Democratic Vice President Al Gore and Republican Governor George W. Bush, won just over 48 percent of the popular vote—with Gore receiving slightly more votes nationwide. Bush, however, won in the Electoral College by five votes (after one of the Gore electors in the District of Columbia abstained).

When the race appeared headed toward a photo finish in the final days before the election, the media began to speculate about how Media-Age Americans would respond in the very plausible instance that one candidate won the nationwide popular vote while the other candidate carried the Electoral College, thus winning the presidency. Even before the virtual dead heat in Florida, the analysts wrung their hands over the "legitimacy" of a president elected under such circumstances. Ironically, the most common scenario mentioned was one in which George W. Bush carried the popular vote while Al Gore became president by virtue of a win in the Electoral College. As they always have (and as they always will), the American people surprised the pundits.

While the recount controversy in Florida spurred attempts to convince three electors pledged to support George W. Bush that the "national interest" required them to vote for the candidate who carried the nationwide popular vote, no groundswell of cries to abolish the Electoral College has emerged. Some people still question the outcome in Florida (even after media recounts have confirmed that George W. Bush would have won Florida under any of the recount scenarios in play during the recount period), but virtually no one has called President Bush's legitimacy into question solely because he won the presidency without carrying the nationwide popular vote.

The continuing genius of the Electoral College rests in its guarantee that a successful candidate for president has garnered support across a broad cross section of Americans. As in prior elections marked by a president's failure to carry the popular vote, such as the elections of 1876 and 1888, Al Gore appealed to voters on a more regional basis than did George W. Bush. In fact, Bush won twenty-nine states, while Gore won twenty-one. Bush carried 2,436 counties nationwide, while Gore carried 676. The regions in which Bush prevailed covered some 2,432,456 square miles of the nation, while the regions in which Gore prevailed covered just 575,184 square miles. Al Gore carried the popular vote by carrying urban areas in the Northeast, the Midwest, and California by huge margins; Bush won the electoral vote by obtaining the support of a majority of voters in states as diverse as New Hampshire, West Virginia, and Arizona.

The Electoral College strikes a balance. It requires a candidate to win a large percentage of the popular vote (by assigning electoral votes to states based on the number of districts they possess in the U.S. House of Representatives, which is determined by a state's population) and demands that a candidate pay attention to every American, not just Americans who live in large population centers (by assigning each state an additional two electors, regardless of population, to ensure sufficient representation, as in the Senate).

Very simply, the framers of our Constitution designed the

Electoral College to protect against what they called "the tyranny of the majority." In other words, it prevents the will of a 50 percent plus one majority from completely overrunning the will of a 50 percent minus one minority. The will of the people does not achieve its most effective expression in the voices of just over half of the people when a candidate may succeed by completely ignoring just under half of the people.

Imagine the following extreme, but possible, scenario if the Electoral College did not exist: a candidate could lose forty-nine states but win the presidency. Imagine the chaos if Candidate A won every state but California. If he won each of those states by a fairly small margin—akin to Bush's margin of victory in Florida—his lead might amount to less than 500,000 votes overall. If Candidate B won California by one million votes, based on overwhelming support in Los Angeles and its suburbs, then Candidate B would win the overall popular vote by 500,000 votes, despite having lost forty-nine of the fifty states. In the Electoral College, Candidate A would win, 525 to 13. But in a direct election, Candidate B would prevail. The checks and balances of the federal system ensure that a candidate cannot get a majority of the votes in only one state and still become president of all fifty.

The total combined population of the *fifteen states* of Alaska, Delaware, Hawaii, Idaho, Maine, Montana, Nebraska, Nevada, New Hampshire, New Mexico, North Dakota, Rhode Island, South Dakota, Vermont, and Wyoming is about 16 million. The total combined population of the *four cities* of New York, Los Angeles, Chicago, and Houston is about 16 million. The smallest of these states, Rhode Island, encompasses a little under 1,500 square miles. The combined area of the four largest American cities is just over 1,500 square miles. In a direct election, the people of just four cities would have about the same electoral clout as the people in fifteen states. Thus, in a direct election, people in large cities would be given preferential treatment by the candidates because it would be less expensive and more efficient for them to spend their time there rather than travel throughout an entire state.

What is a representative form of government if not a qualification of majoritarianism? The brilliance of the American system rests in our recognition of this principle and our institutionalization of it in our Constitution.

PRINCIPLE 8

EMBRACE THE DIFFERENCES

Women and men are different. The culture of the United States is different from the cultures of other nations. Within the U.S., northern culture is different from southern culture, and both are different from California culture. Our world contains rich diversity—as does our nation. We represent different races and genders, religions and creeds, backgrounds and beliefs. Resistance to diversity constitutes the seedbed for all manner of prejudice. In a crisis—as in daily life—the person who is able to appreciate and embrace diversity is most likely to emerge successfully.

We have heard the observation that America is the world's greatest melting pot so often it seems clichéd. But this phrase is oft-repeated for good reason. Men, women, and children have found their way to our shores and into our communities from every corner of the globe. There is no such thing as a typical American. We represent every race, tongue, tribe, belief, and background. (One hundred forty-three different languages and dialects are spoken within the population of Miami-Dade County, Florida alone!) Our rich diversity constitutes our nation's greatest strength.

In America, every person matters. Every human being has inestimable value. Things can be replaced, but there is no replacement for a mother or father, sister or brother, aunt or uncle, teacher, neighbor, or friend.

The pioneers of our republic understood this vital principle, even if their notions of equality suffered from unacceptable limitations by today's standards. They founded our national and cultural institutions upon the ideal of equality. Although our history contains miserable failures to observe this principle, its enshrinement as part of our national creed has kept the fires of our national conscience burning so brightly that when confronted with instances of prejudice and injustice we will continue to forcefully remedy them. The American Revolution persists, even to this day.

The opening refrain of the Declaration of Independence affirms the essential worth of every single person: "We hold these truths to be self-evident, that all men are created equal, that they are endowed by their Creator with certain unalienable Rights, that among these are Life, Liberty, and the pursuit of Happiness. That to secure these rights, Governments are instituted among Men, deriving their just powers from the consent of the governed."

The ideals of life, liberty, and the pursuit of happiness for every person demand that we do not simply tolerate diversity; rather, we must *embrace* it. We must celebrate, protect, relish, and cherish it. In some ways, we can understand American history as a long and epic struggle to defend diversity against blatant discrimination and petty prejudices alike—a struggle carried on from the writing of the Bill of Rights, to the Civil War, to the struggles for civil rights in the 1960s.

For me, the most painful aspects of the post-election storm—from the beginning of the recount controversy to this very day—have been the promulgation of partisan distortions, innuendos, and outright lies that have sought to implicate me in the alleged disenfranchisement of African-American voters during the 2000 presidential election in Florida.

The flaws in Florida's elections system that the 2000 presidential election revealed—uncounted ballots due to undervotes and over-votes, polling places and voting machines that were inaccessible to persons with disabilities, too few resources for voter education, among others—had existed throughout our nation for decades. Before Election 2000, the political will to fix these problems had not arisen in America, as election reform proposals quickly fell victim to competing demands for limited funding. No politician can honestly claim that prior to Election 2000, he or she would have placed elections ahead of education, health care, law enforcement, and other pressing concerns.

For example, even Donna Brazile, who served as Al Gore's campaign manager, implied that prior to Election 2000, she had under-estimated the need for a sustained voter education drive. In her May 2, 2001, speech before the National Press Club, she made the following admission:

> Okay, if I had to do it all over again, I would have forced the DNC [Democratic National Committee]—at the time I did not force the DNC, I "requested." I'm a DNC member, so all I could do was to request—I would have forced the DNC to put more money in voter education. *We had a lot of first-time, inexperienced voters, and that left a mark on me.* That's important, and I'm going to remind the Democratic Party, I'm going to remind the DCCC [the Democratic Congressional Campaign Committee], and everyone else I can remind, *voter education is just as important as turnout.* We've got to make sure that we do that. *So if I had to do it all over again, I would have done that.* (My italics.)

Even had I anticipated the concerns that Election 2000 revealed, I possessed no constitutional authority to address them. In Florida's decentralized system of election administration, sixty-seven independently elected (one is appointed, two are non-partisan) constitutional officers—Florida's county supervisors of elections—exclusively control matters such as the purchase and operation of voter machinery as well as ballot design.

Nevertheless, a majority of the U.S. Commission on Civil Rights, in a politically tainted report that arose out of their blatant violations of due process (which I discuss in more detail as part of Principle 10), ignored the clearly defined, decentralized structure of Florida's system of elections in order to personally attack Governor Jeb Bush and me. As the *Miami Herald* stated in its June 7, 2001, editorial, "the report goes too far in concluding that Gov. Bush and Secretary Harris bear prime responsibility for the problems on Nov. 7. The report should have acknowledged that counties are responsible for conducting elections and that Florida's election machinery was no healthier under Mr. Bush's Democratic predecessor."

In light of this fact, the members of the commission who voted against the majority report, in their published dissent, made a valuable point about the commission majority's charges of widespread discrimination against African-American voters, which the majority alleged was designed to help the George W. Bush campaign:

If anyone was intent on suppressing the black vote or to "disenfranchise" anyone else, it would have required the cooperation of these local officials . . . Thus, it seems natural to inquire about the political affiliations of Florida's supervisors of elections. If the U.S. Commission on Civil Rights seeks to show that the presidential election was stolen by Republicans, led by the governor and the secretary of state, it would be logical to expect that they had the greatest success in those counties in which the electoral machinery was in the hands of fellow Republicans. Conversely, it is very difficult to see any political motive that would lead Democratic local officials to try to keep the most faithful members of their party from the polls and to somehow spoil the ballots of those who did make it into the voting booth . . . Of the 25 Florida counties with the highest rate of vote spoilage, in how many was the election supervised by a Republican? The answer is zero. All but one of the 25 had Democratic chief election officers, and the one exception was in the hands of an official with no party affiliation.

The commission's majority also grossly exaggerated the root and effect of the flaws of Florida's elections system. In an article published in its June 6, 2001, edition titled "Panel's Conclusions May Have Overstated Key Findings," the *Miami Herald* stated that, while the commission's majority report alleged that "blacks were nearly 10 times as likely as whites to have their ballots rejected by counting machines . . . the rejection rate in black-majority precincts was only about four times higher [than] it was in black-minority precincts." Significantly, "the discard rate for about 65,000 undervotes . . . was almost the same for blacks and whites statewide, according to The Herald analysis."

Even the *Herald*'s study fails to take into account a basic truism of every election. *Because of our cherished tradition of the secret vote in America, no one knows whose ballots were disqualified as undervotes or overvotes,* much less the racial identity of these voters. The ratios cited above were the product of debatable statistical studies, which involve such complicated notions as "regression analysis" and "correlation," which are always subject to challenge by someone else's statistical model.

> *Whoever will cultivate their own mind will find full employment. Every virtue does not only require great care in the planting, but as much daily solicitude in cherishing as exotic fruits and flowers; the vices and passions (which I am afraid are the natural product of the soil) demand perpetual weeding. Add to this the search after knowledge . . . and the longest life is too short.*
>
> —LADY MARY WORTLEY MONTAGU

As the commission members who voted against the majority report pointed out in their dissenting report, the majority ignored plausible non-race-correlated explanations for the alleged statistical discrepancies in ballot rejection, such as voter error. For example, the dissenters pointed out, "an important source of the high rate of ballot spoilage in some Florida communities may have been that a sizable fraction of those who turned out at the polls were there for the first time and were unfamiliar with the rules of the electoral process. Impressionistic evidence suggests that disproportionate numbers of black voters fell into this category. The majority report's failure to explore—or even mention—this factor is a serious flaw."

A particularly egregious unfounded attack that the commission's majority report launched against me involved the so-called "purge list" (which, as I shall explain, was a misnomer). Acting on the orders of the Florida legislature, my Division of Elections administered measures intended to reduce voter fraud, which the legislature passed after Miami's mayoral election of 1997. The courts overturned that election due to the decisive votes of ineligible felons and deceased persons.

> *Do unto others as if you were the others.*
> —LEONARDO DA VINCI

The legislature required the Division of Elections to select a private company to compile a comprehensive list of potentially ineligible voters, including felons, whom Florida law prohibits from voting unless Florida's Executive Board of Clemency has restored their civil rights. Under my predecessor's administration, the Division of Elections hired DBT Online pursuant to this mandate.[10]

Contrary to widespread distortions, however, this list was *not* a purge list. Florida law required the state's sixty-seven county supervisors of elections to verify the accuracy of the list. By law, the county supervisors retained exclusive control of the voter registration rolls. They were the *only* officials who had *any authority* to remove the names of citizens from the registration rolls.

The majority of the Civil Rights Commission, however, unfairly attacked the Division of Elections for allegedly not providing Florida's sixty-seven county supervisors of elections with assistance in dealing with the list.

During September 1999, the division conducted five separate four-hour workshops across Florida for supervisors and their staff. The division provided each person in attendance with detailed instruction manuals that contained explanations concerning how each supervisor could conduct verification of the matches set forth on the list. In particular, the manual contained a section with extensively marked examples of errors, called "false positives," that could appear on the list. The manual also included a section explaining a false positive, and how a false positive could occur. The *Miami Herald Report: Democracy Held Hostage* confirmed the care that the Division of Elections exercised in making sure that the supervisors were aware of how they should approach their responsibilities regarding the list, reporting that the division "told [the supervisors] of the list's limitations, that the matches were graded as 'possible' and 'probable,' and that [the supervisors] were responsible for verifying the accuracy of the matches . . . The supervisors were wary from the start."

To develop the comprehensive list the legislature mandated, it was necessary to establish broader matching parameters than an exact match of names. Persons use aliases and different variations of their names in public records, which a procedure that looked only for exact matches of names could not detect. Thus, the list was bound to contain errors. Throughout the time the list was in use, the Division of Elections continued to remind the supervisors that the list contained these "false positives." Further, the division continued to provide the county supervisors with resources to assist them in carrying out their duty to verify the matches.

Undaunted by the facts, partisans continue to skewer me with unfounded myths about the effects of the DBT Online list that continue to multiply. One creative report stated that "Ms. Harris' office drew up a list of more than 700,000 Floridians permanently disqualified from voting . . . because of a criminal past, and sent it to county election supervisors" while another writer ranted hysterically that "173,000 registered voters were permanently wiped off the voter rolls." In actual fact the entire list of possible felons ineligible to vote in Florida contained 42,322 persons, the majority of whom were not removed from the voter registration rolls, according to a study by the *Palm Beach Post*, published in its May 27 and May 28, 2001, editions.

The *Palm Beach Post*, hardly a bastion of Republicanism, found as a result of this study that "thousands of felons voted in the presidential election . . . [who] almost certainly influenced the election" in favor of former Vice President Gore. According to the *Post*, this estimated number of illegal voters far outnumbered the persons who allegedly could not vote because supervisors of elections erroneously removed them from the voter registration rolls. The *Post* stated that "the number of voters wrongly disenfranchised by the felon purge appears to be far less than the 'thousands' its critics have claimed." The *Post*'s study determined that no more than 108 "law-abiding" people of *all races* "were purged from the voter rolls as suspected criminals, only to be cleared after the election."

The *Miami Herald Report* stated that "some . . . claim that many legitimate voters—of all ethnic and racial groups, but particularly blacks—were illegally swept from the rolls through the state's efforts to ban felons from voting. *There is no widespread evidence of that.* Instead, *the evidence points to just the opposite*—that election officials were mostly permissive, not obstructionist, when unregistered voters presented themselves." (My italics.) Most important in light of the Civil Rights Commission majority's libelous charges of racism, the *Palm Beach Post*'s study confirmed the fact that we have always made clear: DBT Online *did not use race* to match names on the voter rolls with felons. In fact, the commissioners who voted against the majority report stated in their dissent that, based on their analysis of Miami-Dade County's use of the DBT list, "the error rate for whites was almost double that for blacks."

The *Palm Beach Post*'s study also claimed that supervisors of elections "cut from the rolls 996 people convicted of crimes in other states, though they should have been allowed to vote." The *Post* based this statement upon its contention that under Florida law, the state of Florida did not have the authority to require felons who had moved to Florida to apply for executive clemency under any circumstances, if the laws of the state where they had been convicted had automatically restored their voting rights.

In its exercise of due caution, the Department of State's Division of Elections *did not* initially direct DBT to match Florida voter registration lists with lists of felons who had been convicted in states that automatically restored their voting rights. In 2000, however, county supervisors of elections raised the question of the eligibility to vote of any out-of-state felon who had not obtained executive clemency from Florida. At the behest of these supervisors, the Division of Elections requested an advisory opinion from Florida's Office of Executive Clemency.

The Office of Executive Clemency, (which answers to a bipartisan executive cabinet that at that time included Democratic Attorney General Bob Butterworth, Democratic Insurance Commissioner (now U.S. Senator) Bill Nelson, and Democratic Agricultural Commissioner Bob Crawford), replied that all felons convicted in another state who could not provide a certificate or order from that state which indicated that their civil rights had been restored were required to apply for executive clemency in Florida before they would be permitted to vote.

As a bipartisan agency, the Office of Executive Clemency has been universally recognized for decades as the preeminent authority on Florida's law and policy pertaining to the restoration of felons' civil rights. Thus, the Division of Elections distributed this opinion to each of Florida's sixty-seven supervisors of elections, relying upon it as an accurate statement of the law in Florida. In further reliance upon the bipartisan clemency board's instructions, the Division of Elections directed DBT to include as many states as possible in compiling its list of felons who were potentially ineligible to vote, as the division's mandate from the Florida legislature required it to do so.

Despite the virtual blizzard of baseless charges and accusations that has surrounded me since Election Day 2000, I have not permitted myself to become sidetracked. Rather than become ensnared in the distortions about my alleged responsibility for election system defects over which I had no control, I purposed to make election reform my top priority in the 2001 legislative session. Although my goals and motives were mocked by some members of the press, who said we could never gain its passage, I proposed the bill that became the election reform model for the nation, due to a remarkable bipartisan effort of the Florida House and Senate. When I testified before the U.S. House of Representatives' Administrative Committee, both Republican and Democratic members of Congress praised our bill.

Not content to rest on our laurels, in 2002 I won passage of legislation that forcefully seeks the inclusion of persons with disabilities as full and equal participants in our elections. When Governor Jeb Bush signed this legislation into law in May 2002, Florida had implemented reforms that addressed the subject matter of nine out of the eleven recommendations in the commission majority's report. (In fact, Florida had addressed the subject matter of eight of those recommendations before the commission majority ever made them.)

It is regrettable that its majority sullied the commission's august reputation by crafting a battle plan for politicians interested in wielding the sword of racial division. Nevertheless, I remain determined to follow the path of principled leadership by trying to dispel myth, distortion, and innuendo. Principled leaders do not allow partisan name-calling and finger-pointing to distract them from pursuing solutions.

DIVERSITY AND THE ARTS: A CANVAS OF CHANGE

Their personal nature notwithstanding, the most disappointing aspect of the recount-related attacks has been their tendency to obscure my intense efforts as secretary of state to promote diversity on an international scale through cultural exchange.

When I became secretary of state, Florida lagged far behind other states in its efforts to build relationships of trust and understanding with other nations. While Florida's leaders understood that our competition with other states for trade and jobs required state government's active engagement on the global stage, they did not fully understand the diplomatic, educational, cultural, and humanitarian foundation that must support this endeavor.

Shortly after the beginning of my term as secretary of state, we moved to fill this void in Florida's global strategy. We obtained the Florida legislature's statutory authorization to conduct several innovative international affairs initiatives, and we assumed management of Florida's participation in five existing programs and international accords by virtue of a Memorandum of Agreement we signed with Governor Jeb Bush.

Today, the Florida Department of State's Office of International Affairs conducts more than thirty programs that employ cultural, diplomatic, humanitarian, and educational tools to help Florida compete and win in the global economy, while promoting international understanding, stability, and security.

In the post-September 11 environment, all nations face a new paradigm into which the traditional assumptions about the international economy and global security do not fit. No nation can guarantee its prosperity or security without first helping to build understanding among nations. Cultural exchange programs provide the primary vehicle for the achievement of this objective.

President Dwight D. Eisenhower, perhaps the greatest U.S. military leader of the twentieth century, understood the paramount importance of promoting prosperity, stability, and security through direct contact, person-to-person and community-to-community, across national boundaries. Thus, he founded the Sister Cities/Sister States program, in which Florida is an enthusiastic participant under the Florida Department of State's direction.

> *I think, at a child's birth, if a mother could ask a fairy godmother to endow it with the most useful gift, that gift would be curiosity.*
>
> —ELEANOR ROOSEVELT

Cultural exchanges provide depth and meaning to these contacts. Visual artists, musicians, actors, dancers, and authors convey thousands of years of heritage through works of art, which transcend the barrier of language and the blockade of politics. In order to create a framework for enhanced cultural exchange opportunities, the Florida Department of State has led Florida's preeminent cultural leaders on missions to Mexico, Japan, Brazil, El Salvador, Chile, Uruguay, and Argentina since 1999, while receiving in excess of seventy inbound missions from more than forty nations during that period.

Many of these contacts have produced bilateral cooperative agreements between entire nations and the state of Florida for the exchange of archaeological and historic sites' professional assistance, traveling exhibits, qualified professors, and professional artists. These agreements have produced substantial economic benefits. Together with the Department of State's International Cultural Exchange grants program, these agreements have produced a marvelous array of displays and performances in Florida and beyond.

Additionally, we recently persuaded the World Olympians Association (WOA) to relocate its headquarters from Monaco to

Coral Gables, Florida. The WOA represents Olympians past and present worldwide. While drawing significant sports events, conventions, and other sports-related business to Florida, the WOA will bring many of its estimated eighty thousand members to Florida, exposing them to our communities, business leaders, and children. Similarly, when Florida hosted negotiations for the Free Trade Area of the Americas (FTAA), the Department of State provided numerous opportunities for these key leaders to become familiar with Florida's culture and heritage.

While working to expand Florida's international ties, I have continued to promote an exciting, nurturing setting for the growth of cultural activities within Florida. The arts provide effective media for creating unity in diversity; through the arts, we communicate our ideas, struggles, aspirations, and dreams with persons from other backgrounds. The arts enable us to become one people who draw strength from the richness of our differences.

UNIFYING PRINCIPLES

I believe in the power of the arts to transcend the cultural differences that might otherwise divide us. Two principled leaders I admire exemplify this power—Maya Angelou and Gloria Estefan. These women overcame tremendous personal and cultural obstacles to forge better lives for themselves, and they have enriched and ennobled us all through their contributions.

Maya Angelou stirred the hearts of the nation on a cold January day in 1993. Already widely acknowledged as one of America's premier literary figures, she became the second poet in U.S. history to compose and deliver a work for a presidential inauguration. Of the millions who heard her majestic voice for the first time on that day, few imagined that, as a child, this regal woman had been mute for five years.

Maya Angelou was born in 1928 into a troubled home. When she was three her parents divorced, and Maya and her brother were sent from California to Stamps, Arkansas, to be raised by their paternal grandmother. Several years later, she was sent back to live with her mother. The move home proved disastrous. Barely eight years old, Angelou was raped by her mother's boyfriend. The crime was discovered, and when the perpetrator was brought to trial, the little girl was forced to testify. A few days after the trial ended, the rapist was found beaten to death. With childlike logic, Maya concluded that her testimony had caused the death of the man, and she resolved to stop talking in public. "I thought if I spoke, anybody might die," she has said.

Maya was sent back to her grandmother's home, where a family friend, Mrs. Flowers, took a special interest in the silent girl and encouraged her to read. Later in her life, Angelou said, "Probably the only way any of us will ever be free of the blight of ignorance and racism is if we read."

Maya Angelou acquired an early fondness for the Bible and the works of Paul Laurence Dunbar, an African-American poet who died in 1906. The simple imagery of Dunbar's "Sympathy" resonated deeply with Maya's own experience. Years later, this poem provided the foundation for Angelou's first autobiographical bestseller, *I Know Why the Caged Bird Sings*.

Returning to her mother's home in California, Maya became a mother at the age of sixteen. She stayed in school, however, studying acting and dance, and graduated with honors. She then took a variety of jobs, waiting tables and even becoming the first woman (and first African-American) streetcar conductor in San Francisco. Though she worked hard to provide for herself and her son, Guy, her heart never strayed from the arts. She continued to develop her skills as a singer, dancer, playwright, and novelist throughout the 1950s.

Angelou's developing political awareness and her love of theater coalesced in 1960 when, after hearing a speech by the Reverend Martin

Luther King Jr., she decided to produce a play to raise money for the Southern Christian Leadership Conference. The success of *Freedom Cabaret* led to her appointment by Dr. King as the northern coordinator for the Southern Christian Leadership Conference, where she became a champion in the continuing campaign for civil rights.

The publication of *I Know Why the Caged Bird Sings* in 1970 was greeted with critical acclaim. In the years that followed, U.S. presidents regularly sought her wisdom and perspective. Gerald Ford appointed her to the Bicentennial Commission in 1975, and Jimmy Carter appointed her to the National Commission on the Observance of International Women's Year in 1978. In 1981 she received a lifetime appointment as the first Reynolds Professor of American Studies at Wake Forest University. Today, she continues to write and lecture extensively worldwide, paying special attention to developing nations, especially Africa, where countless underprivileged women have been helped by her inspirational message and personal touch.

For those who struggle to overcome abuse, discrimination, and prejudice, Maya Angelou's life illumines a dark world. She is a person with whom millions can identify and whom all must admire, a woman who overcame horrific circumstances to become one of the great voices of contemporary literature. Once silent, she now communicates her message of hope fluently and forcefully, not just in English, but in French, Spanish, Italian, Arabic, and West African Fanti.

"Courage," she says, "is the most important of all the virtues, because without courage you can't practice any other virtue consistently. You can practice any virtue erratically, but nothing consistently without courage."

Gloria Estefan has hurdled enormous barriers to become an influential singer/songwriter, with particular accolades for being the first person to take the Latin music influence mainstream. A pioneer of the Latin sound a full twenty years before it exploded on the scene with Ricky Martin and Enrique Iglesias, Gloria and her husband, Emilio, cleared the path while their inheritors were still infants. But Gloria's road to international stardom was jeopardized by an accident that threatened not only her career, but also her life. Though her recovery from a broken back was her most public comeback, the obstacles she overcame early in life helped forge her character so that she has become a Grammy Award-winning and multiplatinum-selling musical artist in addition to being a successful wife, mother, and advocate for freedom.

Cuban born in 1957, Estefan immigrated with her family to Miami when she was a year old, leaving all of their possessions in the homeland. Virtually penniless, the family began afresh in their new country. Even at a young age, the girl had evident musical talents; family members recall that little Gloria Maria Fajardo "loved music since she could talk."

In 1961, her father took part in the Bay of Pigs invasion, the unsuccessful attempt to oust Fidel Castro from power. Castro's forces captured him, and he consequently spent a year and a half in a Cuban prison. During that time Gloria and her mother lived in a Cuban ghetto near the Orange Bowl in Miami.

Upon returning home, Gloria's father chose to serve his new country in the armed forces. Tragically, he was exposed to Agent Orange while fighting in Vietnam and contracted multiple sclerosis. Gloria cared for him until his death in 1980, while her mother worked to support the family. During this difficult experience, a guitar she had been given provided Gloria's one solace. Alone in her room, she would sing for hours.

As a young girl, Gloria was introduced to pop music. In an interview she recalled feeling unattractive and isolated as a child and finding release in music: "When I was a teenager, . . . I was shy, I wore glasses, I had a big eyebrow . . . They were years of torture. It was very depressing and scary for me. Music was the one bright spot in my life. My childhood made me very serious and introverted; music was an escape from that. I sang instead of crying."

In 1975, while still in high school, Gloria joined a band led by Emilio Estefan, the Miami Latin Boys, which played the wedding circuit. With the addition of the talented young female singer, they changed the name to the Miami Sound Machine. A little more than three years later, Gloria married Emilio Estefan and went on to finish her college education.

Well-known in Central and South America, with the spotlight now focused on Gloria, the group released their first English album to U.S. and European markets in 1984. Their crossover was a gigantic success; the Latin rhythms provided an irresistable pop alternative during the mid-1980s.

"I was told," said Estefan, "you're too Latin for the Americans, too American for the Latins. But that's who I am. I'm Cuban American; I'm not one thing or the other. I have an American head and a Cuban heart."

It seemed the sky was the limit for Estefan until the morning of March 20, 1990. Estefan's tour bus was stopped along a Pennsylvania interstate highway shy of the New York border on a snowy night, with Gloria inside. Suddenly, the bus was rear-ended by a speeding semi truck. Gloria's back was broken.

Fortunately, doctors were able to place two 20-cm titanium rods on either side of her spine, necessitating 400 stitches to close the 14-inch incision. The question everyone (including a few of her doctors) were asking was: Will she ever walk, let alone take the stage, again?

"One more millimeter and my spinal cord would have been severed," Gloria remembered. "I was nearly paralyzed. It was pretty bleak. The doctor said I might be able to walk again, but he doubted that I would be able to perform. And then he said, 'It's all up to you. I have seen recoveries that have nothing to do with medicine, [but] everything to do with the person's spirit and desire to get better.'"

Miraculously, with determination, courage, and a lot of physical therapy, within one year of the accident she was performing again.

"I got thousands upon thousands of letters while I was recovering. Many people wrote to say our music had helped get them through difficult experiences. Others were praying for me in the lobby of the hospital. They made me want to come back and, later, I wanted to tell everybody how much the power of people together in a community praying and concentrating on something positive had to do with my recovery," said Gloria.

Furthermore, a little more than a year after her tragic accident she began a world tour, singing with passion to audiences around the globe her newest song, "Coming Out of the Dark," inspired by the accident. The song quickly rose to the number one spot on the charts, and Gloria was on her way to the top once again. In 1993 Estefan released a Spanish language album, *Mi Tierra* (My Country), winning a Grammy Award in 1994.

With a profound appreciation for life and all she had been graced to accomplish, Estefan wanted to use her gift of music to help those in need. In August 1992, tragedy struck the state of Florida. Hurricane Andrew swept through just south of Miami, leaving forty-one people dead, countless people homeless and displaced, and about $15.5 billion in property damage, creating the costliest natural disaster in U.S. history. As a way of giving back, Estefan organized a benefit concert that raised $3 million for the victims of the hurricane.

Estafan's successes have not been related only to her career. She has been married to Emilio for twenty-four years while working in an industry notoriously hard on marriages. Despite the pressures of life on tour, she has remained devoted and active in the lives of her children. Her humanitarian efforts to reach disadvantaged children and youths are now conducted by a foundation that bears her name. And her efforts to raise awareness of the political plight and struggle for freedom by the captive citizens of her homeland, Cuba, led to her being awarded the Ellis Island Medal of Honor in 1993.

The enormity of the obstacles she has conquered is only a secondary testament to the vibrant life and courageous character of the shy Cuban girl who is today universally recognized as one of pop music's divas. She has turned tragedy into triumph by refusing to allow barriers to obstruct her path and by using those challenges instead as stepping-stones to rise above circumstances, refine her talents, and promote the welfare of others. Gloria Estefan has demonstrated the spirit of cultural leadership, not just by her career, but by the totality of her life.

APPRECIATING DIVERSITY

Just as an unvaried diet soon ceases to satisfy, so an unbroken sameness in our workplace, our community, our habits, our friendships, and our recreations invariably leaves us hungry and dissatisfied. We are naturally inclined to experience a wide range of sights, sounds, tastes, ideas, perspectives, influences, and inspirations. Our tired imaginations are reinvigorated when we expose ourselves to people and experiences outside our ordinary, mundane existence.

Regrettably, it is very easy for us to fall into comfortable habits and patterns. How can we overcome the lethargy of sameness and limitation? If we are going to celebrate the diversity that constitutes such a critical part of the genius of the American way of life, we must be very deliberate about it.

1. EMBRACE DIVERSITY

How varied are your interests? How different are your closest friends? Are you exposed to diversity in your workplace? Do you have adequate opportunities to see the beauty and integrity of distinctiveness? What about your children? Are they regularly exposed to the wide variety of peoples, cultures, and perspectives that have made America as great as it is?

For most of us, diversity is something that must be cultivated lest we fall into a routine and live the majority of our lives within the confines of a narrow rut. We must attempt to work at surrounding ourselves with people who are different from us. We have to seek out people with varied perspectives and backgrounds. We have to experience directly the valuable contribution they can make to our outlook and effectiveness. The rewards are worth our effort.

2. EMBRACE CULTURAL DIFFERENCES

Journalist and sociologist James Kunstler has noted that as a result of modern commercial development, a smothering standard of sameness has begun to obscure the wild diversity of the North American continent. Every freeway looks nearly identical—whether traversing the Great Plains or crossing the Appalachians, whether skirting a major urban center or plunging into a national wilderness area. Every mall has the same stores that carry the same wares. Every suburb has the same fast-food outlets with the same architecture and the same menus. Scattered across America at predictable intervals are a series of copycat strip centers and office park developments—all comprising a human environment not actually intended for humans, but for automobiles. Kunstler calls the phenomenon the "geography of nowhere."

There are islands of distinctiveness to be found in the midst of this sea of sameness, of course, but we have to be very intentional in seeking them out. We can go to the cultural festivals, visit the historic sites, frequent the museums. Study the heritage of our communities and those we visit. Take time out for the craft fairs, see a foreign film, or try an ethnic food we've never sampled before. The quest for diversity is wonderful fun—a veritable treasure hunt with a guaranteed payoff.

3. EMBRACE CHANGE

There is a direct correlation between diversity and change. Alternatives are friendly reminders that we do not know it all, and that there are many ways to approach a problem. Change breathes new life into neglected and stale ideas. It can alter our course just enough to snatch victory from the jaws of defeat.

Change also offers unexpected opportunities to draw deeply from the well of life's variety. Many beautiful and unexpected events occur when we alter our routes along the highway of life. The well-trod paths of everyday existence provide stability and security, but an over-reliance on them can engender dependency and stifle originality.

One of the easiest ways to begin embracing differences is through the promotion of cultural heritage, particularly in the realm of the arts. We are a nation of immigrants, and our lives and families repre-sent a largely untapped treasure of diversity. By reading the literature of another time, place, or culture, such as the works of Eudora Welty, Lady Murasaki, Frank McCourt, Toni Morrison, Naguib Mafouz, Gabriel Garcia Marquez, or Isabel Allende. . .by viewing interna-tional art exhibits, both classic and contemporary. . .by listening to the sounds of music shaped by experiences unknown to us. . .by learning another language—we can get a sense not only of the worlds of others, but also our own. We begin to understand not only who we are, but how others might see us.

During the post-election storm, I learned so much from people who were not like me at all. I drew strength from people who differed from me culturally and politically. Thanks to them, my mind has been broadened and my heart softened. Hearing from people all across America, from every walk of life, reinforced my appreciation for America's differences.

The use of racial division to salve or inflict political wounds also reminded me that we still have a long way to go before we are able to fully celebrate our differences for their own sake. It reminded me that while the beauty of America may be our commitment to diversity, it is a beauty that can quickly fade away if we fail to take the appropri-ate initiatives.

PRINCIPLE 9

RESIST THE TYRANNY OF THE URGENT

J. R. R. Tolkien often asserted, "In life, as in literature, most shortcuts actually turn out to be long cuts." Effective leaders stay on task and on message, even when seemingly urgent distractions clamor for their attention. Diversions abound. Illusory quick fixes and magic wands beckon everywhere. Learning how to filter out the noise of life constitutes one of the greatest disciplines we can ever develop.

A merica has endured a number of very heated and torturously close presidential races. While we may have felt that the Election 2000 recount controversy took a harrowingly long time to resolve (thirty-six days), it took *three months* to determine the winner of the disputed Election of 1876 (Rutherford B. Hayes)! Just twelve years after that election, Americans bore yet another agonizingly close race. The Election of 1888 featured one of the most contentious battles for the presidency in American history. But we might never have known it by the demeanor of the Republican candidate, Benjamin Harrison. He remained calm and composed throughout the long ordeal.

No political novice, Benjamin Harrison was the grandson of President William Henry Harrison. He knew only too well how the fickle tides of politics and popular opinion could ebb and flow.

Therefore, he would never allow his sense of worth or identity to be defined by the races he won or the offices he held.

On election night, amidst nail-biting tension at his campaign headquarters, nothing ruffled Harrison's equilibrium. His campaign advisors were concerned that he only seemed interested in the polling results of his home state of Indiana. When, at just after ten o'clock, the official tallies indicated that the state would safely land in the Republican column, he thanked everyone at his headquarters and went home. He slept peacefully all night, though few, if any, of his campaign workers would. The race went down to the wire, and Harrison's victory in the Electoral College (he lost the popular vote) was not certain until very early the next morning.

A day later, one of the new president-elect's dearest friends came by Harrison's home to offer his congratulations. This friend asked him why he had turned in so early—especially when the results still hung very much in the balance. Harrison responded, "I knew that my staying up would not alter the result if I were defeated, while if I was elected I had a hard day in front of me. So a good night's rest seemed the best course in either event."

He later explained his attitude to his new White House staff: "A fellow who fails to take into account the divine is bound to miss a good deal of sleep unnecessarily—it can help but little. Our charge is simply to render our services aright and leave the results to providence."

Harrison could sleep peacefully because he possessed the remarkable ability to resist the tyranny of the urgent. He understood that the truly important must take precedence over the clearly importunate.

According to leadership expert John C. Maxwell, the two most difficult things for people to accomplish are "to think and to do things in their order of importance." But effective leaders, he says, "force these disciplines upon themselves." They understand the vital importance of principles and priorities. They know what is important and what is not, and they are able to order the tasks strategically so that they can productively focus on essentials rather than peripherals. Whenever a storm strikes, whenever problems arise, and whenever crises hit, they are able to stay the course.

All too often, we wrestle with a fragmented perspective of life that hampers our effectiveness precisely because we cannot say "no" to the insistent but insignificant things that constantly crowd into our schedules and grapple for our attention. As a result, the vital things get crowded out. Urgency replaces priority. Thus, when we go home at the end of the day, we think that we were busy all day, but in fact we failed to get anything accomplished that really mattered.

Benjamin Harrison suffered under no such illusions. He had the fortitude and the discipline necessary to differentiate between what really mattered and what really did not.

FASTER AND FASTER

Can you imagine any candidate for political office today having the kind of confidence, patience, or perspective to go to bed before knowing the election results? I cannot. I have been through a nerve-racking election night on several occasions. Believe me, it is not easy to get to sleep even when you feel certain you know what has happened.

These days, we are extremely impatient. We desire instant messaging, rapid transit, speedy recoveries. Many of us enjoy instantaneous access to information on broadband internet. We can conduct business at the speed of light. We prize shiny new electronic toys far above timeworn treasures. Everything seems to move faster and faster.

Speed and efficiency define almost everything that we do. As a result, the urgent tends to overwhelm the important. Our entire culture is rapidly morphing into a mirror image of its mass-produced art, instant entertainment, pop fashion, prefab architecture, and microwaved meals.

This urgency-driven mindset is only exacerbated by the fact that we never really allow ourselves to slow down, to process. We allocate little time to read, think, or reflect. We do not feel we can afford to stop for fear of being passed over—or run over—by the next person. Spend a quiet evening thinking, reading, talking, and musing? Not likely. Have to get up and go. No time to lose.

Not surprisingly, according to social analyst Richard Hoggart, we currently live in a "post-literate society." Many observers share this opinion. It has become commonplace for prognosticators of the future to herald the impending demise of literature, of books, indeed, of the printed word. With the demise of books, they warn, will come the demise of quiet reflection, thoughtful analysis, and measured discernment.

> *I am of certain convinced that the greatest heroes are those who do their duty in the daily grind of domestic affairs whilst the world whirls as a maddening dreidel.*
>
> —FLORENCE NIGHTINGALE

Such dire warnings are not unwarranted. There can be little doubt: the electronic 24-hour-cycle mass media have become the dominant means of conveying and purveying modern culture today. This process occurs at a faster and faster rate—to the point that we are bombarded continually with more and more information, which contains tidbits that mean less and less. In consequence, we think about less, and we respond to less, with every passing day.

During the recount, television commentators urgently pressed for interviews. They would find me on my cell phone, home phone . . . any unlisted phone. I had no desire to "tell my side of the story." I believed the truth would stand. My advisors thought I should appear once or twice, and finally they prevailed. As we were trying to determine with whom we should interview, my husband received a call for me on *his* cell phone! It was Larry King. I teased Mr. King, saying that my husband did not wish for me to appear on his program because the night before, David Letterman had said I was in the middle of my fifteen minutes of fame. The first phase, as he described it, was character annihilation by the media. The second phase would be the beauty makeover (for which I am still waiting.) In the third phase, I would pose for *Playboy*. And in the fourth phase I would become the fifth "Mrs. Larry King." I think I surprised him, because he said that my husband and his wife would both be at the interview if I chose to grant it! Anders and I found the exchange very funny. Disallowing the tyranny of the urgent to govern can result in serendipitous moments!

RECOVERING A SENSE OF PROPORTION

How, then, do we resist the tyranny of the urgent in this hurry-hurry world of ours? Particularly when the storm strikes and the crisis crowds in on us, how do we keep from succumbing to the temptation to frantically react? How do we prevent ourselves from leaping before looking? Can we learn to take time to measure our responses, temper our tongues, and restrain our knee-jerk responses?

When I was a college student, one of the most significant events in my development was the time I spent studying abroad. Amidst the glorious landscapes and lively cities I explored in Europe, I found, and still find, the cathedrals the most impressive sites. In order to place the recount experience in perspective, I recalled those magnificent structures, with their spires, jewel-colored windows, statues, and gargoyles, and concluded that a Gothic cathedral is a vivid expression of humanity's capacity to resist the tyranny of the urgent. Towering above city skylines, cathedrals are testaments to the slow, deliberate, long-range thinking of the medieval mind. Built with painstaking precision and incredibly complex detail, these edifices rose at a protracted pace, generation after generation.

Many may protest that a study of medieval cathedral building is an archaic, off-the-path subject for a leadership book, but we have no better example to contrast with the common exhortation, "just get the job done." Standing almost a thousand years after they began to appear, cathedrals are the antithesis to our fast food, disposable culture. They took forever to build. When finished, they became permanent fixtures in the landscapes they dominated. Because of the astonishing physics of the project, the cathedral builders had to be equally mindful of both the means and the end. Any shortcut would eventually have catastrophic consequences, possibly costing many lives and undoing hundreds of years of work. Patience and safety were the order every single day.

But more than the mechanics and science of it all, consider the psychology of cathedral building. Every successful cathedral project, including modern-day Gothic Revival churches, required supreme leadership ability. It took remarkable "people skills" to build ongoing support in a community. . .to initiate and sustain a project that the original participants, their children, their children's children, and several generations after that would never see to completion. The organizer of the project, whether a bishop, an abbot, or an architect, had to be spiritual leader, project manager, financier, cheerleader, and intergenerational visionary all rolled into one. This leader had to make a dramatic impact to propel the project into the future with sufficient force to ensure the continuation of the project through successive generations. Given the talent, time, and resources necessary to build a cathedral, many who tried, failed.

> *The greatest advances in human civilization have come when we recovered what we had lost: when we learned the lessons of history.*
> —WINSTON CHURCHILL

At best, each cathedral would take a lifetime to complete. The more ambitious the building project, the farther its completion extended into the future, growing more distant from the planners. In glaring contrast to our era of just-in-time delivery, the construction of a cathedral required piercing foresight and unwavering dedication from its planners and builders. As the German poet Heinrich Heine noted, "In the Middle Ages, they had convictions, whereas we moderns today only have opinions; and it takes more than opinions to build a Gothic cathedral."

The Gothic cathedral provides an excellent allegory for leadership. Effective leaders begin with a blueprint for what they wish to construct. Next they build a solid foundation, sufficient to bear the weight of the building. Finally, as the walls grow higher, effective leaders take care to install the buttresses necessary to secure the building against the pressures of wind and gravity that would otherwise destroy it.

Without a detailed strategy for whatever we wish to accomplish, we cannot point ourself in the right direction, much less lead others. Any attempt to rush the project of our life is flirting with disaster. If we fail to ground our projects in our first principles, our endeavors will crumble under their own weight. If we do not engage the support of family and friends, the forces that naturally arise in opposition to any project will bring it crashing to earth.

In embarking upon an endeavor of great magnitude, effective leaders settle in for the long haul, like the visionaries who built the great cathedrals. If we wish to create something of value that will last, we must forsake instant gratification, remaining resolutely focused on the future while working hard in the present. Effective leaders allow the time necessary to find suitable ground for their work. They prepare that ground painstakingly. They build with precision according to plan, refusing to cut corners with ill-advised compromises. Anything less can reduce the most elaborate edifice to a pile of rubble. The right balance of strategy, patience, and vision, however, can produce an enduring legacy that future generations will enjoy and admire.

SCULPTING THE FUTURE

The construction of the cathedrals involved numerous artisans, the vast majority of whom are unknown to us today except by the individual characteristics of their work. One man, however, is universally recognized for both his sculpting and painting in churches all over Italy during the Renaissance—Michelangelo Buonarroti. While his name and work are familiar around the world, the story of his persistence in the commission of his art is not. Michelangelo would customarily labor for years on pieces of marble in his effort to bring an image to life. Speaking of the visionary, yet tedious, nature of his art, Michelangelo once described the process of sculpting: "I saw the angel in the marble and carved until I set him free." His work was not to be rushed.

Michelangelo's greatest accomplishments are the ceiling paintings of the Sistine Chapel, one of the most spectacular achievements of a glorious era. Originally designed as the location of papal elections, the architecture of the Sistine Chapel paralleled its spiritual significance. Commissioned to paint the ceiling by Pope Julius II, Michelangelo single-handedly executed the task by laboring persistently in less than perfect conditions.

Initially, the artist objected that the job was intentionally designed to be impossible. The Sistine Chapel, built on a foundation that bears the exact dimensions of Solomon's temple, boasts a ceiling that soars a stunning sixty feet at its apex. These dimensions provided Michelangelo's first hurdle.

The architect Donato Bramante was hired to build a scaffold for Michelangelo that would allow the painter to comfortably reach the ceiling, but Michelangelo, sensing that Bramante did not have his best interest at heart, discarded the deficient structure for his own. Erecting a one-of-a-kind flat wooden scaffold supported by brackets above the chapel windows, with a unique maze of ladders allowing for the transport of materials, Michelangelo put himself within arm's

> *You can never dictate the future by the past—you may, however, ameliorate its illest effects and heighten its greatest delights by its remembrance. People will not look forward to posterity who will not look backward to their ancestors.*
>
> —EDMUND BURKE

length of the five-thousand-square-foot ceiling.

Michelangelo also protested that the Sistine Chapel commission would distract him from his real forte—sculpting. Nevertheless, Michelangelo transferred his love of sculpting to his painting with both theological and artistic precision. At first he commissioned other painters to assist him, but soon judged their abilities as too inferior. Reportedly, he locked these artists out of the Sistine Chapel while he worked alone.

With no one but laborers to daily prime the sections of ceiling and to haul supplies whenever he needed them, Michelangelo spent the better part of four years at his task. The inconveniences were innumerable, from kinks in his neck to paint in his eyes to the mildewing of his frescoes.

Michelangelo's paintings on the ceiling's nine panels recount nine stories from the book of Genesis. By the time he finished *The Last Judgment,* painted on the wall above the altar (the largest fresco of the sixteenth century), Michelangelo had painted more than three thousand figures—an immense commission for just one man, regardless of the time involved. The project cost Michelangelo his health and his eyesight, as well as the postponement of many of his unfinished sculptures. Had he lacked fortitude, the momentous task and its exacting toll could have easily disillusioned Michelangelo. While he had many opportunities to cut corners, he did not succumb to such temptations. Rather, he remained focused on creating a legacy that has lasted for centuries.

The examples of Michelangelo and the cathedral builders are monuments to persistence. They beckon all leaders to persevere, even when the task is monumental and the path is tortuously long. Dramatic challenges elicit our greatness. While we may have to traverse a lonely and thankless course, if we can bear up to the end—even if we have to pass on the project to our successors—the results of our life's work can be magnificent and benefit generations to come. That legacy constitutes our reward for rejecting the tyranny of the urgent.

We are supported in our efforts to resist the tyranny of the urgent when we nurture these critical disciplines in our lives:

I. KNOW YOUR HISTORY

Bartok Havic, the Czech historian, has stated, "History's record is clear: a people who cannot look past the moment, past the fleeting pleasures of fleshly indulgence, will be a people whose culture vanishes from the face of the earth." In the current cultural situation, we must hearken to the voice of experience. As the literary critic Donald Davidson aptly commented, "The past is always a rebuke to the present; it's a better rebuke than any dream of the future. . . because you can see what some of the costs were, what frail virtues were achieved in the past by frail men."

We need to come to terms with our heritage if we are to move ahead with confidence and effectiveness. Our best chance to resist the tyranny of the urgent is to slow down, take a deep breath, and take stock of where we are and where we ought to be; to learn the lessons of the past and to pay heed to the specific wisdom of experience.

> *History must be our deliverer not only from the undue influence of other times, but from the undue influence of our own, from the tyranny of the environment and the pressures of the air we breathe.*
>
> —LORD JOHN ACTION

The English author and lecturer John H. Y. Briggs has poignantly argued that a historical awareness is essential for the health and well-being of any society: it enables us to know who we are, why we are here, and what we should accomplish. He wrote, "Just as a loss of memory in an individual is a psychiatric defect calling for medical treatment, so too any community which has no social memory is suffering from an illness."

If we take the time to look beyond the present horizon, we will be better able to resist the tyranny of the urgent and to embrace the permanent things that really matter in the long run. Such an inquiry can be deeply satisfying and enjoyable. We can read, travel, visit a museum or tour a historic site. Reconstruct our family tree. Interview relatives or seniors in our communities to listen to and/or write about their stories. Take a course in history or the classics. Restore an antique. We must discover the remarkable lessons of the past—and then apply these lessons to the present with an eye to the future.

2. GET A LIFE

Contrary to the assertions of typical self-help manuals, we cannot manage time. The clock just keeps ticking no matter what we do. We can, however, manage ourselves. We can manage our thoughts, our priorities, our feelings, our ambitions, our actions, and our use of time. Self-control is in rather short supply in the modern world, but it is one of the greatest assets we have at our disposal. It is also the very best means of resisting the tyranny of the urgent.

Go home. Spend time with your family. Tell stories around the dinner table. Build a fire in the fireplace. Barbecue in the backyard. Kayak down a river. Write a letter to your favorite teacher, find him or her, and send it. Take a watercolor painting, photography, sculpture, or calligraphy class. Go bird watching or study a regional botanical guide. Learn a new language. Write a poem to someone you cherish. Take a walk in the woods or along the beach or in the park or just down the street. Give a present you made to a friend for no reason. Stop for a moment to relax. Listen to the music and hum a few bars. Slow down and smell the roses.

3. PLANT A GARDEN

If you're going to take time to smell the roses, you might want to consider actually growing them. From the very beginning of time, human beings have felt at home in a garden. We find solace from the wearying effects of this difficult world among the flowers and herbs, trees and vines, vegetables and fruits—despite the intrusions of weeds, insects, tares, and thorns.

> *The recollection of the past is only useful by way of provision for the future.*
> —SAMUEL JOHNSON

Gardening has been rather artlessly defined as little more than an enjoyable leisure activity, a means to produce food or enjoy herbs, or as a way to create beautiful landscapes with pleasantly arranged flowers, shrubs, trees, and lawns. To be sure, for some gardening is a form of exercise, a means of saving money on food, or a way to ensure that fruits and vegetables are free from pesticides or other chemicals. But gardening has also always been more than that.

Gardens are invariably serene and therapeutic. They serve as havens where we can think, refuges from the helter-skelter of our daily routines, sanctuaries where we can pray, reflect, and ponder. Throughout history some of the greatest advances, keenest insights, and most creative efforts have been born in meditative moments in gardens. Beyond colorful, sweet-smelling ornamentation for homes or churches or public places, gardens have always provided space for bodies and souls to explore the frontier of truth and freedom. Thus could Benjamin Disraeli assert, "How fair is a garden amid the trials and passions of existence."

Live in an apartment? Plant a garden in pots and set them on the sill or in a window box. Start a terrarium. Place fragrant bouquets you have learned to arrange throughout your home. Take time to smell the roses—whoever may have grown them.

I always try to practice what I preach, but the hectic pace of my schedule precludes me from maintaining a garden. My solution? I visit a farmers' market every Saturday morning. While I enjoy the fresh flowers and vegetables I find there, this routine offers me a refreshing opportunity to rest, relax, and recharge. The cares that have beset me during the previous week melt away as I take in the fresh air, the pleasant smells, and the vibrancy of the crowds of people who, if but for a few hours, have also declared their freedom from the tyranny of the urgent. If you wish a more intellectual challenge, consider learning the botanical names of all the horticulture that surrounds you. My grandfather could recite the Latin nomenclature of every plant we encountered—and that covers a lot of vegetation in Florida. My mother also knew every name of every tree, shrub, plant, flower, and weed in our environs. They are very tough acts to follow!

* * *

MYTH CONCEPTION:
RELUCTANT REVOLUTIONARIES

Posterity: you will never know how much it has cost my generation to preserve your freedom. I hope you will make good use of it.
—JOHN QUINCY ADAMS

There is a profound difference between a revolutionary and a reformer. Perhaps the most notable aspect of the American Revolution is that its leaders were disinclined to revolution. Virtually all of the patriotic founders—from the familiar luminaries like George Washington, John Adams, John Hancock, Thomas Jefferson, and Patrick Henry to the lesser known heroes like Richard Henry Lee, James Iredell, Samuel

Chase, and John Dickinson—were careful, conservative, and constructive men. They were reformers, not revolutionaries. They resisted even the idea of radicalism and loathed the disruptions of violence—whether rhetorical, political, or martial.

As Paul Johnson has pointed out in his magisterial *History of the American People,* the founding fathers were largely faithful sons of colonial gentry. They were devoted to all the conventional Whig principles of political stability, including the rule of law and the maintenance of corporate order that they had inherited from their English forebears. They had worked hard to engender a law-abiding, settled, and peaceful society. They wanted nothing to do with the raucous upsets and tumults of agitation, insurrection, and unrest.

Even in the face of increasing pressure from Parliament and Crown, they were reticent to protest, much less rebel. They were determined to exhaust every possible legal course of action before they would countenance the thought of armed resistance. For more than a decade they sent innumerable appeals, suits, and petitions across the Atlantic to Westminster authorities. Even after American blood was spilled at the Boston Massacre, they were willing to negotiate a settlement.

> *To be genuinely wise, one must make haste slowly.*
> —BENJAMIN FRANKLIN

It took more than the conflicts of Lexington and Concord, more than the full-scale battles of Bunker Hill, Falmouth, and Ticonderoga to provoke the patriots to commit themselves to a course of independence. War had raged between Britain and the colonies for over one year, but as late as the first week of July 1776, there was not yet a solid consensus among the members of the Continental Congress that "such an extreme as full-scale revolt," as John Dickinson dubbed it, was necessary.

When the Declaration of Independence was drafted by a committee composed of Benjamin Franklin, Roger Sherman, Robert

Livingston, John Adams, and the young Thomas Jefferson, the resolution was defeated twice before it was finally adopted. Even then the cautious delegates decided to keep the document secret for four more days before releasing it to the public.

Our Founding Fathers were, at best, reluctant revolutionaries. What, then, ultimately convinced them to set aside their native conservatism and steer the thirteen colonies toward war and independence?

Again, according to Paul Johnson, it was their very traditionalism—their commitment to a settled life of freedom—that drove them to arms. They fought against Britain in order to preserve everything Britain had always represented.

John Adams wrote in his manifesto *The Rule of Law and the Rule of Men* that it is the "duty of all men" to "protect the integrity of liberty" whenever the "laws of God," the "laws of the land," and the "laws of the common inheritance" are "profligately violated." Justice demands, he argued, "a defense of the gracious endowments of Providence to mankind," including "life, liberty, and property." To deny this duty is to ensure the reduction of "the whole of society" to the "bonds of servility."

Sometimes principled leaders must fight, not because they like the fighting, but because by fighting they hope to prevent the necessity to fight continually. Patrick Henry asserted that only a "grave responsibility to God and countrymen" compelled the peace-loving people of America to fight. He believed that the tyranny and corruption of the British Imperial system had all but ensured that "an appeal to arms and the God of Hosts" was "all that was left" to the patriots. "Is life so dear," he asked, "or peace so sweet, as to be purchased at the price of chains and slavery? Forbid it, Almighty God! I know not what course others may take, but as for me: give me liberty or give me death."

Thus was America's great experiment in liberty begun—and only thus can it possibly endure.

The Belloc Song

It all boils down to affection,
We will flee from what we abhor.
It's clear upon further reflection,
We are defined by the things we adore.

With all of the millions of voices
Fighting for room in my head,
I could be paralyzed by all these choices
So I'll let time do my sorting instead.

When I am dead
I pray it will be said,
His sins were scarlet
But all his books were read.

I'll join the everlasting conversation
Read of places I've never been,
Read for my mind's emancipation
From the tyranny of fashions and trends.

In love and worship I transcend myself,
And I am never more myself than when I do,
When I lose myself in a book or another
I find myself from a truer point of view.

Written by Wes King. © 2002 Wes King/Lotterthanme Music (ASCAP).
   Wes quotes author Jane Hamilton on this one: "I really believe you can't build a self without books. You get an inner voice by listening to someone else's words in your ear."

PRINCIPLE 10

Be Broken, Be Bitter, or Be Better

*We cannot always choose our circumstances, but we certainly
can choose how we respond to them. In today's society, we
perpetually face the temptation to revolt against maturity.
But difficult times demand substantive responses. Mature
leadership emerges in a time of conflict with uncanny calm,
while immaturity recedes trembling into the background.*

No one in his or her right mind actually wishes for adversity, sickness, conflict, or scandal. No one wants to cope with pain, struggle, or loss. Trials and tribulations, grief and woe are never welcome companions for the journey of life.

Even so, to varying degrees, every soul on earth becomes well acquainted with all the deleterious consequences of living in an imperfect world. No one—rich or poor, famous or obscure, strong or weak, educated or ignorant, wise or foolish—has ever escaped distress, sorrow, and bother.

Not only is adversity inescapable, but amazingly it can become quite beneficial. There is no school quite like the University of Hard Knocks. No situation teaches us more. Nothing provokes us to greater maturity, focuses us upon the things that matter most, and sharpens our sense of purpose like hardship. Suffering either makes us or breaks us—but when it makes us, it makes us more compassionate and sensitive than ever before, more attentive and patient toward conditions we had not previously noticed, and less likely to jump to conclusions or make snap judgments. Sorrow often softens us. Trouble can temper us. Given the choice in the aftermath of trauma to turn back the hands of time, often we would decline to do so, for we are better off for having endured.

We cannot choose our circumstances; but we can choose how we respond to those circumstances. Everyone suffers. But some people suffer well—and this process improves and strengthens their lives in any number of ways. Others face heartache and permit themselves to break over it. Still others face the same kind of heartache and become embittered through it. In times of calamity, some people wither under the white-hot intensity and never fully recover. Some are refined by the fire and come back better than ever. The difference is not in the nature of the trouble but in the nature of our response.

Our troubles will not ultimately define who we are. But how we handle our troubles will shape our calling and destiny. Our reaction to adversity, our growth and maturity in light of our problems and grief, will make the most significant difference in our lives.

Principled leaders do not enjoy difficulty more than anyone else. But they do view hardship as an opportunity to advance and to prove their mettle. In tough times, they develop resolve. They rise to the occasion. They not only grab hold of life; they grab hold of all that life offers—the bad as well as the good—and they make the most of it. It is not just that they are thinking positively, putting on a happy face, and looking for the proverbial silver lining; leaders believe deeply that all things work together for good—somehow, some way. This sincerely held principle allows effective leaders to avoid wasting time lamenting their ill fortune, casting blame, or wallowing in guilt. Principled leaders suffer pain as do all others, yet keep moving toward the future.

BEARING UP

To be certain, I have enjoyed a blessed life. Even so, like everyone else, I have had my share of sorrows. I have lost friends and loved ones. I have known disappointment, doubt, disease, and discouragement. I have known the heartache of ruptured relationships in my family over such temporal issues as money and property. I have suffered through abusive, dysfunctional relationships. I have lived through the shame and sorrow of a failed marriage.

Thus, when the post-election storm blew into my life with all the destructive bluster and fury of Hurricane Andrew, I was no stranger to the specter of hardship. Still, I was unprepared for the range of emotions I would feel as I was buffeted by the political fury that ensued.

In order to manage the crisis properly, my staff and I erected a firewall that denied all strategic access to *either* of the battling presidential campaigns and their respective political party organizations, thereby preserving the independence of our decision-making. Nevertheless, we evenhandedly performed our ministerial duties and answered all elections-process and legal questions directed our way. We were still besieged with media queries, legal challenges, court battles, and ideological squabbling, however.

Some Republicans, who felt I was not always acting in the best interests of the party, attacked me. Their accusations were accurate; I was, after all, trying to enforce the law, regardless of whom enforcing the law benefited.

It is a matter of public record that I had expressed a definite preference in the campaign. Everyone had a preference. I was, in fact, one of the eight co-chairs of the Republican presidential campaign in the state of Florida. This position had no bearing on my intention or ability to uphold the law. Contrary to the implications the media continued to raise by fixating on that role, members of Florida's executive cabinet, including my predecessor as secretary of state, have long served as state chairs or co-chairs for presidential candidates.

My colleague on the cabinet, Attorney General Bob Butterworth, actually ran Al Gore's campaign in Florida as chair of that campaign. Moreover, as the *Washington Post* reported in its book on the recount, titled *Deadlock*, while Al Gore debated whether to proceed with his public concession of the election after the networks had projected a Bush victory, Attorney General Butterworth provided legal advice to Gore campaign National Chair Bill Daley on Florida's automatic recount provision. According to the *Post*, Daley asked Butterworth, "Are you sure we have an automatic recount?" Butterworth answered, "I'm the attorney general . . . I'm sure." Further, the *Post* reported that at the time Butterworth decided to release an official Attorney General Opinion contradicting the statutorily authorized opinion on manual recounts in Palm Beach County that my Division of Elections had issued, he "had kept in touch with the vice president's team throughout the dispute—he remembered chatting once with Daley, a couple of times with Gore attorneys Mitchell Berger and Kendall Coffey, and several times with officials of the state Democratic party."

> *Often the same thing that makes one person bitter makes another better.*
>
> —J. C. RYLE

In addition to the ire of Republicans who thought I was not favoring the Bush campaign, I drew the fire of Democrats who assumed that I would do anything within my power to harm the cause of the Gore campaign. They automatically called into question my integrity, reliability, and objectivity, and assumed that I would be cavalier in my application and enforcement of the law. And so they came out with all guns blazing before I took any action whatsoever.

Despite the pressure I received from both sides of the political fence, I refused to break—or even bend—the law for the sake of my candidate *or* for Al Gore's sake. (The latter seemed to be the only means of passing the media's test for impartiality.)

The attacks, and the manner in which they were carried out, grew particularly vicious after the recount ended, and disappointed Gore partisans trained their fire on me. As part of Principle 8, I described the deep injustice a majority of the U.S. Commission on Civil Rights inflicted via their "report" on the 2000 presidential election in Florida. The process and manner by which the majority commissioners, led by Chairperson Mary Frances Berry, performed their work constituted almost a worse injustice than the rampant falsehoods contained in the report itself.

I testified during the commission's first set of hearings in Tallahassee in January 2001. (The commission later held another round of hearings in Miami.) Under detailed questioning, I confessed that I was not aware of every daily action and telephone conversation of my cabinet staff and the 681 full-time employees throughout the seven divisions of Florida Department of State. Furthermore, our legal counsel felt strongly that much of the information being asked of me should be addressed by the division director—who was seated next to me and who actually had the conversations in question or led these actions—particularly because these were the subject of numerous lawsuits.

Chairperson Berry assailed me, bragging that she had "run" a division with "thousands of employees," and that she had "felt it was [her] duty to inform [herself] so that" she could answer "questions about every aspect of the operations and the policies" of that division. Chair-

> *God often digs the wells of joy with the spades of affliction.*
> —ISAAC WATTS

person Berry launched this broadside attack and accused me of failing to accept accountability, despite my statement *no less than three times* during my testimony before her that day that I accepted full responsibility for all the actions of the Florida Department of State's Division of Elections.

When Chairperson Berry authorized, either tacitly or otherwise, an unapproved draft of the commission's report that was filled with false and libelous statements, the shoe landed snugly on the other foot. Appearing on national television, Chairperson Berry disingenuously stated that she had "no responsibility" for the work of her staff. Nevertheless, during the same period of time, the commission's acting general counsel appeared on national television to defend the leaked report's false attacks on me.

The leak constituted a shameful and fraudulent violation of due process. On May 24, 2001, the commission's acting general counsel, Edward Hailes, sent us a letter that contained the following statement: "Prior to publication, the Commission provides to government agencies . . . an opportunity to comment on the accuracy of those portions of the report pertaining to that agency or organization . . . Enclosed for your review and comments is a copy of the *relevant* portions of the draft report." (My italics.) The letter further specified June 6, 2001, as the deadline for our response, at which time the commission would supposedly consider that response for publication as part of its report.

As we prepared our response to the scattered portions of the draft report we had received with the above-referenced letter, my office received a call from a reporter with the *Washington Post*. He asked whether we wished to comment on the commission's report, which he claimed was highly critical of me. As became apparent during the next twenty-four hours, someone associated with the commission had leaked another report to the *Post*, the *New York Times*, and the *Los Angeles Times*. Shockingly, the statements about Governor Jeb Bush and me that appeared in those papers the following day had not even appeared in the "relevant portions of the draft report" that Mr. Hailes had purported to send to my office. This statement, which appeared in an Executive Summary, said, "The state's highest officials responsible for assuring effective uniformity, coordination, and application of the election were grossly derelict in fulfilling their responsibilities and unwilling to accept accountability."

Since the commission clearly had *not* provided us with all "relevant portions of the draft report," we postponed our response until we received the opportunity to view, and rebut, the *entire* report. The June 6 deadline came and went; we did not receive the report.

I was not the only party affected by this leak, of course. The commission's majority did not provide the two Republican appointees on the commission with a copy of the report until *one day after* the leak to the press. Nevertheless, the majority moved forward with its approval of the report on June 8, three days later, even though one of those Republican appointees, Commissioner Russell Redenbaugh, is visually impaired and had little or no time to have the report read to him.

Once we had time to review the entire report (since the commission never sent us a copy, we obtained the report from the commission's website), we issued a thirty-six-page response that thoroughly rebutted every aspect of the report. We submitted that response to the commission, citing federal regulations that require that if a report "tends to defame, degrade, or incriminate any person, the report or relevant portions thereof shall be delivered to such person" at least *thirty* days before it is made public, allowing a *twenty*-day period for a response, which the commission *shall* append to the report.

Clearly, a statement that accused me of being "grossly derelict" in my duties was defamatory and degrading when no evidence cited in the report supported that statement, and when much of the evidence cited in the report contradicted that statement. We had not received all relevant portions of the report; we had not received *any* portions of the report until we received the May 24 enclosure from Mr. Hailes (thus violating the federal thirty-day requirement, as the report became public just eleven days later, with its June 4 leak to the press); and obviously, the commission did not give us the required twenty days to file a response.

In light of all of these violations of federal regulations, we at least expected the commission to meet the requirement that it append our response to the report. Instead, we received a shocking reply from Mr. Hailes. Ignoring the June 4, 2001, leak, Mr. Hailes noted that we had "declined to comment" by the original June 6 deadline while still insisting that he had sent us all "relevant" portions of the report. Moreover, Mr. Hailes made the following statement about the Executive Summary that contained the "grossly derelict" comment (which we had obtained from the *Washington Post*'s website): "The document you obtained from the *Washington Post* website *was not, is not, and will not be a part of the Commission's report*. The staff is in the process of preparing an Executive Summary for the report that was approved on *June 8, 2001*." (My italics.)

> *To scale great heights, we must come out of the lowermost depths. The way to heaven all too often leads through hell.*
>
> —HERMAN MELVILLE

Sure enough, the Executive Summary that now appears with the commission's report *does not* contain the "grossly derelict" language. Meanwhile, Chairperson Mary Frances Berry or whoever leaked the report on June 4, 2001, had accomplished their purpose. According to Mr. Hailes, the absence of the "grossly derelict" comment from the "report that was approved on June 8" relieved the commission from its legal duty to publish our response with the report. Nevertheless, the "grossly derelict" comment became the statement from the report *most widely quoted in the press*. The malicious purpose of the leaked report, as well as the retracted "grossly derelict" comment contained therein, was to poison public opinion before *anyone* had a chance to thoroughly examine the full report to see if it supported that accusation.

So, what of Chairperson Berry's statement that she was not associated with the leak (and, by implication, we might assume she was denying any association with the "grossly derelict" statement, since Mr. Hailes suggested that the leaked Executive Summary was, in fact, a rogue document that had no association with the commission's report)?

Chairperson Berry wrote a letter to the editor of the *New York Times,* which was published on July 19, 2001, in which she referred to her "view that *dereliction of duty and leadership by the state's highest officials plagued the system.*" (My italics.)

I invite you, the reader, to draw your own conclusions.

Through this attack and others like it, the political prognosticators predicted that I would not be able to bear up under the pressure, that my career would be derailed, that I would surely melt into a little puddle, leaving only my broomstick behind. Through it all, I had to keep reminding myself that I could be broken, be bitter, or be better.

The new legions of reporters who scrutinized my every move following the recount controversy did not realize that I had overcome vicious and unfounded attacks on my integrity since the beginning of my political career. During my 1994 campaign for the Florida state senate, I unknowingly became one of seventy Democratic and Republican candidates for office who became entangled in a thicket of campaign contributions made illegally by Riscorp, a southwest Florida insurance company. When I discovered this problem three years later, I became the only candidate out of the above-mentioned seventy who repaid the entire amount of improper contributions to my campaign—$20,000— out of my own pocket. (Contrary to media reports, I was never required to do so.)

Regrettably, these same media sources have conveniently forgotten that this controversy involved any other public official but me. Most egregiously, when they attack me on this issue, they fail to mention that Democratic U.S. Senator Bill Nelson received at least $75,000 in illegal campaign contributions from Riscorp during the same time period—*while he was running for election as Florida's Insurance Commissioner and would soon be in charge of regulating Riscorp.*

Neither I, nor do I believe the dozens who accepted these contributions, had any idea what activities, illegal or otherwise, were transpiring at Riscorp's headquarters. To accuse me of such would be tantamount to saying that a candidate who received a donation from Arthur Anderson or Enron knew what was going on behind closed doors.

Even during the month prior to the 2000 presidential election, I faced disingenuous media attacks concerning my legislatively approved international travel budget, which triggered an avalanche of misinformation that has continued to fester to this day. Contrary to the absurd claims that my international travel budget has reached $3 million per year, that budget has averaged $11,000 per year over the three years I have served as secretary of state (or .006% of the annual budget independently appropriated by the Florida legislature for the Florida Department of State's annual budget).

Not content to rest with their distortion of my international travel budget, media sources have reported that I fly first class at state expense, when I *never* have done so. Further, they have often misread my hotel bills, reporting the bill for several nights as the rate for one night, or reporting the bill for two persons as the rate for one, thereby inflating the cost of my hotel stays. In all of this breathless "investigative reporting," media reports have also usually neglected to mention that during the course of two years, my predecessor as secretary of state spent more money traveling on the taxpayer-funded state airplane than my entire budget for transportation, lodging, conferences, meals, and all other expenses relating to domestic and international travel during a comparable period.

Despite the constant frustration I have experienced concerning these distortions and falsehoods, I have resolved that they will not break my desire to serve. They will not embitter my faith in the people to see through the haze of misinformation. I have thus decided instead to become a better person, a better public servant, a better wife, and a better friend. Even when I feel that the media or a political adversary has ventured beyond the pale, I strive to remain accountable to the following maxim: never begrudge your adversary's good fortune, nor rejoice in their downfall. Despite our differences, we must all strive to work for the betterment of our nation and our world. That effort begins in the heart and mind of each of us.

VISION AND VALOR

One of the most fascinating and enduring figures in American history is Theodore Roosevelt. Countless books on leadership mention his role in the charge up San Juan Hill and his apt use of the "Bully Pulpit" while occupying the highest elected office in the land. Yet few relate how he was consistently able to pull triumph out of the depths of tragedy. When facing utter personal despair, he not only endured, but submitted himself to the hand of Providence and looked for the lessons that only dire hardships can teach.

While eagerly expecting the birth of his first child with his wife, Alice, Teddy Roosevelt saw his joy turn to overbearing agony when life suddenly went awry. Roosevelt had enjoyed a rich and full family life as he was growing up. He desired to continue that legacy with his own children. After three years of marriage, Alice became pregnant. Preparations immediately began for a grand house that would shelter and nourish the many children Roosevelt planned to have. Land for the house had been purchased and much of the preliminary planning was under way for a spacious home that would overlook Long Island's Oyster Bay.

The plans continued, and so did Roosevelt's political career. Called back to the capital of Albany, Roosevelt left his wife in New York City, where she struggled through the pregnancy, her frail constitution magnifying the miseries common to her condition. During that time Alice developed a renal ailment that would worsen over the course of her pregnancy, but would not be detected until after she gave birth to their first child.

On February 12, 1884, while Roosevelt was in Albany, Alice prematurely delivered a healthy baby girl. But the next morning a series of telegrams requested Roosevelt's immediate return to New York City. Upon his arrival, he was struck with more bad news than he had reckoned. "There is a curse on the house," his brother told him. "Mother is dying and Alice is dying too." Roosevelt's mother, Martha Bullock Roosevelt, was in the final stages of typhoid, which had appeared as the onset of a cold a few days earlier. Alice's dire situation had been discovered, and her health was declining rapidly. Just after midnight Roosevelt's mother died. Less than twenty-four hours later, Alice, at the delicate age of twenty-two, also died. Valentine's Day, 1884, was among Roosevelt's most grim times.

> *Hardship reveals some of the most vital matters in life in particular ways that almost nothing else ever really can. Prosperity, for instance, is full of friendly acquaintances and smiling ne'er-do-wells; real friendship is shown in times of trouble and in days of adversity.*
>
> —ABRAHAM KUYPER

But the day after Roosevelt buried both his wife and his mother, he celebrated the baptism of his new daughter, Alice Lee. A young rose grew from the thicket of misery.

As Teddy Roosevelt faced his darkest days, he sold his possessions, left his daughter with his sister, and moved to the Dakota Territories. But while he regrouped, he never surrendered his spirit, regardless of how dark and murky life got. And the sun eventually reappeared in his life. He married his second wife, Edith, with whom he raised five more children in addition to Alice. He soon was catapulted first to the governorship of New York, and then to the position of vice president. Assuming the helm of state after the assassination of President William McKinley, Teddy Roosevelt was able to boldly lead America into the twentieth century because he was grounded in a firmly established set of principles that allowed him to act consistently and comprehensively regardless of the situation he faced.

Despite achieving great feats of statesmanship, which included brokering the peace between Russia and Japan, earning him the 1906 Nobel Peace Prize, having a vigorous family life with a wife and six children who loved him, and engaging in a host of intellectual pursuits and wilderness adventures, disappointment was never far off. After Roosevelt left office his chosen successor, William Howard Taft, abandoned many of the programs and policies that President Roosevelt had implemented during his tenure. Making a third-party presidential bid for a third term in 1912, Roosevelt narrowly survived an assassination attempt that required him to sit out the last three weeks of the campaign—dashing his hopes for reelection. Woodrow Wilson, the Democratic Party candidate, was elected instead, with only 41 percent of the vote.

Even greater heartaches were to come. In 1917, at the beginning of America's involvement in World War One, all four of Roosevelt's sons were sent to the front lines. His son Archie was seriously wounded in March 1918. His youngest son, Quentin, was shot down and killed in July of that same year—a tragedy from which Teddy Roosevelt never had time to recover, as he died just six months later on January 6, 1919.

No one has ever accused Teddy Roosevelt of dwelling on his misery, despite the regular tragedies he encountered. He lived life to the fullest and addressed his problems head-on, as they came. Even as the storms crossed his path, he never stopped fully applying himself and excelling in everything he did. He understood one of the most profound truths of life: difficulties invariably will attend our way. Our friends and loved ones will die, and we, too, have a day appointed for us. But troubles and death are part of our existence. They are the bumps and valleys that form the texture of our humanity. Teddy Roosevelt's ability to deal with and overcome the vagaries of living helped him to maximize the opportunities he encountered in his personal and professional lives. His success was universally acknowledged. Thus, in 1925, it was no surprise when his image was chosen to accompany Washington, Jefferson, and

Lincoln on the Mount Rushmore monument—where he takes his rightful place among America's greatest presidents.

From the austere granite face of that South Dakota memorial to the remote jungles of equatorial South America, we again see that when beset by troubles, we have but three choices: become broken, become bitter, or become better. The inspiring story of a quiet missionary's resolve not to let tragedy be her master is one of my favorites. Elisabeth Elliot's example teaches us that we are in control of the extent to which our circumstances can control us. As a youngster I was deeply moved when she and Carrie Ten Boom visited our summer camp to speak with us.

Elisabeth Howard met Jim Elliot in March of 1947 at Wheaton College in Illinois. They were attracted to one another at once, but their individual plans to become missionaries took priority over romance. In May 1948, a long talk ended with a bittersweet conclusion: they loved each other, but must wait to see if marriage would help, not hinder, their plans for missionary work.

From 1948 until 1952, Jim and Elisabeth prepared themselves separately for missionary work in Ecuador, where several indigenous cultures would benefit from medicine, sanitation, literacy, and peacemaking with other tribes. There, Jim worked among the Quichua in eastern Ecuador, while Elisabeth worked in western Ecuador among the Colorado tribe. Circumstances and Elisabeth's demonstrated commitment to a self-sacrificial lifestyle finally convinced Jim that marriage would help, not hinder, the missionary effort in Ecuador. In 1953, Jim formally proposed the marriage—a proposal Elisabeth accepted happily. Jim and Elisabeth waited for a need to arise among the Quichua for a married couple to direct a mission outpost. A flood in August 1953 created that need. Finally, after years of wondering, waiting, and praying, the couple married on October 8.

Although they enjoyed each other's company, life at the mission outpost was not easy. In addition to the hardships common to a primitive lifestyle, the Elliots had to overcome the indigenous people's fear of them. Elisabeth later learned that some tribes, including one that became of special importance, the Aucas, thought that all foreigners were cannibals. The Elliots courageously lived with the kind of fervency of commitment to their mission that enabled them to accept death as a possibility, perhaps a necessity, before the indigenous peoples would welcome the presence of strangers among them.

Elisabeth bore a daughter, Valerie, in 1955. The Elliots transformed their lonely outpost into a bustling mission center operated by four other missionary couples. As the mission continued to expand, five missionaries decided to attempt contact with the nearby Auca tribe, reputedly savage killers who lived in isolation from any outside influence. The mission embarked upon exploratory flights over Auca territory, dropping gift packages and shouting words of welcome and friendship in native languages. Several times, the Aucas attached return gifts, one of them a live parrot in a bright woven basket. This encouraging response prompted the missionaries to take daring action: they would land and camp in Auca territory.

On January 2, 1956, Jim Elliot left with four fellow missionaries for Auca territory, planning to maintain regular radio contact with the mission station. Radio conversations reported no contact with the tribe until January 6, when one Auca man and two women arrived to inspect the camp and remained for the better part of one day. The missionaries took photos of the Aucas and excitedly anticipated friendly exchanges with the rest of the tribe shortly. On January 8, however, without warning, the Aucas returned in force, speared the missionaries, and left their bodies on the beach. A search party composed of soldiers, missionaries, and journalists sought the five men and found their bodies riddled with spears, a destroyed plane, and a camera.

On January 16, the search party returned and met with the grieving families to confirm the missionaries' deaths. Elisabeth wept and grieved and questioned, as any woman who loved her husband would.

Because she had no answers to the smaller questions of what was to come next, she remained in Ecuador, continuing Jim's work and remembering his credo: "He is no fool who gives what he cannot keep to gain what he cannot lose." Elisabeth also prayed for the Aucas who had killed her husband. Instead of allowing her loss to gnaw at her soul with thoughts of anger and revenge, she forgave and loved. She stated, "The fact that Jim loved and died for the Aucas intensifies my love for them."

> *A wise man will make more opportunities than he finds.*
>
> —FRANCIS BACON

In November of 1957, almost two years after Jim's death, an opportunity arose for Elisabeth to meet two Auca women who had left their tribe. Quickly traveling to a nearby Quichua village where the women were staying, Elisabeth gained their trust and persuaded them to stay with her for a time. For a year she clothed and loved them, tending to their every need, from aching teeth to hurting souls. In return, they patiently taught her their language. When the year ended and the women desired to return to their Auca village, they invited Elisabeth and Valerie to go with them. Elisabeth accepted.

So it was that the Auca women left to prepare the way for Elisabeth and Valerie, and Rachel Saint, a sister of another of the slain missionaries. Two years and nine months after Jim's fatal journey, Elisabeth entered the Auca village. She lived among the natives, tending their hurts, recording their language, and carrying on Jim's desire to reach the Auca people. She survived this daring act of faith.

Many called Elisabeth foolish. They mocked her resolve. They accused her of putting herself and her daughter in harm's way without regard for Valerie's innocence and potential. But these critics did not know the fire that had burned deep in Jim's soul for the Auca people—a desire that was branded on Elisabeth's heart as she learned how deeply Jim was moved by the needs of the remote tribe. Now back home in the United States, this courageous woman has continued her missionary work as a noted author and radio host.

The stories of Teddy Roosevelt and Elisabeth Elliot show us that, while lessons learned in life's garden of roses do at times last a lifetime, it is the harsh schoolmaster called tragedy whose tests produce the most enduring character qualities. Such is the story of one of my favorite authors, C. S. Lewis.

Lewis was closely acquainted with tragedy from quite early in his life. His father, Albert, and mother, Flora, both Northern Irish Protestants, married in 1894. Warren, Lewis's older brother, arrived in 1895, and Clive Staples Lewis ("Jack" to his family), followed in 1898. The boys spent a quiet Victorian childhood in Belfast, complete with a nurse and summers at the seaside.

Although Jack's mother left much of the daily care of her sons to their nurse, she did personally attend to their illnesses, vacations, and schooling. Especially after his best friend and brother, Warren, left for boarding school in 1905, Jack became quite attached to Flora and shared her voracious appetite for books. Physically, Flora was never very strong or hale. She frequently suffered from headaches and fatigue. In 1908, Flora was finally diagnosed with cancer, and for the greater part of that year she grew steadily more ill. Despite the best medical care available, including an operation to remove the tumor, she died in August, on the morning of her husband's birthday.

Albert, grieved by the loss of his wife as well as the deaths of his father earlier in the year and his brother ten days after Flora, sent Jack away to school the next month.

Thereafter, Jack was to have a miserable boyhood and adolescence. His protected childhood had ill prepared him for the savage, competitive world of boarding school. The loneliness and grief of losing his mother, while simultaneously adjusting to the insensitivity of the other boys and the cruelty of some schoolmasters, was almost unendurable.

When Jack was sixteen, he escaped boarding school life. Albert arranged for the private tutor under whom he had studied, William Kirkpatrick, to prepare Jack for university entrance exams. Jack soon mastered Greek and French, in addition to polishing his public school Latin and gaining an understanding of German and Italian. Life with Kirkpatrick was pleasantly scheduled, with breaks for substantial meals and independent thought or recreation interspersed with the arduous academic work. Back in the cozy, domestic environment of his childhood, Lewis excelled.

Jack did equally well at Oxford before being called away to serve in World War One. He was wounded by shrapnel and sent home in 1918. During his war service he made the acquaintance of Paddy Moore, whose mother, Janie, and sister Maureen would become a huge part of Jack's life. Jack and Paddy agreed to care for each other's parents should one of the boys die in battle. Paddy did die, and Jack faithfully cared for Mrs. Moore, even sharing a home with all of its attendant chores and obligations, from 1919 until Mrs. Moore's death in 1951. Although rumors arose that their attachment was romantic, it was far more likely that the mother grieving for her dead son and the son grieving for his dead mother found solace in a parent-child relationship.

Immediately after his graduation from Oxford, Jack began teaching philosophy, and a year later, English, at Oxford's Magdalen College. Known as a demanding tutor and a fascinating lecturer, a life centered upon stories and words suited his nature and tastes to perfection. At Oxford he befriended J. R. R. Tolkien. Their association grew into the Inklings, a group of writers who met to read and discuss original and classic works. Jack wrote several scholarly works while teaching at Oxford and, after his religious conversion in 1931, produced a number of spiritual works as well.

The middle years were not easy for Jack, however. His brother, Warren, retired after a career in the army and came to live with Jack. The two brothers enjoyed a close friendship, but Warren did not share

Jack's appreciation for Mrs. Moore. His loved ones' obvious distaste for each other distressed Jack, as did Warren's alcoholism. Warren went on drinking binges, after which he was frequently ill and depressed. In addition, Mrs. Moore grew ill in the years prior to her death.

Hard on the heels of Jack's loss of one woman came his gain of another. Joy Davidman Gresham quite literally invaded Jack's life in 1952. She began a correspondence with Jack in 1950, but her visit two years later was one of desperation. Joy's husband, William Gresham, was an alcoholic and a womanizer. Joy sought advice about the course of her life from the wisest person she knew. While visiting Lewis in Oxford, Joy received a request from her husband for a divorce. Jack advised Joy to grant the divorce, and Joy went back to America to finalize the details.

In 1953, she returned to England with her two sons, David and Douglas, and settled in London. She saw Jack occasionally over the next two years, during which time he accepted a post to teach at Cambridge. Joy assisted him with writing *Till We Have Faces,* and Jack came to appreciate and depend on her. As they saw each other more often, Joy's feelings of romantic attachment grew quickly, while Jack's remained ambivalent. In 1956, Jack married Joy secretly in a civil ceremony—solely for the purpose of facilitating her English citizenship, as Jack told the few people who must know of the marriage.

But in October of that year, a familiar evil touched Joy. Cancer claimed Joy's health and shocked Jack into realizing his love for her. He publicized the marriage that December and began debating with clergymen about the morality of marrying a divorcee. A former pupil agreed to perform a church marriage ceremony in March 1957. For the next three years, Jack tenderly and devotedly cared for his fragile, brave wife. He ensured that her sons would remain in England after her death, and he took advantage of her periods of remission and recovery to travel, garden, remodel—anything to bring her pleasure. The fifty-nine-year-old bachelor had fallen in love at last, and he adored his wife with a sincere and generous passion. His oldest friends, though puzzled by his choice, acknowledged that Joy made Jack feel happy and complete. Perhaps the knowledge that their married life would be short caused both partners consciously to cherish it in an extraordinary way.

The gleam of happiness that Jack found with Joy dimmed in the spring of 1960. After one last trip, an exhausting, yet longed-for vacation to Greece, Joy declined quickly and steadily. She lived for three weeks in a nursing home, courageous and spirited to the last, before she died in July of that year.

Jack grieved deeply, pouring his confusion and sadness into a small but incredible volume, *A Grief Observed.* In it, Jack describes the process of bereavement and the relationship married partners continue in memory and reflection after one of them dies.

Jack lived for three years after Joy's death, years during which he read and studied and wrote, but with a difference. His friends found his personality to be gentler and more compassionate. Even a book on studying literature, *An Experiment in Criticism,* shows Joy's influence in its softer tone. He also took more time to answer letters personally, especially when he sensed someone in need. In opening himself to the tragedies of his lost mother and wife, he was himself enriched in love and patience.

Life is riddled with troubles. They are inevitable. But the absoluteness of trouble's existence does not necessitate our surrender to it. For some, tragedies inspire greatness, encourage resolve, and deepen devotion. It is from the bleakness of tragedy's undoings that rebirth appears most spectacularly. What can we learn from those who have borne their tragedies well?

1. TROUBLES CANNOT BE AVOIDED

We do not need to go looking for trouble; it will find us. Alfred Lord Tennyson wrote, "Sadness and sorrow attach themselves to all, there are

> *What is in this world but grief and woe?*
> —WILLIAM SHAKESPEARE

no exceptions, there is no escape, such is the Adamic bequest to all who dwell upon this terrestrial ball."

Thus, the principled leader does not become obsessed with caution or compulsive about risk prevention. The principled leader instead reasons the possible and proceeds with the business of life—knowing there will be interruptions, disruptions, and difficulties no matter what precautions are taken. In brief, the principled leader is realistic, not fatalistic or naive. The principled leader has a clear estimation of the character and nature of this world, but is stirred to constructive action by this understanding rather than being lured into a slumber or frightened into a stupor by it.

2. TROUBLES CAUSE US TO DESPAIR OF IRRELEVANCY

Adversity leaves no room for false illusions. Rather, adversity awakens us and delivers greater clarity and focus. As September 11 deeply reminded each of us, trivial issues cease to matter much in the face of the harsh realities of suffering and loss. When crises with life-and-death implications intrude upon our daily routines, we rightly turn our attention from irrelevant matters. We no longer place much stock in temporal desires. We concentrate on family, friends, and faith. In the days and weeks following the terrorist attacks on Washington and New York, we awoke as if from a dream to the value of permanent things. Likewise, when a family member suffers an automobile accident, a coworker is diagnosed with cancer, a neighbor goes through divorce, a local teen is arrested for drugs, or a friend loses her job, we gain a perspective and are afforded an outlook that changes not only how we empathize and act, but also who we really are. Thomas Wolfe observed, "There is nothing quite like calamity to reinforce reality." The principled leader, therefore, lives in the real world.

3. TROUBLES DRIVE US TO OUR FRIENDS AND FAMILY

When difficulty strikes, we turn to our friends and family. It is then that we discover how precious they really are. Winston Churchill said, "In prosperity a man may accumulate a plethora of acquaintances. But it is only in tribulation that a man is able to distinguish his friends from his throng." We turn to our friends for comfort, assurance, and solace, for perspective, vision, and counsel. We turn to our friends, and as a result, we are more than we were before our troubles began—more substantive, more balanced, and more mature.

> *The duration and depth of sorrow in one's grief is often in direct relation to the durability and breadth of one's friends.*
> —SAMUEL JOHNSON

4. TROUBLES ARE THE HEART OF OUR STORY

People who talk incessantly about all their successes are braggarts. People who continually tell us about their most significant feats, greatest joys, and fondest memories are bores. People who are never vulnerable, never wounded, and never open are fakes. Our greatest difficulties in life will actually open up more opportunities than our greatest accomplishments. What we have overcome makes us interesting to others because what we have overcome makes us more approachable, compassionate, and wise. According to Charles Spurgeon, "It is the wounded friend who is the most helpful friend when we find ourselves wounded." Friendship is not just a matter of empathy; people who have faced trials and tribulations and prevailed become emblems of hope to others. Their testimony becomes an inspiration. The greatest adversity they faced becomes the widest bridge to span the gap between lonely souls.

I would never wish upon anyone the struggles and attacks that I endured in connection with Election 2000. Nevertheless, I would not let anyone take that experience away from me. I have grown through this experience more than I could have ever imagined. I have learned much. I am a different person in many ways.

And for that I am deeply thankful.

* * *

COMBATING THE MEDIA MYTHS

As I indicated earlier in this book, I have not sought the spotlight during my years in public service. Thus, I have generally eschewed developing a "media strategy." Despite the misreporting and bias I encountered prior to the 2000 presidential election, I generally endeavored to do my job to the best of my ability, with the expectation that at some point in time, the truth would finally triumph over the distortions. My office did not issue many press releases. I wrote few letters to the editor calling a particular reporter to task for sloppy, inaccurate, or biased reporting.

The 2000 presidential election changed everything. While we survived the recount controversy due to the extraordinary efforts of Ben McKay and Adam Goodman, media scrutiny of every move we made continued to ratchet upward in the months thereafter. We had to develop a strategy for coping with the brave new world in which Election 2000 had deposited us, and we needed to find someone to implement this strategy effectively.

After a nationwide search, we finally found the right person. During May 2001, David Host became our new communications director. A native Kentuckian who had served as media assistant for U.S. representative Larry J. Hopkins (R-KY) nine years earlier, David was practicing law in Dalton, Georgia, during the time of the recount. He had followed the recent controversial battles closely in both the courts and in the media.

David's political acumen and legal background, as communicated through his extraordinary writing skills, have enabled us to turn the tide that the media storm pressed upon our shores in the wake of the 2000 presidential election. I would feel comfortable matching him against anyone in the business.

We now answer every attack with strength and resolve. We prefer to be not bitter, but better. We have discovered that allowing such distortions to pass without a response allows one more myth to become part of the popular lexicon that are repeated again and again. I hope this book will serve as an aid and inspiration to those facing adversity, and perhaps as a myth buster as well.

This Is Your Time

It was a test we could all hope to pass
But none of us would want to take.
Faced with the choice to deny God and live,
For her there was one choice to make.

This was her time.
This was her dance.
She lived every moment.
Left nothing to chance.
She swam in the sea.
Drank of the deep.
Embraced the mystery of all she could be.
This was her time.

Though you are grieving and mourning your loss,
Death died a long time ago.
Swallowed in life so her life carries on,
Still it's so hard to let go.

This was her time.
This was her dance.
She lived every moment.
Left nothing to chance.

She swam in the sea.
Drank of the deep.
Embraced the mystery of all she could be.
This was her time.
What if tomorrow?

What if today?
Faced with the question,
What would you say?

Fall on the mercy and hear yourself saying,
Won't you save me?

This is your time.
This is your dance.
Live every moment.
Leave nothing to chance.
Swim in the sea.
Drink of the deep.
Embrace the mystery of all you could be.
This is your time
This is your dance

"Every generation has to find out for itself that this is not Paradise, but Paradise Lost," Wes writes. "For this generation, one of those reminders will always be the tragedy at Columbine High School. Still, there will always be a Jim and Elisabeth Elliot, a Winston Churchill, a Martin Luther King. As Jim Elliot said, 'He is no fool who gives what he cannot keep to gain what he cannot lose.' This song was inspired by the life of Cassie Bernall and dedicated to her memory."

PRINCIPLE 11

ACT AND RISK ENMITY; TO REMAIN POPULAR, DO NOTHING

Leaders risk. They do not play it safe. Leaders lead. They do not wait until the path is already clear ahead. Leaders get things done. They do not simply preserve the status quo. They actually work rather than occupying their time with mere rhetorical appearances or photo ops. As a result, leaders simply cannot please everyone all of the time.

G. K. Chesterton once commented, "If a thing is worth doing, it is worth doing badly." By that statement, he did not intend to sanction mediocrity. He simply meant, "If a thing is worth doing, it is worth doing." If a thing is worth doing . . . but for the lack of resources . . . but for the lack of reward, admiration, or popular support . . . but for the lack of practical experience, adequate facilities, sufficient funds, or any other material convenience, *it is still worth doing*. Of course, this philosophy is guaranteed to dramatically complicate one's life.

Anyone who acts on principle will surely attract criticism. Anyone who pursues a determined course of action is bound to meet equally resolute opposition. The nature of the course of action and its attendant decisions does not matter. People can argue only with a person who has taken a position. Critics can rail only against actual programs. Opponents must have something to oppose. Thus, if you wish to remain in everyone's good graces, do nothing whatsoever, decide nothing whatsoever, and stand for nothing whatsoever. Abandoning that which is worth doing is always a safer and more popular course of action. Of course, it is also wrong.

Teddy Roosevelt proclaimed, "Better faithful than famous. Honor before prominence." Likewise, President James A. Garfield asserted, "It is a greater honor to be right than to be president—or popular, for statesmanship consists rather in removing causes than in punishing or evading results—thus, it is the rarest of qualities." Both men would have wholeheartedly agreed with Chesterton's maxim. As a result, both men were reviled by some. Indeed, assassins ultimately gunned down both men. Garfield succumbed to his wounds while Roosevelt survived.

Doing the right thing is dangerous. It is bound to rankle the ire of some and enrage others. It is bound to provoke a ferocious reaction. It always has; it always will.

I have been in politics long enough to have learned this lesson. Sometimes, the facts do not matter. Sometimes, logic seems irrelevant. Sometimes, the merits of programs and policies are beside the point. Sometimes, public servants can draw withering attacks simply for doing their job.

Add the stakes of the 2000 presidential election to that routine state of affairs, and you have a prescription for some particularly mean-spirited assaults. Regardless of what decisions I made, I was bound to come under fire. I became a target the moment that I decided I would not try to fly below the radar and do nothing. I became vulnerable to attack the moment I decided to decide. This fact stands as a universal principle of life, a principle that is evident throughout the whole of human history and a lesson that dominates the entire story of American politics through the centuries.

A panoply of armchair quarterbacks continue to suggest that since

I served as one of several honorary co-chairs for the Bush campaign, I should have recused myself from making any decisions regarding the recount. Could I have avoided the stress, the threats, and the infantile name-calling had I done so? Absolutely. Would I have remained true to my oath of office and set the proper precedent for persons who find themselves in my position in the future? Absolutely not.

Many people in positions of public trust expressed their preference in the 2000 presidential election. Former President Bill Clinton endorsed Al Gore. Did that fact preclude him from making presidential decisions that could have been perceived as helping the former vice president's candidacy (such as raiding our nation's emergency oil reserves to stem the tide of higher gasoline prices)? Florida Attorney General Bob Butterworth served as chair of Al Gore's campaign in Florida. Should that fact have disqualified him from issuing an official attorney general opinion supporting the Gore campaign's request for a manual recount in Palm Beach County (particularly when his own website proclaimed that "questions arising under the Florida Election Code should be directed to the Division of Elections in the Department of State," and the Division of Elections had already ruled on this matter)?

> *Learn all you can, but learn to do something, or your learning will be useless and your vision will depart.*
>
> —BOOKER T. WASHINGTON

Even more to the point, should the four justices of the Florida Supreme Court who ruled in favor of the Gore campaign twice[11] have recused themselves, particularly when the Gore campaign's lead Florida attorney who appeared before them in both cases, Dexter Douglass, had played a major role in their appointments to the court by Democratic governors?

I choose to believe that each of the individuals I mentioned had honorable intentions behind their decisions. When we stand for most elected offices, the people choose us as Democrats, Republicans, the candidates of a third party, or independents. They know our politics, but they expect us to leave partisanship at the door when the interests of our state or nation are at stake. By avoiding the hard decisions our sworn duties require us to make because our political interests might collide with these duties, we abdicate one of the primary responsibilities of leadership. Some associates of Al Gore and, indeed, some members of the media would have labeled me a "partisan hack" unless I bent or broke the law in their candidate's favor at every turn.[12]

Despite the combustible, corrosive rhetoric that continues to be hurled in my direction, however, no one yet has pointed to any instance where I failed to follow the law in administering the recount controversy. Even the Florida Supreme Court's decision countermanding my refusal to extend the deadline for certification was vacated by a unanimous United States Supreme Court (in their first of two rulings they made regarding the 2000 presidential election).

NEVER THE TWAIN SHALL MEET

The two most dominant American political figures during the second and third decades of the nineteenth century were John Quincy Adams and Andrew Jackson. Bitter rivals and diametrically different personalities, the two men were identical in their commitment to act rather than temporize.

One was from the East, and the other was from the West. One was refined, classically educated, and sophisticated, while the other was of coarse stock, barely educated, and simple. One was an intellectual, and the other was an adventurer. One was an urban gentleman whose family represented the closest version of American royalty in that age, while the other was a rural scrapper whose background stood in diametric opposition to that day's notion of American respectability. One was a diplomat, and the other was a soldier. One took pride in being a Boston Brahmin and insider, and the other took pride in being a Tennessee renegade and outsider. They distrusted each other. Indeed, some said they genuinely despised each other. To be sure, they spent most of their careers fighting each other, personally and politically.

Yet despite these very obvious and glaring differences, the two men shared an essential nature. Both men were decisive. Both men acted on principle. Both men were doers. And both men endured rabid opposition as a consequence.

James Monroe was the last member of the Virginia Dynasty to serve in the White House. The person who succeeded him was the last president from the Massachusetts Dynasty—the Adams family of Braintree. John Quincy Adams, though not born to royal purple, was certainly born to patriotic red, white, and blue. He literally grew up with the young nation: as a boy, he watched the Battle of Bunker Hill from an outlook near his home. By the end of his life, he had held more offices than any earlier president.

> *Speak softly and carry a big stick; you will go far. It sounds rather as if that were but a homely old adage, yet as is often the case with matters of tradition, this truism is actually true.*
>
> —THEODORE ROOSEVELT

The only son of a president to reach that office until the election of George W. Bush, Adams followed a career that closely resembled his father's. Both father and son attended Harvard; studied law; were successful diplomats and peace commissioners in Europe; were elected president for only one term; and both became embroiled in partisan conflicts that caused them to spend their least successful years in the White House.

Brilliant, studious, and precise, Adams was a more successful diplomat and statesman than a politician. As President Monroe's secretary of state, he negotiated with the Spanish for Florida and was largely responsible for the document that became known as the Monroe Doctrine. He spoke more than a dozen languages, was widely traveled, and was remarkably well-read. Indeed, he may have been the most intellectually precocious man ever to serve as president, with the possible exception of Teddy Roosevelt.

Adams reached the presidency through the convoluted events that marked the election of 1824, the second presidential election in American history to be decided in the U.S. House of Representatives. (The first was the election of Thomas Jefferson in 1800.) While Adams had finished second to Andrew Jackson in electoral votes, Jackson had not received the necessary constitutional majority. Adams prevailed in the House after Henry Clay, the Speaker of the House who had also run for president in the same election, threw his support to Adams. Jackson supporters charged that Adams had forged a "corrupt bargain" with Clay, since Adams soon appointed Clay as secretary of state. Adams and his nascent presidency never recovered, and Jackson defeated Adams handily in their 1828 rematch.

Adams met with much greater success in Congress, where he served for his last seventeen years. There, he distinguished himself through his dedicated fight to remove the gag rule, which prevented Congress from considering any antislavery petitions. After fourteen years of struggle, he finally prevailed. He served in Congress until he collapsed on the floor of the House of Representatives in 1848, sixty-six years after he had first served his country at his father's side.

Jackson's administration marked the emergence of a new kind of politics. The dynastic, elitist leadership of the past had finally given way to Jackson's more egalitarian and democratic orientation. Nevertheless, Jackson still had to reconcile those principles with the problems of an expanding economy in a growing country. Like Thomas Jefferson's election to the presidency twenty-eight years earlier, Jackson's ascendancy constituted a quiet revolution in American democracy.

> *If we take the generally accepted definition of bravery as a quality which knows not fear, I have never seen a brave man. All men are frightened. The more intelligent they are, the more they are frightened. The courageous man is the man who forces himself, in spite of his fear, to carry on.*
>
> —GENERAL GEORGE PATTON

A child of the western frontier, Jackson was as rough-hewn as the log walls of his birthplace. From his earliest years, struggle marked his life. At fourteen, he fought in the Revolution. On the frontier he studied law and gradually rose in Tennessee politics, representing the new state in Congress before he became a state Supreme Court judge. He gained his greatest fame not as a politician, however, but as a military hero. In the War of 1812 he commanded the American forces that soundly defeated the British at New Orleans.

Tall, with a commanding presence, Jackson had a large, devoted personal following. His decisive victory over Adams convinced him that he was the champion of the people. He was determined to act on their behalf. And he was determined to do so boldly and decisively. Indeed, he exercised his authority with a firm hand. He asserted the supremacy of the federal government when South Carolina tried to nullify tariff laws, and in his most dramatic act, he boldly vetoed the recharter of the Bank of the United States, the half-private bank that had become powerful enough to threaten the government itself. Jackson proclaimed that the government should not "make the rich richer and the potent more powerful" at the expense of the rest of society.

Both Jackson and Adams took bold stands on a host of issues. While they were not that far apart on most substantive policy concerns, their contrasting styles and their clear and definable positions attracted opposition—from each other and from others.

Adams remained as decisive, determined, and confrontational as ever as a member of the U.S. House of Representatives. Near the end of his life he said, "My object has ever been to stand on principle and principle alone. Had my purpose and motivation been to attract a popular following, I would have done little that I have done—and little else besides." He knew that the best way to remain popular was to do nothing.

> *Things just don't turn up in this world until someone turns them up.*
>
> —JAMES A. GARFIELD

Likewise, in his later years, Jackson described his veto of the national bank as the action of a man "who cared not for popular acclaim, but rather for principle. Had I wished for ease in office, I would have whiled the hours away in amiable discussions rather than in arguable decisions." He also knew that the best way to remain popular was to do nothing.

These two men were as different as they could be. Nevertheless, they were able to lead—and engendered great controversy—because they were willing to do what was worth doing. They remain enduringly popular precisely because they were willing to be unpopular.

DOING WHAT'S WORTH DOING

Principled leaders are controversial. They stand for certain things; they necessarily stand against certain things. This causes them to stand out, rendering them more than a little peculiar in this plain vanilla world of smothering uniformity.

To maintain a sense of equilibrium, the principled leader must keep several things in mind as he or she does what is worth doing.

I. TO AFFIRM ONE THING IS TO DENY ANOTHER

It is not possible to take a stand without calling into question another stand. To some people, this simple truth is invariably offensive. "Why do our leaders fail to unite and do what is right?" they despair. Of course, one person's concept of what is "right" may constitute an anathema to other individuals. In a healthy, deliberative democracy, there is no way around vigorous and even sometimes fiery debate.

> *He that wrestles with us strengthens our nerves and sharpens our skill. Our antagonist is our helper*
>
> —EDMUND BURKE

Principled leaders are always careful. They try to measure language, maintain collegiality, and moderate extremes. No matter how hard they may try, however, someone, somewhere, somehow will take umbrage and level the charge of partisanship. Andrew Jackson admitted, "I know if I were to say the sky was blue, someone would take great offense."

2. ACCEPT THE NATURE OF THE STRUGGLE

Our world is inclined to polarization. People take sides. And since there are at least two sides to every issue, people will inevitably hurry onto opposing sides in order to join the fray. This state of affairs might not be a desirable component of a perfect world, but it is reality. The effective leader assesses the situation as it actually exists—not as it ought to be or used to be or one day might be. John Quincy Adams confessed, "It is never my desire to fight but it is always my intention to do so. I am resigned to such a posture only because I know the nature of man is contention and not conciliation. Thus, the vast majority of the moral work which needs to be done will be accomplished only after the clash and clatter of conflict."

3. IF YOU HAVE TO FIGHT, FIGHT FAIRLY

In joining the fight principled leaders must heed ethical restraints. We may be forced into conflict against our will, but we need not become cheap-shot artists against our will. We can stick to the point. We can avoid personal attacks. We can be accurate. We can maintain decorum, respect, and integrity. We can fight fairly. In fighting for what is right, of equal importance is to fight in the right way. How can we fight for justice, if not to fight justly? If we are fighting for what is good and true, the least we can do is to use goodness and truth as the ground not only of our ends but also of our means.

4. ADMIT THE MYSTERY AND COMPLEXITY OF THE WORLD

Some people seek to reduce everything in the world to basic formulas. They believe that leaders should always produce simple solutions, regardless of the complexity of the problem. They expect leaders to summarize everything in an easy-to-grasp shorthand.

Hollywood's portrayals of politics and politicians compound this problem. Like the presidential impostor in the 1993 movie *Dave*, who solves the nation's budget crisis in a few minutes by uttering a few simple platitudes, some individuals believe that only conspiracies, corruption, and incompetence prevent our leaders from "doing the right thing."

Certainly, principled leaders must sail in a definitive direction while communicating clarity of purpose. They must not become hamstrung by the complexities of issues to the point of inaction and paralysis. While tending the tiller, leaders must make course corrections based on new information, without permitting the shifting gales of popular opinion or the musings of political "analysts" to push the boat off course.

In his reaction to the September 11 attacks, President Bush demonstrated this delicate balance of principled leadership. He issued bold, clear statements that informed our terrorist enemies and their state sponsors that the United States will no longer tolerate their activities. He unambiguously warned other nations that they must choose sides. Then, rather than immediately hurl missiles, he bided his time. He carefully built the necessary alliances and waited for the opportune moment to launch a properly measured attack. President Bush continues to demonstrate extraordinary leadership in the face of some of the most difficult foreign policy challenges any American president has ever confronted.

The decisions I faced when the recount controversy landed on my desk were much simpler. I held fast to this immutable principle: We would follow the law regardless of the result that course might produce.

Not every crisis presents us with clear solutions. Thankfully, the hard work and support of so many extraordinary people ensured that I plotted a steady course through the recount controversy. Although coping with the personal attacks was at times difficult, following the law was simple. I did not aim to win a popularity contest, so I felt the unmitigated freedom to follow the dictates of my conscience. While I have not enjoyed the venomous assaults that have resulted, I would not trade places with the public officials who bind themselves to the fickle whims of opinion polls. As my husband said, I would have to live with my decision the rest of my life.

* * *

MYTH CONCEPTION:
STICKS AND STONES

During the post-election storm, I found myself garnering international attention. Though most of the individuals who weighed in on my character, my politics, my family, my ambitions, and my motivations had never even heard of me a few weeks earlier, that small detail did not restrain them from unleashing a scathing barrage of name-calling.

They called me everything in the book: "Commissar Harris," "Comrade Madam Chairman," and the "electoral Czarina of the South." "Vampira," "Morticia," and "fodder for a latter-day Brothers Grimm." And these pearls of juvenile humor were some of the kinder things that Gore staffers, late-night lampoonists, and journalists offered!

Ah, the joys of serious analytical journalism. Forget for a moment that I rarely wear much makeup, or that when people meet me they exclaim in surprise at how different I look from the photographs they have seen. Forget about bias or inaccuracy. How about a simple lack of anything substantive to report? How about the desperation of resorting to the playground bully tactic of name-calling—the politics of personal destruction?

> *Nothing is ended with honor which does not conclude better than it began.*
> —SAMUEL JOHNSON

I suppose the authors of this prattle intended to belittle and marginalize me. But instead, they belittled, marginalized, and cheapened themselves. Rather than exposing my deepest motives and character, they exposed their double standards and doublespeak while utterly destroying their credibility.

As Shakespeare famously averred, when your critics "protesteth too much," they actually give themselves away. By boiling down their assessments to bite-sized media McNuggets, they sadly reveal their own limitations.

Spin You 'Round

Just beneath the surface,
Just on the other side,
There is a deeper meaning
Less said and more implied.
For what we get from these five senses

Is only part reality.
The real is really made up
Of what the eye can't see.
So learn to listen to the silence,
And a part of you awakes,
Sets your soul to dancing,
To the music that it makes.

Let it spin you 'round.
Let it lift you right up off the ground.
Let it open up your eyes.
To a beautiful surprise.
When your imagination will believe,
You will be free.

All the things that just don't add up,
The things you can't explain.
Every thing means something,
The pleasure and the pain.
All the alleys all the mystery,
The brick walls and the breaks,

Somehow work together,
There is no mistake.
Let it spin you 'round.
Let it lift you right up off the ground.

Let it open up your eyes.
To a beautiful surprise.
When your imagination will believe,
You will be free.

You are Christopher Columbus
As you fight the raging sea.
With the courage of King Arthur
You are bound by chivalry.
A child, wide-eyed with wonder,
You want to see the world,
And be a part of changing
this wide, wide world.

Written by Wes King and Fran King. © 2001 Dayspring Music, Inc. (BMI) & Father Brown Music (Admin. by Dayspring Music, Inc.) (BMI). All rights reserved. Used by permission.

"I pray with all my heart for the preservation of my children's innocence," writes Wes. "The older Fran and I become, the more we are dizzy with the wonders of life. This song was inspired by *Orthodoxy* by G. K. Chesterton." He adds a quote from George Macdonald: *Convert my imagination, and baptize me with wonder.*

PRINCIPLE 12

UNSTRING YOUR BOW

There is a time for battle, for confrontation, and for
engagement. But when the clash has passed, it is essential
that we know how to relax and enjoy life.
A bow that remains perpetually strung loses its elasticity—
and thus its effectiveness. Marriage, family, and friends
ground us, secure us, and preserve us. Faith, hope, and love
are the things that matter most.

At the end of the thirteenth century when they began to pioneer the powerful new military technology of the longbow, the Norman English bowmen found that the more elastic and flexible a bow remained, the more useful it was in battle. As a result of this discovery, they developed a host of new maintenance techniques, including the use of fine herbal oils to rub into the wood, leather sheaths to seal out moisture, and storage niches far from the drying effects of the hearthside. But they also learned that the best precaution a bowman could take in caring for his weapon was to unstring the bow when it was not in use. The simple practice of releasing the tension, relaxing the pressure, and relieving the strain not only enabled the bow to last longer; like exercising a muscle, it conditioned the bow to snap back faster and set arrows farther into flight. A bow that was never unstrung would quickly lose its effectiveness. A bow that was never relaxed became useless as an offensive weapon.

The same principle applies to us. If we stay on red alert at all times, our longbows arched and arrows poised to strike, we will soon lose our conditioning. To be effective in our work and in our calling, we need to be fresh, rested, and ready. In particular, each of us must learn how, and when, to release the tension, relax the pressure, and relieve the strain.

> *To every thing there is a season and a time to every purpose under the heaven: A time to be born, and a time to die; . . . A time to kill, and a time to heal; a time to break down, and a time to build up; A time to weep, and a time to laugh; a time to mourn, and a time to dance; . . . a time to embrace, and a time to refrain from embracing; A time to get, and a time to lose; a time to keep, and a time to cast away; . . . a time to keep silence, and a time to speak; A time to love, and a time to hate; a time of war, and a time of peace.*
>
> ECCLESIASTES 3:1-8 (KJV)

We need to blow off steam, remembering how to laugh, to dream, to think, to have some fun, and to turn our mind to something other than the crisis at hand. We need to refuel, refresh, and recreate.

Unfortunately, we do not unwind easily, especially in a time of crisis. A leader who wrestles with the demands of principles will likely feel guilty for not focusing on the problem constantly. We tend to think that due diligence means exceeding our reasonable physical and mental capacities.

Certainly, I felt that way during the maelstrom of the recount period. While my staff and I worked steadily to address the myriad of issues we faced day after day, we felt that we were somehow shirking our duties if we took a break to eat or sleep.

Though there are times when we must work longer and harder

than normal—and we did during that post-election storm—at some point we reach the limits of our physical and mental endurance. At that point, if we fail to rest, our performance will suffer. During the thirty-six days of the recount controversy, I received over 750,000 emails, thousands of faxes and letters, and hundreds of flower arrangements that covered every available surface and poured from our offices to line the corridors. This encouragement greatly sustained me. On Friday evenings, I and my staff divided into teams and delivered these arrangements to nursing homes and hospitals. We placed the beautiful larger arrangements in the foyers and took the smaller ones to patients and residents throughout these locations.

I will never forget one particular resident, a tiny elderly lady who was very kind to me. She exclaimed that she recognized me from television, but thought I was much taller. I explained that I once was very tall but the recent attacks had beaten me down a few inches. As I was leaving her, she said she would call her children to speak of our visit together. We finished delivering the flowers, and as we left this home her nurse came running after us—laughing. She said this gentle lady's son had just called, very concerned that his mother must be over-medicated; she had moments ago called to tell him that Katherine Harris had brought her flowers, and had sat on her bed and talked with her!

I received many other gifts during that period as well, including a cobalt-blue Chinese fighting fish (named Chad) that became our office pet; a stuffed white Siberian tiger (also named Chad); a locket containing loose chads, which I was tickled to wear; and an extra-large-sized men's athletic supporter (which I did not wear!).

The lighthearted humor that pervaded our office helped us bear the strain. At times, we still work around the clock at the Department of State, in a seeming endeavor to live up to our motto: "We will sleep when we die." On occasions, I have still attempted to deliver eighteen speeches in a day. We are striving, however, to become more balanced in our approach, while maintaining our perspective through humor.

Fortunately, history provides us with wonderful models of effective leaders who better understood the principle that very hard work, very long hours, and very great stress must ultimately be balanced with rest and relaxation. Otherwise, the weapons of our intellect and our will become stiff and useless, and when push comes to shove, they will break, not bend.

> *The best prize that life offers is the chance to work hard at work worth doing.*
> —THEODORE ROOSEVELT

A REFUGE FROM THE STORM

One of the most remarkable heroes and leaders of the twentieth century was Sir Winston Churchill. As the forces of totalitarianism rolled unimpeded across the European continent, and England was subjected to blistering bombings killing tens of thousands of innocent civilians, Churchill was the man to whom the English people turned to change the course of the battle and, eventually, history.

His almost immediate ascension to prime minister constituted a massive comeback. At the time, his political future had appeared to have completely evaporated, as he had not held office for more than a decade. During the time that he spent out of public office, however, he had been one of the most fervent prognosticators of the looming Nazi threat. His warnings had gone unheeded, however, while the British government under Prime Minister Neville Chamberlain pursued a feckless strategy of appeasement toward Adolf Hitler. Churchill vividly described this policy as "feeding a crocodile hoping it will eat you last." The eruption of World War II provided Churchill with a tragic form of vindication. Yet, this singular crisis in history enabled him to return to the political scene, where the world became witness to the awesome power of his will and the captivating character of his leadership.

> *The art of life is to know how to enjoy a little and to endure much.*
>
> —WILLIAM HAZLITT

Under the considerable stresses and strains of the war, Churchill remained stable and balanced, a constant beacon of hope for the British people. His constancy was the product of his repeated bouts with and victories over adversity. He had fallen from grace during World War I, later returning to serve in the government of Prime Minister Stanley Baldwin. Churchill's decade-long absence from politics began in 1929 with the fall of Baldwin's government, as a result of the worldwide depression that had ground British economic life to a halt. Thus began what Churchill called "the Wilderness Years."

Despite the financial hardship that had befallen Churchill as well by this time, his departure from political life allowed him time to devote to his writing, which proved to be a wild success and provided the means for him to return to his beloved home in Kent, Chartwell. While Churchill had purchased this refuge from the storm several years earlier, in 1922, just days before the birth of his child, Mary, the house had been closed while he pursued his political ambitions in London. Churchill and his family returned to Chartwell so he could regroup and refocus his life, unknowingly preparing for his "finest hour."

> *Friendships ought to be founts of joy. Therein we find not only our truest companions but our truest selves. Therein we tap into the source for an authentic happiness, for it redounds to a providential provocation of all that is good and substantial and true. Let us not therefore take for granted or neglect for the sake of business this matter of friendship.*
>
> —JANE AUSTEN

Despite his exile from public life, Churchill's days at Chartwell were far from inactive. He spent his time reading and writing, working in the garden and tending to his animals, as well as painting and building new amenities for the house. For Churchill, his home reflected his active life and mind. "I cannot separate who I am, what I do, and how I think from where I live," he would later write. Chartwell mirrored Churchill's energetic character and his multifarious interests, and he would dive excitedly into shaping the house according to the dictates of his tastes. Philip Tilden, who was hired to remodel the house, recalled, "No client that I have ever had, considering his well-filled life, has ever spent more time, trouble, or interest in the making of his home than did Mr. Churchill."

Like its owner, Chartwell was in constant motion. "I lived mainly at Chartwell where I had much to amuse me," he said. "I built with my own hands a large part of two cottages and extensive kitchen garden walls, and made all kinds of rockeries and waterworks . . . Thus I never had a dull or idle moment from morning till midnight." As his daughter, Mary (later Lady Soames), attested: "Chartwell was the center of [our] family life, and the place my father . . . most liked to be in the world."

For Winston Churchill, Chartwell was more than a home; it constituted a personal expression. Understanding the importance of home space and creating an atmosphere in which he could thrive, Churchill would later assert, "We shape our dwellings and afterwards, our dwellings shape us." When we prepare a place of refuge, we must create a space that reflects who we truly are to serve as a reminder of our essential being when we experience self-doubt.

Chartwell was an ideal setting for Churchill to engage in another of his great loves—painting. A convert late in life to the art, he nonetheless embraced it with enthusiasm and built a painting studio at his home so he could indulge his interest. Artwork would help him overcome his moments of gravity, solitude, and self-doubt: "Happy are the painters for they shall not be lonely. Light and colour, peace and hope, will keep them company to the end, or almost to the end, of the day." He painted to soothe his soul, not to win public acclaim, which is why his paintings were rarely shown during his lifetime and two of the early exhibitions of his work were conducted under pseudonyms.

This pastime was born out of the depths of his adversity. Having been blamed for the failed naval attack on the Dardanelles in 1915 at a great cost of life, he was removed from his position as First Lord of the Admiralty, which prompted him to resign from the navy for a position as colonel in the army during World War I. Preparing to leave for the front lines in France—an open and public defeat of sorts—he first took up the paint and brush, launching a passion that would remain with him for the rest of his life. Lady Soames later related of those dark days, "It was at that moment when he was right down that the Muse of Painting came into his life. She picked him up and took him by the hand and opened a new world that brought Papa in contact with wonderful, clever, interesting, and gifted people. I do think that this had an enormous effect on his capacity to bear great trials and tribulations."

She also pointed out that his newborn obsession nearly had fatal consequences. When he was stationed in Flanders in 1916, his men found him in harm's way utterly immersed in his art: "Painting gave him tranquility, even close to battle . . . A few miles from the front lines, Papa was having a go at his newly-found occupation. His junior officers were amazed to see their commander sitting in a broken-down chair in the wreckage of an old Flanders farm, with shells exploding not very far away,

> *Our age finds it difficult to come to grips with Churchill. The political leaders with whom we are familiar generally aspire to be superstars rather than heroes. The distinction is crucial. Superstars strive for approbation; heroes walk alone. Superstars crave consensus; heroes define themselves by the . . . future they see it as their risk to bring about. Superstars seek success in a technique for eliciting support; heroes pursue success as the outgrowth of their inner values.*
>
> —HENRY KISSINGER

painting away, entirely absorbed by the problems of perspective and colour."

Painting for Churchill was not a distraction or an escape; rather, it allowed him to remain fully cognizant of and engaged with his surroundings. His artwork informed and complemented his other pursuits, affording him a broader perspective of his life and the life around him. We should not be surprised, however, that his paintings rarely focused on people. "Trees don't complain," he tellingly noted. But he never intended his painting to attract criticism—or praise, either. "I do not presume to explain how to paint, but only how to get enjoyment," he said. "Do not turn the superior eye of critical passivity upon these efforts . . . We must not be too ambitious. We cannot aspire to masterpieces. We may content ourselves with a joy ride in a paint-box. And for this Audacity is the only ticket."

He pursued his painting aggressively, as he did all of his other interests. Over the last forty-eight years of his life, he produced more than five hundred paintings, many of which he would give away as gifts to his friends. With dedication and practice, he grew quite accomplished. John Lavery, the Glasgow artist whose wife assisted Churchill in developing his art, wrote of his skill in his *Life of a Painter*: "I know few amateur wielders of the brush with a keener sense of light and colour, or a surer grasp of essentials . . . Had he chosen painting instead of statesmanship I believe he would have been a great master with the brush."

While painting gave expression to Churchill's senses, his writings best communicated his thinking. He would eventually combine the two talents in an essay written for the *Strand Magazine* in 1921, titled "Painting as a Pastime." In one sense, writing was a self-serving activity for Churchill. "History will be kind to me for I intend to write it," he once said. Writing was his primary means of supporting his family during the winter years of his political exile. But he also saw it as a way of relating his philosophy of life: "I have been a journalist half my lifetime and I have earned my living by selling words and I hope thoughts."

Writing was Churchill's method of reflection and examination, his way of describing the world as he saw it. When Churchill was out of government and public life, it constituted his means of staying fully engaged with the events of his day. But as with painting, he saw the joy and privacy he could achieve away from competitors and critics. Speaking to the 1906 annual dinner of the Authors' Club, he said, "Authors are the happy people in the world, whose work is pleasure . . . I have sometimes fortified myself amid the vexations, vicissitudes and uncertainties of political life by the reflection that I might find a secure line of retreat on the pleasant, peaceful and fertile country of the pen, where one need never be idle or dull."

Through the fertile country of the pen, Churchill could relive his youth and career, rehabilitate his image, and recover his spirit. But he also found that wrestling with the past, the present, and the inner sanctum of the mind could prove a formidable task. "Writing is an adventure," he said of the process. "To begin with, it is a toy and an amusement. Then it becomes a mistress, then it becomes a master, then it becomes a tyrant. The last phase is that just as you are about to be reconciled to your servitude, you kill the monster and fling him to the public."

Despite the high level of combat regularly required of his writing, he would author volumes regarding his travels and his adventures, his political philosophy, and his wartime experiences, from the Boer War to the Cold War. His *Marlborough: His Life and Times* remains one of the premier political biographies of all time, and his epic four-volume *History of the English-Speaking Peoples* contains many statements of adoration for his distant half-home, America (his mother, Jennie, having been an American citizen). Having played an active role in the two great military contests of his day, World Wars I and II, he gave considerable attention to the multi-volume serials, *The World Crisis,* which comprises his personal recollections from the period of 1911 to 1928, and *The Second World War,* regarding which he said, "This is not history; this is my case." These, combined with his many other books, essays, and speeches, attest to the fact that he was always ready to communicate to posterity what he thought of his world and his time.

Like most writers, Churchill was an avid reader, and he made certain that Chartwell's sprawling house and grounds were custom tailored for that side of his life as well. He believed different types of reading demanded different types of spaces. Thus, the house featured great open hearths to read near in the winter and sun-exposed window niches to read near in springtime. There were leather club chairs in the library and overstuffed couches in the living areas. And there were bright lamps throughout the house so the great man could wander from room to room, book in hand, never interrupting his ever-fertile mind. He liked to read newspapers, magazines, and political dispatches in his working study. He preferred to read history and biographies in his formal library; his wife Clementine's downstairs breakfast room seemed best suited for reading verse. He rehearsed speeches and rhetoric aloud in his beloved gardens near the fishpond. He perused the Bible as he walked along a wooded path that circled the estate. He read fiction in his painting studio.

In addition to his passionate pursuits of painting, writing, and maintaining his home at Chartwell, Churchill was always prepared to enjoy the smaller vices of life; these afforded a window into his rebellious and playful streak, and he made sure to incorporate them into his daily rituals: "I must point out that my rule of life prescribes as an absolutely sacred rite smoking cigars and also the drinking of alcohol before, after, and if the need be during all meals and in the intervals between them." He was also quick to admit that he was not suited to every vice, including indulgence in rounds of the ancient game: "Golf is an ineffectual attempt to direct an uncontrollable sphere into an inaccessible hole with instruments ill-adapted to the purpose."

> *Only the man able to rest and relax, to laugh and play will be able to fight and struggle, lead and guide. Only the man who knows when he has come to the end of his energy will be able to expend even greater energy.*
>
> —ROBERT TAFT

Churchill's personal quirks and vices were the subject of many of his jokes. They spoke of his humanity, his earthiness, and his desire to modestly tweak popular sensibilities and confront cultural haughtiness whenever the occasion demanded it. Churchill knew his limits, but didn't mind challenging conformity. His rough, but usually mild, mannerisms were a welcome relief in an age in which temperance and prohibition were the social rage. But with a few notable exceptions, his witticisms were not intended to bring others down as much as to level the playing field.

Churchill clearly loved life, his family, his home, his work, and especially his play. "His zest for life was one of his most attractive characteristics, of which those of us who were fortunate enough to be close to him were the luckiest benefactors," recalled Lady Soames. "For he was such fun to be with, and his spontaneous enjoyment of so many things [was] infectious. In a life packed with action and arduous work, my father nearly always found time for what he called 'my toys.'"

Churchill's humor and quick wit were testaments to the vibrancy of his soul, while his relentless work as a statesman, an author, and a painter was an indicator of what Teddy Roosevelt had earlier called "the strenuous life." The endurance he achieved in the years leading up to and during World War II, and the dramatic victory to which he led the country, helped to ease the sting of his Conservative Party being voted out of office in 1945, swiftly on the heels of V-E Day. That event, however, set the stage for him to become an international statesman and to mount another political comeback as prime minister in 1951.

As leaders, we are rarely faced with trials as difficult and ominous as what Churchill faced upon becoming prime minister in 1939. The enormity of the challenge necessitated that he maintain a balanced life and a private sanctuary. His strength, stability, and joys outside his political career were the products of years of intentional development. When the time came for him to assume leadership during one of the premier ordeals of world history, he was perfectly primed and ready to rise to the challenge. Churchill understood that the quiet life and the active life were of equal importance; he attended to the solitude of his soul just as much as the counsel of his advisors; he was as comfortable in his garden as in the halls of state; and he was as easily at home with his poodle, Rufus, his famous black swans, or his marmalade office cat at Chartwell as standing among the glitterati of British society.

Of all the stories of the remarkable exemplars I've chosen for this book, I love Churchill's the most. I deeply identify with his insistence on a balanced life—public and private, demanding and restful, among family and constituents, with varied, yet complementary interests. I respect and honor his readiness to spring into action when called to serve and his ability to settle joyfully into periods of quiet retreat. His use of Chartwell as a three-dimensional canvas for self-expression reminds me of my relationship with our home in Tallahassee. No matter my choice of design and decoration to fill these rooms, this home is permeated with its own ambiance and beauty. I have always found it a perfect refuge; every corner hosts a purposeful arrangement of furnishings and appointments from our heritage that never cease to delight and calm my heart. As a photorealist painter, I have even displayed some of my work, while the numerous photographs of family and friends, past and present, that adorn every room provide me with constant reminders of what really matters to me. Only a three-minute drive from the busy neighborhood of the Capitol, the surroundings are replete with trees and plant life that astonish us in every season: dozens of varied Camellia trees, fifteen feet tall, bloom two and three times a year; purple and white wisteria weave through the looming treetops; the amaryllis surprise us every Easter; the vivid azaleas and fragrant gardenias as well as the delicate grandfather's beard and dogwood blossoms remind us we're in the Old South; and the fragile resurrection ferns on the magnificent live oaks, which appear wilted beyond all possibility, revitalize after every rain. I shall miss this lovely escape dearly.

Churchill's witness to us today is to take life as it is, to live it fully in all of its various dimensions, and not to make it more complicated or difficult than it already may be. We need to cultivate the ability to bend without breaking. To that end, we would do well to take Churchill's advice and "go into the sunshine and be happy with what you see."

UNSTRESS YOURSELF

Effective leaders generally understand the critical necessity of priorities. Like the rest of us, however, they, too, tend to give faithful lip service to their need for family time, vacations, adequate rest, health, and exercise, while watching passively as the daily grind of their schedules squeezes these vital activities out of their lives.

Even when we choose to address these needs, we are often multitasking. I have been known to work out on an eliptical machine with a newspaper, a book, and a highlighter, my calendar, and a pencil and pad handy to extend my task list for the day, a vital bottle of water at my side so I can address all the necessities, all at one time.

Paradoxically, as we grapple with serious responsibilities, we find we lack the energy to relax. I know I do. Yet I am beginning to understand that my ultimate effectiveness will depend on how well I master the skill of "unplugging."

These disciplines, which are no less important than any of the others I've been exploring through the rest of this book, help us to make life—even in the hardest circumstances—livable:

I. LAUGH OUT LOUD

Laughter is always the best medicine—especially when times are rough, when the going gets difficult, and when the pressure is on. A sense of humor is our best defense against bitterness, anger, and frustration. When issues connected with the Election 2000 recount threatened to overwhelm me, when the court cases seemed to pour into my office every two to three minutes, and when we felt that the press was about to pound the door down, I truly discovered the conquering power of laughter.

G. K. Chesterton emphasized, "Laughter makes men merry. Merry men are wise men. Wise men are productive men. Therefore make your workers laugh and they will prosper your enterprise." Thankfully, perhaps due to the amazing volume of prayers that people offered on my behalf, I became uncharacteristically calm during the pressures of the recount. I began to joke with my staff, cutting through the thick fog of tension that had enveloped us. To my everlasting surprise, they actually thought my jokes were funny! This development prompted Maureen Garrard, a member of our staff who knew me long before I entered the public arena, to ask, "Where is Katherine Harris, and what have you done with her?"

We all had to laugh when one group of over one hundred fourth graders arrived to see me during the recount. Normally, when I ask children if they know what the Secretary of State's responsibilities entail, the typical answer is, "You answer the Governor's telephone calls." Yet this particular day, attended by the press, all the students enthusiastically raised their hands, and when I called upon a young girl, she answered, "You get to pick the President of the United States!" I winced inwardly—she had clearly been watching those inaccurate news reports—but couldn't help laughing. Kids say the darnedest things.

2. GET PHYSICAL

Making certain to take care of myself is one of the lessons I have learned from the many effective leaders I have been honored to encounter. Three years ago, Anders and I resolved to spend quiet, hidden weekends together. We kayak, work out, walk on the beach, read, and enjoy our closest friends; (and Anders loves golf—I've promised after the campaign to begin playing again.) We returned to ensuring I receive eight hours sleep every night, and I have continued this practice with the exception of the three to four hours each night I could garner during those thirty-six days and during the writing of this book. However, after a year and a half of attempting to develop thicker skin, the weight of the relentless personal attacks began to sink into my psyche. So when I began working on this book, I made a commitment to exercise, eat right, and, after twenty-five years, to return to my first loves, tennis and painting. (I had played the number one position in tennis on my high school and college teams and painted my way through life until I left college.) During this period, I did not have the time to return to my cherished Outward Bound Program, but I permitted myself to take a restful five-day holiday (except for working on this book for six hours each night.) For the first time since the recount, I allowed myself the luxury of focusing exclusively on myself, in an attempt to get back in shape and finally take that annual physical I had postponed for the last three years. At last, I ate delicious proper meals (albeit 1000-1200 calories a day), gloried in sports (seven to eight hours per day of tennis, aerobics, boxing, weight-lifting, "boot camp", dance and swimming); explored the beauty of the outdoors (hiking, biking, and bird watching); delighted in an occasional massage or sauna; completed my physicals . . .and gained three pounds! Nevertheless, I returned feeling refreshed and restored with an entirely different outlook. The results amazed me: I felt better, I thought more clearly, and I had more energy.

Many of us remember the images of Ronald Reagan, the leader of the free world, at his Rancho del Cielo: riding with ranchhands, wiping his brow, chopping wood, repairing a fence. Some of history's greatest writers and poets—including Wordsworth, Coleridge, Scott, Tennyson, Yeats, and Kipling—discovered their greatest inspiration and their most productive bursts of creativity following intense physical exertion.

Of this phenomenon, John Buchan said, "The mind and the body are of a part. One cannot be as it ought without the other. Therefore, just as there is an intellectual side to being physical, there is a physical side to being intellectual." Whether it is scheduling time to get to the gym or taking a walk to clear the mind, we need to acknowledge the role of a healthy body in relation to a healthy psyche. If we lack the energy to work consistently at the top of our game, we rob not only ourselves but also our colleagues and employers of our best effort.

3. SURROUND YOURSELF WITH BEAUTY

I love beautiful paintings and sculpture, stirring concerts and dance performances, excellence in the athletics of Olympic sporting events, a thought-provoking play or a period film (well, maybe any good film), the quilts of Faith Ringold, handicrafts and folk art from the diverse cultures of the world. I extol the variety of human creativity and the breathtaking glory of nature—whether an exquisitely fit, exotic animal in its natural habitat, the beauty of an Andalusian horse, or my Springer spaniels bouncing through the water. I am amazed by life and our artistic renditions of it. I once studied in Israel when my camera broke. This accident forced me to resort to drawing what I witnessed. The sketches I made of these lands and its artifacts during our field trips remain my most prized of any artwork I have ever produced. The presence of beauty around me has an instantaneously relaxing and refreshing effect. When I am working in an urban setting, my memory lingers on our walks on the beach and Florida's unparalleled sunsets. Claude Monet said of his exquisitely peaceful gardens at Giverny, "When beauty compasses me round about, I am not only in a better frame of mind, I am in a better frame of life." This has been my experience as well.

The positive impact of the arts upon all dimensions of life has driven my passionate commitment to the expansion of arts education opportunities for children. A Getty study has shown that exposure to the arts expands their logic and deductive reasoning skills. This finding is confirmed by additional studies reporting that children who have had exposure to arts education score higher on the SAT by an average of 68 points on the verbal section and by an average of 32 points on the math section.

The arts have enabled some of our children-at-risk to experience incredible opportunities to learn and develop. For example, the Tallahassee Boys Choir engages 120 young men at risk. They sang at our inaugural ball, and they remain the hottest ticket in town today. These outstanding young men are mentored, taught math through music and dance, and must maintain a "B" average. The Pope invited them to sing last year in Italy, while President George W. Bush bestowed upon them one of our nation's highest cultural honors. The arts have transformed their lives forever.

We are surrounded with alternatives to our fast-food sitcom culture, opportunities to experience beauty and depth. Re-route your drive to take the scenic route instead. Visit a museum, gallery, botanical garden, or children's exhibit. Experience a ballet or opera. Watch an uplifting movie. See a play. Nothing will ennoble your mind and soothe your sentiments like a musical: the conflict and tragedy of *West Side Story*; the magic and pageantry of Andrew Lloyd Webber's *Phantom of the Opera*;

the joy and exuberance of *The Lion King;* the passion and truth of *Rent;* the romance and mystique of *South Pacific;* the humor and sadness of *The King and I;* the depth and pathos of *Miss Saigon;* or the spectacle of Victor Hugo's *Les Misérables.* You will never forget the impact of the profound lyrics and incredible music. We all sometimes need the drama on the stage to replace the drama in our lives.

4. SIMPLIFY

Most of us tend to clutter our lives with much that is unnecessary. We have too many collections, too many commitments, too many distractions, (never too many books, though!) When I am able to clear away the competing concerns, the trivial disruptions, and the clanging alarms of my crowded life, I find that I am much better able to do the things I am called to do. I remain in a much brighter state of mind.

> *The accumulation of mere stuff is often a dead weight that hampers our freedom to move, to go, to do what we have always known that we should.*
>
> —THOMAS CHALMERS

One practical step we can take as leaders is to delegate. If we have managed to surround ourselves with quality, competent, trustworthy people, we must utilize and empower them. But as a leader, it is also our responsibility, and certainly in our own best interest, to make certain that they do not become buried with the inconsequential. We have to know and gauge our limits and assess those of the people working with us so they can attend to critical details while keeping the bigger picture in mind.

Another lesson is to learn to say "no." We often become overwhelmed with obligations due to our inability to admit that our plate is full. We should never fear new challenges, but if we have permitted our life to become a detached maze of disconnected interests, we must politely decline, so that we may sort through our commitments in order to determine what is necessary, what is valuable, and what is not. We must secure very private downtime to process our thoughts.

5. TAKE THE TIME TO DEVELOP NEW AND INTERESTING FRIENDSHIPS

During my recent vacation, I met three amazing women who hailed from backgrounds completely unlike my own. We had as much in common as the extremes of north, south, east, and west. We spent an extraordinary time together, sharing our different perspectives on many matters, often laughing together until we cried.

> *I would have written a shorter letter if I had had more time.*
>
> —OSCAR WILDE

The breakneck speed of our world has encouraged us to become increasingly narrow-minded and atomized. We fall back upon the familiar and the comfortable, thereby depriving ourselves of the rich experiences new friends can bring to our lives.

This disturbing trend of insularity increasingly manifests itself at all levels in the world of politics. Where our nation once stood as relatively unique among the world's democracies for the collegiality and friendships that routinely developed across party and ideological lines, we continue to backslide into the abyss of "us" versus "them." Without question, this phenomenon has impacted the effectiveness of government while perhaps contributing to the coarsening of our society.

As principled people, we can fight vigorously to advance our cause without demonizing the person who would dare oppose it. Despite the mythology of partisanship that surrounded me during the recount, I have always maintained a reputation for working well with Democrats and Republicans alike throughout my tenure as a state senator, as secretary of state, and now as an author. (Yes, more than one staunch Democrat offered valued counsel on this book.) I work well with people of divergent opinions because I approach them as colleagues or friends, not bitter adversaries.

6. FIND YOUR "SAFE PLACE"

We all need a place of refuge when we are buffeted by the storms of life. This is not merely escape; it is, rather, where we go to find the peace and perspective necessary to evaluate our situation and to decide what to do next. It does not have to be an exotic location on the other side of the planet; it can easily be a spot at home that is uniquely ours where we can create a restful environment. We need only a room or corner that we can arrange in a manner that makes us feel serene. Alternatively, we might find a weekend getaway or even a pleasant area of a nearby park or beach or trail where we can walk, think, sit, and unwind.

Usually, these safe places coincide with where our loved ones are. Perhaps the greatest gift my husband affords me is the haven of the caring, considerate support he provides, regardless of where either of us are in the world. When we are together, I feel loved and secure, simply because of him. When we are apart, he calls me daily to awaken me, and his voice is the last sound I hear before I fall asleep at night. The moment I see him again, all is right with the world. I know that I could not and would not wish to accomplish the challenges that routinely land before me without his support.

We must also cultivate methods to unstring our bows wherever we are and whatever circumstances confront us. Even in the turmoil of absolute crisis, we need to have the composure to take a moment and make sound decisions.

Composure is as much an attitude as it is an ongoing exercise, one we soon find is infectious. If our subordinates find us to be unsettled, they will mimic our behavior and exacerbate the problem. But if they believe we are calm, poised, and confident, regardless of the situation, they will have a level of assurance that will relieve some of the tensions.

We must realize that those who look to us for leadership—especially our children—will take their cues from our demeanor and behavior. We must be mindful of our actions and reactions.

7. COUNT YOUR BLESSINGS

It is important for me to stop and deliberately recall what I have been given. I take so much for granted—my faith, my family, my friends, my health, and my work. I live so much of my life at such a rapid pace that I often must force myself to slow down and remember the multitude of blessings I enjoy. I must stop to appreciate God's good gifts and make certain that I am honoring my most deeply held principles. Do my time commitments, my creativity, and my energy and ideas properly reflect my understanding of my calling? Where have I "laid up my treasures"? Am I invested merely in the here and now, or am I working with the future in mind? This process relates the order of my priorities to the state of my heart. When I contemplate how fortunate I am, the dilemmas I face seem less imposing. I do not focus upon what I cannot control because such fixation interferes with my ability to focus on what matters most.

8. FORGIVE

Lady Soames related about her father, Winston Churchill, that "someone once said of him, 'Winston is a very bad hater.'" She agreed, saying, "I would say that he could be a very good hater, but he could never keep it up for long!" Probably nothing else in life frees us to unstring our bows as much as learning how to forgive others. To forgive unilaterally, completely, and unconditionally constitutes one of the most liberating experiences in life. It literally sets us free. Forgiving enables us to move on. It permits us to build bridges of reconciliation. And it refreshes the heart and soul with inestimable joy. "A man who cannot forgive," Charles Spurgeon wrote, "is a poor fellow indeed, for he punishes himself for the sins of others."

Earlier this year, Brent Bozell's Media Research Center hosted the well-attended Media Dishonors Awards. Awards were presented to those members of the news media whom this organization believed had demonstrated the most bias during the previous year. (The evening also featured a salute to the media's exemplary coverage of the September 11 tragedy.) When it was learned Dan Rather could not be present to accept his award, I was invited to accept the top award on his behalf, which he was to receive in honor of his "news" cast concerning my certification of the 2000 presidential election, according to law. A film clip was shown of Mr. Rather stating the following:

"Florida's Republican Secretary of State is about to announce the winner—as she sees it and she decrees it—of the state's potentially decisive twenty-five electoral votes."

"The believed certification—as the Republican Secretary of State sees it."

"She will certify—as she sees it—who gets Florida's twenty-five electoral votes."

"The certification—as the Florida Secretary of State sees it and decrees it—is being signed."

—DAN RATHER live on CBS News,
November 26, 2000

These are excerpts from my response:

I am honored to join the ranks of luminaries who have earned this venerable anchor's scorn: Richard Nixon, Ronald Reagan, George Bush (41), Barry Goldwater, Connie Chung, and Bernard Goldberg. Some of you may know me only as Cruella de Ville, the partisan hack, the corrupt lackey of the Bush brothers who single-handedly stole the election by taking the inflexible, unfair, outrageous position that the law said

what it said—not what the media *wished* it said . . . I am honored to certify that Dan Rather has *won* this award. But, perhaps Mr. Rather will
request additional recounts before he believes me!

As professionals, we are expected to conduct ourselves according to
the law and without bias. Unfortunately, in elected office, working
with those persons who do not adhere to the same standards of professionalism goes with the territory. Yet, like Churchill, I am a bad
hater. I try never to dislike anyone (certainly not for very long.) Being
a slave to emotions of hatred, fear, or blame is far more destructive to
ourself than it is to the object of our disdain. Instead, we must try to
recognize others' shortcomings . . . know the facts, but expect the
best. In the wake of the recount crisis, I do not have any ax to grind
nor any compulsion to "get even."

As former Democrat strategist Bob Squires once said, "if you don't
have an enemy in a conflict, create one." According to Ann Coulter
in her latest book, *Slander—Liberal Lies About the American Right*, "Al
Gore advisor Mark Fabiani later explained the Democrats' attacks on
Harris, glibly telling the *New York Times*, 'We needed an enemy.' He
said 'attacking Harris was the right thing to do, and it worked.'"

In his book, *At Any Cost*, Bill Sammon wrotes that during the
recount controversy, less than a week after the Democratic attorney
general of Florida had offered his unsolicited opinion that strongly
vouched for my integrity and honesty:

> Gore personally instructed his team to smear Florida's chief elec-
> tions officer . . . The vice president of the United States . . . was
> now directly involved in the politics of personal destruction. Al
> Gore told his deputy director Mark Fabiani and press secretary
> Chris Lehane "to plant damaging press stories that would dis-
> credit Harris as a Bush partisan. Team Gore went after Harris
> with chilling efficiency . . . Unable to criticize Harris over her

enforcement of Florida law, the press resorted to hurling personal invective.

I feel badly for those who have fallen victim to the divisive misinformation perpetuated to fan the partisan fires. I recognize by their own words they made me their scapegoat. Yet, I know I can live with myself without any doubts or regrets or excuses or second-guessing because I was faithful to the law.

9. BALANCE

Poet and journalist Albert Johnson has argued that the chief characteristic of a principled leader is balance: "It is not simply the ability to make wise decisions in the midst of great pressure in accordance with ethical standards that makes a leader effective. Rather it is that intangible combination of virtues and disciplines that we once called common sense that will set him apart." This sort of personal balance includes a multitude of critical worldview attributes—from stick-to-itiveness and a learner's heart to humility and courage. But it must also include the ability to unstring the bow. Otherwise, the work of the leader will make short work of the leader. Otherwise, the other virtues will all be for naught.

If we live a balanced life, we will be prepared for the day the inevitable storm hits; we will be able to hold our ground, retain our dignity, remember our vision, and support others until such time the tempest passes into the dawning of a new day.

TOP TEN LIST:
Movies

If a picture is worth a thousand words, a moving picture is surely worth ten thousand.
—JEAN RENOIR

When I am wound as tight as a top and I can't even curl up with a good book, Anders has the perfect solution for me: he takes me to the movies. When the stress levels begin to threaten my health and well-being, he knows that this outlet will enable me to relax long enough to return to an even keel. Over the years, we have watched many great films, from the classics to contemporary comedies. Here are some of my favorites:

1. *Casablanca*. I love so many of the classics. One cannot over-praise the mastery of a Hitchcock thriller, the style of a Cary Grant romance or Gene Kelly musical, the wit of Katharine Hepburn, the sheer beauty of Audrey Hepburn, or the elegance of Grace Kelly. For sheer entertainment, however, nothing compares to Bogart and Bergman.

2. *Citizen Kane.* This epic work by Orson Welles is one of the most influential films of all time, shaping the vision of at least two generations of filmmakers from Steven Spielberg and George Lucas to Ridley Scott and Ron Howard. It is evocative and brilliant.

3. *My Left Foot.* Daniel Day Lewis's performance was so extraordinary that I emphatically asserted I would never be able to see him as any other character. Then I saw *The Last of the Mohicans,* which had a profound impact upon my life. I did not recognize Lewis, but instantly thought the same thing: I will always see this actor as this

character. Later I realized that it was the same actor in both roles. Amazing!

4. *Fiddler on the Roof.* Like *Dr. Zhivago, Camelot, The Sound of Music, West Side Story,* and *South Pacific,* this classic musical unfolds on such an epic scale and encompasses so many emotions that it seems more like a cultural landmark than a mere movie experience.

5. *Greystoke* . This movie could strike one as relatively innocuous, but the Tarzan stories remain forever etched in my mind, from my early experiences reading Edgar Rice Burroughs to the times my mother, sister, and I enjoyed early Saturday morning viewings of Johnny Weissmuller swinging through the trees in a landscape much like my native Florida. This story remains a classic portrayal of passion and pathos as the confounded young man returns to British "civil" society.

6. *Braveheart* . I know that Mel Gibson and Randall Wallace combined historical facts, conflated legends, and tinkered with the chronology of events in this film—much as in *The Patriot.* Even so, this marvelous work provides a critical lesson in what constitutes true heroism, and Mel Gibson is at his best.

7. *Chariots of Fire.* From the Vangelis soundtrack to the sweeping cinematography, from the fabulous screenplay to the luminous themes, this is one of the most inspirational films ever made.

8. *Shadowlands* . This movie combines C. S. Lewis's life story and Sir Anthony Hopkins, perhaps one of the most extraordinary actors of our day.

9. *Life Is Beautiful.* For the first fifteen minutes, I wondered what all the fuss was about; then this movie completely

drew me into its passion. Of course, by the end, I was utterly in tears. This film is guaranteed to make you laugh, make you cry, and make you better. It may be my all-time favorite.

10. *Brazil*. Based on the quirky Thatcher-era British novel *The Last Election,* this madcap film is rather like what I would imagine Orwell and Huxley might have created if they had been staff writers for Monty Python. Eye-popping visuals and profound philosophical inquiry combine with slapstick humor to create a film like almost no other—save perhaps *Beetlejuice* or *Mars Attacks*!

Laugh

Ain't it funny
Now we're laughing
We're photographing
And buying toys
Ain't it something
Now we're asking
Have you ever seen such beautiful boys
Laughter always heals the hurting heart
Springing up from faith to give a
Brand-new start
Father, we pray
For the laughter that we need today
Like manna breaking through the clouds of gray
No matter what we're going through
Or how much time we have
May we never forget
To laugh
It's ironic
God would wait and
Promise Abraham so late in life
He would father
Many nations
His descendants would outnumber
The stars up in the sky
Sometimes laughter wears a sad disguise
Sneaking up on you and hits you

By surprise
Father, we pray
For the laughter that we need today
Like manna breaking through the clouds of gray
No matter what we're going through
Or how much time we have
Lord, let us never forget how
To laugh

Solemnity flows out of men naturally;
but laughter is a leap. It is easy to be heavy; hard to be light.
—G. K. CHESTERTON

EPILOGUE

The experience of writing this book has been both educational and cathartic. When I was thrust into the center of an unexpected political maelstrom, the rush of events quickly swept aside any private doubts I might have had concerning my capacity to stand against the tide of expediency. I discovered that by drawing upon the lessons of my past experiences, I could summon the strength to do what was right and just. My simple determination to act with integrity and uphold my oath, while affording me peace and resolve, constituted an insufficient guide to the practical challenges I faced.

When I attempted to return to my regular duties as secretary of state after the recount ended, I found that the landscape had changed dramatically. Every decision I made, no matter how routine, faced enhanced scrutiny. In light of the mountain of tasks we faced in striving to reform Florida's elections system, as well as unfinished projects in other areas, I could not afford to let these circumstances distract me from the objectives that had provided my calling to public service. I needed a philosophical framework that would lend perspective to our goals and suffuse us with vision and energy.

At every turn I found myself reaching deep inside to find the resources I needed to press on—and at every turn I realized the examples of admirable people in my life, and in history, increased my inner peace and resolve. The extraordinary individuals whose stories I have shared with herein faced decisions and obstacles far beyond any challenge I experienced during the storm of Election 2000, or in its aftermath. Nevertheless, their examples gave me the strength to move deliberately forward. It is my sincere hope that their stories will provide you with a similar spark of inspiration when you are called upon to face an unexpected crisis.

As parents or children, siblings or friends, teachers or students, supervisors or co-workers, public servants or entrepreneurs, each of us learns from the examples of principled behavior that we witness in our daily lives—just as each of us is given the opportunity to exercise principled leadership every day. Exemplary leaders are not only the revered and famous people who populate these pages, but are also to be found among the ordinary people in every community who practice their deeply held principles in their daily lives.

The most important lesson I learned from the self-examination I experienced in writing this book was to remain profoundly grateful for the principled leadership and example my parents set for me. They gave me the foundation that prepared me for this test. Of all the heroes I have described herein, they are the most important to me.

AFTERWORD

On August 5, 2002, days before this book went to press, my tenure as Florida's secretary of state came to an end. I had considered resigning for several months. As the primary grew closer, the need to devote my full attention to my congressional campaign became more apparent. I needed to spend all of my time walking door to door and listening to the concerns and challenges of the people of Florida's 13th Congessional District. While the prospect of leaving a post I had cherished caused me considerable heartache, my knowledge that we had accomplished much for the people of Florida in three and one half short years fortified me as I approached the decision I had to make.

I had planned to resign at the August 13 meeting of the executive cabinet, one day after we had made our final presentation to Governor Jeb Bush's transition task force. As we prepared for that announcement, however, I came to a difficult realization. Under the terms of Florida's "resign to run" law, absent a letter of resignation submitted by the date I qualified to run for Congress (July 15), my resignation had become automatically effective on that date.

I was familiar with the resign to run law, having addressed its ramifications under other circumstances during my administration. The intent of this law was to require elected officials who choose to run for another office to announce their resignation at a time when potential candidates could still run for the ensuing vacancy. As a result of a 1998 amendment to Florida's Constitution, however, the office of secretary of state will become an appointed position in January 2003. Because the resign to run law was so clearly designed to apply to an elected office, I wrongly assumed that I was not required to submit a letter of resignation.

Ironically, Florida's chief legal officer and its highest-ranking Democrat, Attorney General Bob Butterworth, made similar assumptions about the resign to run law. He reasoned that because term limits prevented him from running again for Attorney General in 2002, the resign to run law did not apply to him even though he had decided to run for the Florida Senate.

I had a momentous decision to make. I could have joined Attorney General Butterworth in relying upon the gray areas of the law. In fact, I could have made a stronger argument. The office of attorney general will remain an elected office, whereas my situation was unique. Attorney General Butterworth's circumstances were not unique, in that any term-limited elected official seeking another office with an overlapping tenure could adopt his argument. While it would have been more palatable politically, ignoring the clear letter of the law would have violated every principle for which I have ever stood. I had to apply the same exacting standards to myself that I had applied to others.

Therefore, instead of staying until August 13 as I had planned, I acted immediately, disclosing in an August 1 press conference that because of the resign to run law, my resignation had automatically taken effect on July 15. Contrary to various reports, I had violated no rule, and certainly not the law. Moreover, under the terms of Florida's Constitution, I was still legally entitled to act as secretary of state until Governor Bush appointed my successor.

In the aftermath, the state, national, and international media had a field day. Every drop of venom they had reserved for me since the recount controversy gushed forth in a torrent of insults, with no comparable attack on Florida's Democratic attorney general, who had made a similar error—but who still refused to admit that the law applied to him.

I believe principled leadership in times of crisis must demand the character to admit when you have erred and to follow the same rules that apply to everyone else regardless of the political consequences or how much it hurts. After all, if you do the right thing—and that is what matters most, the integrity of the process—then the future will take care of itself when you find yourself in the center of the storm.

KATHERINE HARRIS

Sarasota, Florida

August 11, 2002

Notes

1. All of the previous names were Holland & Knight attorneys—quite the "H&K" neighborhood as well.

2. Under federal law, a state wishing to protect its chosen electors from being challenged in Congress must have concluded all contests of the 2000 presidential election in that state by December 12. As the U.S. Supreme Court released its decision in *Bush* v. *Gore* after 10:00 P.M. Eastern Standard Time on December 12, the five-justice majority of the U.S. Supreme Court concluded that no time remained for the Florida Supreme Court to correct the violations of the U.S. Constitution that seven justices of the U.S. Supreme Court had identified.

3. During my first session in the state senate in 1995, the chairman of the Commerce Committee proposed a bill to replace Florida state government's economic development agency, the Department of Commerce, with a public/private entity. In making decisions concerning business expansion and economic growth, I thought it made a great deal of common sense to have the private sector involved, rather than just government bureaucrats. I supported this new approach to stimulating the growth of domestic and international business in Florida, with its emphasis on diversifying Florida's economy. Florida had plummeted woefully behind other states, ranking forty-second as a state in which to start or grow an existing business.

   Nevertheless, due to the overarching impact of personalities and politics, this particular bill possessed fatal flaws. The bill appeared to contain *no provisions*: (1) that established appropriate reporting requirements for some $30 million in taxpayer money that state government would pour into this public/private entity charged with assisting economic development endeavors—in other words, no accountability; (2) that required private matching funds; (3) that established performance measures for private entities receiving public funds; (4) that provided opportunities for small business (a category that contains almost 90% of Florida's businesses); and (5) that provided any incentives for

Florida's businesses to expand into the international trade arena (except for Florida's largest businesses).

While I was not a member of the Commerce Committee, I fought to have these five shortcomings addressed, as they constituted my objections to the bill.

Perils abounded as powerful political and business personalities weighed in. The state senate's leadership supported the chairman's bill, as did the governor. One high-profile leader stated that he had spent three years of his life working on this legislation, and threatened that he would spend the next three years working against my reelection unless I agreed to support the bill. However, I found welcome support among my colleagues in both chambers of the Florida legislature.

The bill passed the senate that year over my lone dissenting vote. Undeterred, I continued to work with the legislators who had supported my position. The following year, the senate revisited my five points, passing legislation that addressed them over the Commerce Committee chairman's objections.

In the fall of 1997, the new senate president, Toni Jennings, appointed me as the new chair of the Commerce and Economic Opportunities Committee. She encouraged me to launch the domestic and international economic initiatives I believed were important to Florida's future as long as they were pro-environment and pro-consumer.

Landmark commerce legislation was proposed and passed by Republicans and Democrats alike. Within two years Florida moved from forty-second to first in the nation as the best state in which to start a new business or grow an existing one. From 1991 to 2000, Florida doubled its trade, growing from nearly $34 billion to just under $74 billion. According to the U.S. Department of Commerce, each $1 billion increase in new exports supports 20,000 new jobs. On average, these new jobs pay from thirteen to eighteen percent more than other important industries, such as agriculture and tourism, and helped sustain Florida's economy during the economic turndown of 2001 and particularly after the terror attacks of September 11.

In retrospect, even those politically powerful individuals who opposed my amendments have thanked me, stating we would have suffered scandals and lost important opportunities had the changes I advocated not passed. The moral: Stick to your guns! This story also illustrates what we can accomplish when we don't know any better. No one told me a freshman shouldn't challenge a senior legislator's bill!

4. How silly, in retrospect, for these media accounts to seize upon the constitutional amendment as "proof" that the office of secretary of state was "inconsequential." Imagine the media making the same statement about the office of commissioner of education, which received the same treatment under the constitutional amendment.

5. Counties that used precinct level counters (instead of transporting all ballots to a central location for tabulation) experienced a 0.83 percent rate of uncounted presidential votes, compared to the 2.86 percent rate Florida experienced statewide. (All of these counties used marksense voting systems, although counties employing punch card systems could have obtained precinct level counting technology for a comparable cost.)

6. In Chapter 3, I explained in detail how my decision to follow the law did not preclude the possibility of further manual recounts.

7. As part of Principle 8, I will address the "report" the U.S. Commission on Civil Rights issued regarding the 2000 presidential election in Florida.

8. I will also address this matter in detail as part of Principle 8.

9. I discussed this myth as part of the Myth Conception, "Military Ballots, War Rooms, and Hard Drives, Oh My!" which appears in Principle 1.

10. The bill that created this requirement was sponsored by two Democratic legislators, Senator Ron Silver and Representative Kendrick Meek, an outspoken civil rights advocate who is now a state senator and a candidate for the congressional seat presently held by his mother, U.S. Rep. Carrie Meek. The provisions of this legislation made my predecessor's hiring of DBT Online a virtual certainty.

11. As I explained in Principle 3, these four justices ruled in favor of the Gore campaign *notwithstanding* the fact that the legal reasoning behind their first decision *directly contradicted* their legal reasoning in the second decision.

12. Even though, as I explained in Principle 3, had I bent the law as the Gore campaign demanded, Al Gore's legal rights under Florida Election Law would have been prejudiced.

ACKNOWLEDGMENTS

Amidst my continuing duties as secretary of state and my rigorous campaign for the United States Congress, I could not have produced this book without the hard work and support of countless individuals. These people—liberal Democrats, avid Independents, and conservative Republicans—assisted me in this project in their professional capacities as researchers, editors, and consultants although in no fashion do we necessarily embrace one another's political views. I am grateful for their support and input, for it is our joint hope that this book will serve as a constructive aid for people in crisis, rather than as the typical "slash and burn" character assassinations that other publishers had hoped I would write.

Each chapter includes a number of different elements: application and resource lists, practical explanations of common misconceptions, and dozens of quotations. The quotes are taken from my reading through the years as well as from epigrammatic anthologies. Each chapter also includes a wide variety of historical examples, vignettes, profiles, and stories.

I wish to recognize the contributions of George Grant, who first taught me how to analyze the various currents that my experience during the 2000 presidential election recount created in my life. He shared with me his historical research, resources, and writings, and the work of his associates and students—Rodlyn Davis, Brian Goodwin, Robert and Sharilyn Grayson, Nathan Larkin, Patrick Poole, Elizabeth Robbins, Kelly Sullivan, and Duane Thomas—who helped him select the material from lectures, tapes, notes, articles, and books, all of which is used by permission.

The lyrics and their explanations at the end of each chapter are from the music of my brother-in-law Wes King. They were selected with the composer's help and are used by permission.

I also wish to thank David Host, who sacrificed weekends and vacation time to provide me with invaluable assistance with the revision and editing of the manuscript, and Karen Anderson for her stellar research, editing, and meticulous proofing of the manuscript. Carol Gaskin is a godsend. Her superb editing, her insightful wisdom, her softened candor, and her dry sense of humor kept this project on track. Carol's wise fact checker, E. V. Hill, found numerous opportunities to be profoundly helpful with her excellent research skills.

For the entire length of my career in public service as Florida's secretary of state and as state senator, I have relied most heavily upon Benjamin McKay, my chief of staff. Ben and I have fought the great battles, lost a few and learned a lot, yet scaled the heights of achievement together. Every person who enters public life should be so fortunate as to enjoy the confidence and support of someone who has Ben's good judgment, wit, integrity, and fundamental decency.

Likewise, my Assistant Secretary of State, Dave Mann, is the rock of stability and touchstone of wisdom and integrity that anyone in public service should seek to emulate. His unparalleled knowledge of the Department of State, its seven divisions and its history as well as his administrative expertise have served as invaluable resources, particularly when we sailed on the roughest seas.

Every member of my staff at the Department of State is exceptionally committed to their work; for most, their job constitutes both their vocation and their avocation. I am deeply honored to have served with them. Most endured the 2000 presidential election with me. I would not have weathered the storm very well without them, nor would my tenure have been as successful or enjoyable were it not for their amazing efforts over the years.

Our Florida Department of State division directors are among the best in the nation in their particular fields, and I am very grateful for their commitment, expertise and passion concerning their responsibilities: John Russi, Hal Lynch, Barratt Wilkins, Clay Roberts, Jan Matthews, JuDee Pettijohn, and Jay Kassees.

The members of the executive staff have endured the stress of the daily spotlight that the recount generated. While they did not play a role in the creation of this book, it would not exist if not for their incredible support, encouragement, and sense of humor during those thirty-six days and those that have followed: Lillie Goodson, Debby Kearney, Karema Tyms, Rivers Buford, Hugh Simon, Roy Hunt, Suellen Cone, Bonnie Kidd, Jennifer Kennedy, Kerey Carpenter, Gerry York, Heidi Hughes, Chris Schons, Alicia Shirah, Kim Grippa, Trey McCarley, Jenny Nash, Brewster Bevis, Monica Pickel, Melissa Moon, Michael Pilver, Jane Anderson, Laura Council, Jean McElveen, Amy Woodward, Melanie Solomon, Cara Martin, Angie Revel, Kerry Knap, Hanne Robbins, and Jennifer Chester.

One member of my staff who deserves special mention is Rivers Buford, my Legislative Affairs director since early 2001. Rivers has been tremendously effective in achieving passage of my legislative priorities, the most notable having been Florida's nationally acclaimed Election Reform Act of 2001 and the Voter Accessibility Act of 2002. (Rivers achieved an amazing 100% rate of passage for the bills we proposed during his first legislative session with us.)

I have also benefited immensely from the friendship and professional association of two eminent historians, Dr. Janet Matthews and Dr. Roy Hunt. Their knowledge and creativity have inspired me to reach ever farther in my quest to see Florida achieve recognition as a unique model for many preservation initiatives. They always make certain to point the compass of that endeavor back to what matters most.

Our "soirees" at Roy's "humble abode" provided an intellectual oasis. Jan's husband, Lamar, and their family have served as an extended family to me. I cannot count the times our paths have crossed at the most unlikely moments of our greatest joys and deepest heartaches. We have learned together through difficult challenges what matters most.

Cliff King has served as my legal counsel for this book, working diligently to help make this project viable. Cliff and his wife, Mary, became some of my earliest friends when I moved to Sarasota well over a decade ago. They were my first campaign volunteers (Cliff served as my treasurer) when I first ran for the Florida state senate in 1994. We spent countless hours in our early thirties playing beach volleyball on Siesta Key every Saturday and Sunday afternoon. Those were the days!

Heloisa and Charlie Jennings, and Connie Holcomb and Wally Serwatka are among my husband Anders' dearest friends. The men play golf together and the women occasionally have the wonderful opportunity of traveling with them on their golfing adventures. Charlie and Heloisa have been extremely important in my life. They renewed their vows with us on our fifth anniversary. Thank goodness they accepted me! Passing a Brazilian's (Heloisa's) scrutiny was an important milestone in our courtship. She is very special to me; we cherish their friendship.

Wally and Connie introduced me to Anders, for which I shall always remain indebted to them. They engineered a blind date for us on the opening night of the Sarasota Opera's *La forza del destino* (*The Force of Destiny*) by Verdi. And so it was! As if that were not enough, Connie and Wally were instrumental in the publishing of this book, having served as high-level executives in the publishing industry. They have encouraged me every step of the way, not only in my writing, but my art as well.

Margaret and Bill Wise, Sue and Murf Klauber, Michael Saunders, and their extended families were dear friends long before politics surfaced on our radar screen. Yet these friends have remained among our staunchest supporters through thick and thin. I admire each of them immensely—they all serve as my role models.

I have a very special group of women friends. Some are friends of the heart, some are outrageously funny, but all are kind and supportive. We meet for birthdays, holidays, just about any day we can manage balancing successful women's busy calendars. I thank them for keeping me sane, for making me laugh, for guarding my confidences, and for being the dearest friends: Charlene Heiser Wolff, Suzann Soran, Katie Moulton, Graci McGillicuddy, Marianne McKay Smith, Eileen Curd, Kathryn Carr, Susan Kelley, Jeanne Russell, and Brenda Johnson. We count our blessings, for we are married to some amazing men, and we really appreciate our lives because of them! Phillip Wolff, Bob Soran, Michael Moulton, Dennis McGillicuddy, Gary Smith, Howard Curd, Bob Carr, Bill Kelley, Tom Russell, and Brian Johnson have been very good friends to Anders and me—many, many thanks.

I also wish to thank the beauty, ambiance, and energy of the city in which I am graced to live. Sarasota is a veritable paradise, with the whitest sand beaches in the world, the highest level of quality arts organizations per capita, outstanding education from kindergarten through graduate level, extraordinary provisions of social services, and among the best healthcare facilities in the nation. The quality of life is so stellar due to the innovative ideas and financial commitments of Sarasota's best asset—the people!

My congressional campaign staff never bargained for such a monolithic distraction as this book became; honestly, neither did I. Nevertheless, they kept a wonderful, encouraging outlook during all its trials and tribulations while dealing with the challenges of the campaign as well. For their incredible support and belief in me, for their dedicated work ethic and terrific attitudes, for their outrageous sense of humor (just don't ever hide my Roger Staubach football!) and their strong principled values, I thank them and their spouses.

My campaign has definitely been a family affair: Dan and Aimee

Berger have helped me since I first began, and they've made all the difference. We have been through everything together, and no words can begin to thank them enough; Miguel Romano, his mother Carmen, and his extended network throughout Sarasota have cheered us forward. As for his fundraising acumen . . . well, you have read the results; Rori Patrise Smith and her parents and Robby have been such an encouragement, and Rori has taken Sarasota by storm all by herself; Hartley Etheridge and George O'Brien are an amazing couple, so much fun; yet I would put Hartley up against anyone for her competency, knowledge, skills and initiative; Nancie, Rachael, and Nathan Kalin and Chip Parmelee are a wonderful family who carry off grand events and excruciating schedules without a hitch and with grace and charm; Aimee and Michael Fortney—our energizer bunny/outreach coordinator to the Hispanic community and direct mail coordinator/cheerleader—and our sunshine Michala Fortney are a very special family; Zeb Portanova and his wonderful mother Linda and extended family throughout the U.S. for their support and for his efforts in keeping the campaign strong, offering amazing finesse on the issues and leading rock-solid town hall meetings; Brewster Bevis for his yeoman's efforts in always keeping me on time and making certain that I have everything required for every meeting or speech while he covered the district with my signs. Jessica Furst, the most quoted journalism major in the land and a wonderful person, and her parents Bill and Darla; and our good luck maven who has helped me on every campaign and holds us together, Marilyn Libby—thank you. Matt Keelan has become a great friend. He possesses extraordinary talents. Our volunteers throughout the district have become our extended campaign family, and we couldn't make a move without them.

My childhood camp friends remain among the most cherished friends I know; my counselors, Nancy Jackson Davis, Peggy O'Kelly Roberts, and Cindy Taylor Brown, will long stand as having the strongest and best impact imaginable on my life, save my family.

I want to thank the people at Calvary Chapel, Pastor Carl Dixon, and Sandra Kravitz for their guidance and prayers.

My family has given the most—Anders, Louise—thank you for your love, patience, and support. Mom and Dad—thanks for your life-example, your encouragement, and your strong belief in your children such that we accomplished goals we never dreamed possible. Walt, Fran, and Wes, you are the best brothers and sister anyone could hope for. You've given me so much and have been there for me like no others. I thank God we are so close; I am so fortunate. Harrison and Mitch, thanks for your conversations that thrill me, put everything in perspective, and always remind me of what matters most.

Finally, my thanks to the countless individuals who, through whatever means, have provided me with encouragement and support. Their goodwill continues to remind me that near every storm, there exists a calm harbor of refuge and kindness.

About the Author

KATHERINE HARRIS has been in public service for almost eight years, four as a state senator and four as Florida's secretary of state as of January 2003. In the wake of the 2000 election controversy, Harris was a leading proponent of election reform legislation, particularly with regard to voting accessibility for persons with disabilities. As Florida's secretary of state, Harris exercised the most expansive responsibilities of any state-level secretary of state in America, sharing executive power with the Governor of Florida and five other independently elected officials in a cabinet that exercises authority over matters such as education, law enforcement and the environment. She also presidesd over the Florida Department of State, which consists of seven diverse divisions, overseeing art and culture, libraries, historical resources, licensing, corporations, international affairs, and elections. Before entering public service, she was a marketing executive for IBM and vice-president of a commercial real estate firm.

A lifelong supporter of the arts, Katherine Harris is a graduate of Agnes Scott College and holds a Masters Degree in Public Administration from Harvard University's John F. Kennedy School of Government. She is a fourth generation Floridian and lives in Sarasota with her husband, Anders Ebbeson, and daughter, Louise.